Jean-Jacques Rousseau

Jean-Jacques Rousseau

☾

A Friend of Virtue

Joseph R. Reisert

CORNELL UNIVERSITY PRESS

Ithaca and London

First published 2003 by Cornell University Press

Printed in the United States of America

Library of Congress Cataloging-in-Publication

Reisert, Joseph R.
    Jean-Jacques Rousseau : a friend of virtue / Joseph R. Reisert.
        p.   cm.
Includes bibliographical references (p.   ) and index.
    ISBN 0-8014-4096-3 (cloth)
    1. Rousseau, Jean-Jacques, 1712–1778—Ethics.   2. Virtue—
History—18th century.   3. Ethics, Modern—18th century.
I. Title.
    B2138.E8   R45   2003
    170'.92—dc21   2002152061

Cornell University Press strives to use environmentally responsible suppliers and materials to the fullest extent possible in the publishing of its books. Such materials include vegetable-based, low-VOC inks and acid-free papers that are recycled, totally chlorine-free, or partly composed of nonwood fibers. For further information, visit our website at www.cornellpress.cornell.edu.

Cloth printing   10 9 8 7 6 5 4 3 2 1

for my parents

Contents

Preface

WHENEVER I READ ROUSSEAU, I feel that he is speaking directly to me—not in the way that all great thinkers who address universal human concerns necessarily speak to each reader because they speak to all—but in a more personal way. That feeling has persisted from my first encounter with Rousseau down to the present. I still wince when I read his assault on the vanity of intellectuals in the *Discourse on the Sciences and Arts*; I still cringe when I read his critique of avarice in the *Discourse on Inequality*; I still thrill to the dream of freedom when I read the *Social Contract*; I still cry when I read *Emile*. Others, of course, respond differently—sometimes with anger, indignation, or even outrage. But no one can read Rousseau and be unmoved. That is just as he wished.

Rousseau addresses each of his readers personally because he addresses the concerns, small and great, that each of us must confront for ourselves, in our own daily existence. He writes about the everyday challenges of the moral life, about how hard it can be to live up to our own ideals, and about what steps we can take in order to live happier and better lives. He writes about the everyday challenges of our living together in political community, about the difficulty of preserving our freedom, both from the powerful, institutional forces that threaten to overwhelm us from the outside and from our own vices, which threaten to destroy our liberty from within. And Rousseau addresses these concerns—my concerns—with passion and intensity, as if they matter more than anything else in the world.

Rousseau takes with utmost seriousness the ancient idea that we reflect about action, not primarily for the sake of understanding, but for the sake of acting well. This conviction shapes all his works and accounts for their peculiar duality. On the surface, the seductive beauty of Rousseau's prose beckons toward an easy acceptance of the moral advice he offers. But with the brilliance of his ingenious paradoxes Rousseau invites—demands—a measure of philosophical reflection. On first reading, Rousseau's books tell us how to live and show us how we are failing to live as we know we ought. On subsequent readings, if we attend carefully to his arguments, we find that they also articulate and defend a model of human nature that explains why we find it so hard to live as we ought and shows us how we can be moved to do what reason requires. My aim in this book is to explain this duality in Rousseau's writings, first by reconstructing Rousseau's account of human nature and retracing the arguments by which he seeks to vindicate it, then by showing why that model leads to the conclusion that human beings cannot live well without virtue, and finally by explaining Rousseau's approach to moral education both in theory and in practice.

There can be danger in writing about virtue—as Rousseau discovered to his sorrow, when his critics sought to refute his arguments by demonstrating that he had never lived up to the demands of the virtue he preached. Rousseau perhaps invited the critique by portraying himself as a character in his own works and by endowing that character with virtues he knew himself not to possess. In Rousseau's defense, it must be said that he found himself driven to that unusual expedient because his understanding of the human heart led him to the conclusion that moral education is only possible in a relationship with a friend of virtue. In the hope of inspiring his readers to love virtue, Rousseau wrote a pair of didactic novels (*Emile* and *Julie*) in which the title characters acquire virtue through their encounter with a wise and virtuous friend; in each case, that friend is an idealization of Rousseau himself. Rousseau the author invites us the readers to emulate the eponymous hero and heroine of his novels and to accept the proffered friendship of the ideal Rousseau as an aid in our quest for virtue.

In this book, I have endeavored only to explain Rousseau's thought, to demonstrate the soundness of a few of his leading ideas, and to illustrate some consequences of those ideas. Needless to say, I make no particular claim to possess the moral virtue described here; whether this book demonstrates any of the virtues of thought, I must leave the reader to judge. I would not, however, like to be judged guilty of ingratitude: in the course of writing this book, I have contracted a number of debts, both personal and intellectual, and it is now time to repay with my thanks the institutions and the people who have aided me in my work.

I am grateful to the National Science Foundation for the Graduate Fellowship that supported me during the early years of my graduate career, when I began the inquiry that culminates in this book, to the Program in Ethics and the Professions at Harvard University for a Graduate Fellowship during which I began in earnest to write the Ph.D. dissertation from which this book has evolved, and to the U.S. Department of Education for the Jacob K. Javits Fellowship that supported me until the dissertation was completed. To Colby College, I am doubly grateful. First, for support during the sabbatical year that enabled me to revise my approach to Rousseau and to write this book. Second, for the Wiswell Chair in American Constitutional Law, which has provided me with research funds that have greatly facilitated my work. Finally, I am grateful to Harriet Sargent Wiswell and George C. Wiswell Jr., for the gift to Colby of the professorship I am so privileged to hold. To study lives of the great political theorists of the past is to be reminded of the good fortune we scholars today enjoy: Rousseau felt obliged to reject a royal pension because he sensed that the king supported only those whose ideas he favored. Happily, my government and my employer impose no such constraints: the views expressed herein are my own and do not necessarily represent those of the institutions or persons who have supported my work.

Rousseau thought that words could never fully express the feelings one has for one's friends, but he also saw that sometimes one must have recourse to the cold mediation of language and trust that one's friends would recognize the sentiments behind the words. I must thank all of my friends, whose powerful—and, I hope, beneficent—influence on my life first led me to think about friendship in connection with political philosophy.

I am grateful to my teachers in the Department of Government at Harvard, Harvey Mansfield, Michael Sandel, and Peter Berkowitz at Harvard for their help at every stage. They patiently endured my early missteps, carefully read and thoughtfully criticized numerous drafts, and suggested to me fruitful avenues for further inquiry. Judith Shklar, whose seminar on the Enlightenment taught me what graduate school should be, provided the initial inspiration for this project; I regret that I did not have the opportunity to absorb more of her wisdom. Jon Fullerton and Louisa Lund read several preliminary drafts and offered much helpful advice and encouragement. My erstwhile Colby colleague Sammy Barkin read an early draft of the whole manuscript and helped me to find ways to make the argument more accessible to nonspecialists. I owe a profound debt to Andy Sabl, who read a draft of the entire manuscript as it neared completion, and in several long and thoughtful conversations, responded to my argument with sympathetic and penetrating insight. His guidance has saved me from several serious errors and led me to a deeper appreciation of alternatives to the Rousseauian approach to ethics I have defended here.

I thank the good people associated with Cornell University Press, who have worked so hard to make this book a reality. My editor, Catherine Rice, has been supportive throughout the process and has been most tactful at explaining that shorter is often better. The two anonymous readers of the manuscript carefully attended to the argument and raised several significant issues, and the book is better for my having addressed them. I am grateful to Susan MacKay for her careful editing and to Teresa Jesionowski for her assistance in preparing the final manuscript for publication.

Words do fail to express the extent of my gratitude to my wife Susan, not least for her willingness to share our home with Rousseau, whose friendship she neither sought out nor requires. Finally, to my parents, whose love and friendship I will always cherish, I express my thanks for the invaluable gift of their complete confidence and deepest affection. I dedicate this work to them.

Joseph R. Reisert

Waterville, Maine
October 2002

Abbreviations

WORKS BY JEAN-JACQUES ROUSSEAU

C   *Confessions.* Translated by Christopher Kelly. In *The Confessions and Correspondence, Including the Letters to Malesherbes.* Edited by Christopher Kelly, Roger D. Masters, and Peter G. Stillman. Vol. 5 of *The Collected Writings of Rousseau.* Hanover, N.H.: University Press of New England, 1995.

CC   *Correspondance Complète de Jean-Jacques Rousseau.* 51 vols. Edited by R. A. Leigh. Geneva: Institut et musée Voltaire. 1965–1995.

CP   *Constitutional Project for Corsica.* In OC 3.

D   *Rousseau Judge of Jean-Jacques: Dialogues.* Translated by Judith R. Bush, Christopher Kelly, and Roger D. Masters. Vol. 1 of *The Collected Writings of Rousseau.* Edited by Roger D. Masters and Christopher Kelly. Hanover, N.H.: University Press of New England, 1990.

D1   *Discourse on the Sciences and Arts.* In EPW. Referred to in the text as the *First Discourse.*

D2   *Discourse on the Origin and Foundations of Inequality Among Men.* In EPW. Referred to in the text as the *Discourse on Inequality.*

DV   *Discourse on the Virtue Most Necessary for a Hero.* In EPW.

E   *Emile, or, On Education.* Translated by Allan Bloom. New York: Basic Books, 1979.

EPW   *The Discourses and Other Early Political Writings.* Edited and translated by Victor Gourevitch. New York: Cambridge University Press, 1997.

ES   *Emile et Sophie, ou, Les Solitaires.* In OC 4.

GM   The Geneva Manuscript of *On the Social Contract.* In LPW.

GP   *Considerations on The Government of Poland.* In LPW.

J   *Julie, or the New Heloise: Letters of Two Lovers Who Live in a Small Town at the Foot of the Alps.* Translated and annotated by Philip Stewart and Jean Vaché. Vol. 6 of *The Collected Writings of*

Rousseau. Hanover, N.H.: The University Press of New England, 1997.

LA *Letter to M. d'Alembert on the Theatre*. Translated by Allan Bloom. *In Politics and the Arts: Letter to M. d'Alembert on the Theatre*. Edited by Allan Bloom. Ithaca: Cornell University Press, 1960.

LAR *Letter to the Abbé Raynal*. In EPW.

LB *Lettre à Christophe de Beaumont*. In OC 4.

LF *Letter to Franquières*. In LPW.

LM *Letter to Malesherbes*. Translated by Christopher Kelly. In *The Confessions and Correspondence, Including the Letters to Malesherbes*. Edited by Christopher Kelly, Roger D. Masters, and Peter G. Stillman. Vol. 5 of *The Collected Writings of Rousseau*. Hanover, N.H.: University Press of New England, 1995.

LO *Letter to D'Offreville*. In LPW.

LPW *The Social Contract and Other Late Political Writings*. Edited and translated by Victor Gourevitch. New York: Cambridge University Press, 1997.

LSR *Last Reply*. In EPW.

LV *Letter to Voltaire*. Translated by Victor Gourevitch. In LPW.

ML *Moral Letters*. In OC 4.

MP "Mon Portrait." In OC 1.

MT *Lettres Ecrites de la Montaigne*. In OC 3.

O *Observations*. In EPW.

OC *Oeuvres Complètes de Jean-Jacques Rousseau*. 5 vols. Edited by B. Gagnebin, M. Raymond, J. Starobinski, et al. Paris: Bibliothèque de la Pléiade, 1959–1995.

OL *Essay on the Origin of Languages*. In EPW.

PB Preface of a Second Letter to Bordes. In EPW.

PE *Discourse on Political Economy*. In LPW.

PN Preface to *Narcissus*. In EPW.

RW *Reveries of the Solitary Walker*. Translated by Charles E. Butterworth. Indianapolis: Hackett, 1992.

SC *On the Social Contract*. In LPW.

SW "The State of War." In LPW.

Jean-Jacques Rousseau

1 The Problem of Virtue

The shortest and surest way of making men happy is not to adorn their cities, nor even to enrich them, but to make them good.

—*Last Reply*

It's the Preachers' job to exhort us with *Be good, be virtuous*, without much concern for the results of their sermons; the citizen who is concerned about them should not foolishly exhort us with *Be good*; but make us love the estate that helps us to do so.

—Second Preface to *Julie*

WHAT ARE THE VIRTUES of human beings and of citizens? How can these virtues be taught? Who is able to teach them? Phrased in this manner, these questions may seem to exude a faintly archaic air. It is true that they are ancient questions, asked long ago by Socrates, but they are no less important for that. We might hesitate to use the word "virtue" to denote the nature of our concern, but, just as in ancient Athens, concerned parents today continue to think about the talents, skills, beliefs, and values they should try to pass on to their children, and we wonder how it can be done, and whether we or someone else can best accomplish the task. So also do thoughtful young people continue to ask similar questions on their own account. This book aims to articulate and, in large measure, to defend the answers to these questions developed by Jean-Jacques Rousseau, who styled himself not only "citizen of Geneva" but also—and more enduringly—a "friend of the truth" and "a friend of virtue" (LB 931, 968; E 110).

When Socrates first asked these questions of his fellow citizens, they were laden with political significance in addition to the personal and human weight they naturally bear. When he put these questions to his interlocutors, he found that they generally could not give an account of these matters, about which they had previously supposed themselves knowledgeable. Their newly exposed ignorance was disturbing enough to his interlocutors as individuals. But Socrates' inquiries were also viewed as politically subversive because they were taken to imply that his fellow citizens and the laws were failing in what they themselves professed to regard as a fundamental duty: to educate the Athenian youth to be excellent men and citizens. In his *Apology*, Socrates explained to the men of Athens that his *daimonion*—his conscience—called him to a nobler citizenship and a higher piety than those his fellow citizens recognized, which required him to seek true knowledge about virtue. The Athenians pressed him to choose between his conscience and his city: he must either abandon philosophy or leave Athens to go into exile. He refused to make the choice, and for that refusal he was made to pay with his life. The Athenian jury did not have the last word, however. Plato's *Republic* contains a posthumous defense of Socrates' refusal to sacrifice either his citizenship for the sake of his conscience or his conscience for the sake of his citizenship. That work quietly vindicates Socrates' practice of philosophizing in private with a few, select friends as an effective means of teaching them how to be better men and citizens even as it depicts the extraordinary and terrifying measures of civic education that would be required to order a whole city in accordance with true or philosophic virtue.

It may be thought that the advent of modern liberalism has drained these ancient questions of all their erstwhile political significance. Modern liberalism rejects the classical idea that the end of the state is to cultivate virtue, maintaining instead that its purpose is the protection of individual freedom. By guaranteeing a generous set of basic rights for all, the liberal state creates a private sphere that is relatively free from state control and within which individuals may lead their own lives substantially as they see fit. The great and intensely controversial questions about the ends of human life are, so far as is possible, taken out of politics and entrusted to this private sphere by such means as the disestablishment of state religions and the recognition of the liberty of conscience. As a consequence of these and other measures, thoughtful parents in liberal societies are free to educate their children very largely in accordance with their own wishes. Parents have great freedom to decide which virtues they wish to cultivate in their children, and they remain at liberty to decide for themselves whom to entrust with the task of imparting those virtues to their offspring. To the public authority of the liberal state is entrusted only the responsibility to cultivate those all-purpose skills, talents, and dispositions that assist those who possess them to succeed in whatever form of life they choose to adopt.

The establishment of a liberal polity does not, however, make virtue politically unnecessary, even as liberal ideals impose sharp limits on the means that may be used by the state to teach it. In fact, as scholars such as William Galston,[1] Stephen Macedo,[2] and Peter Berkowitz[3] have observed,

1. William A. Galston, *Liberal Purposes* (Cambridge: Cambridge University Press, 1991).

2. Stephen Macedo, *Liberal Virtues: Citizenship, Virtue, and Community in Liberal Constitutionalism* (New York: Oxford University Press, 1990).

3. Peter Berkowitz, *Virtue and the Making of Modern Liberalism* (Princeton: Princeton University Press, 1999).

citizenship in a modern liberal republic demands great and often difficult virtues. Where those virtues cannot be found in sufficient measure, a liberal regime cannot long preserve its liberal character. That polities whose aim is the protection of individual liberty should impose great duties on their citizens may seem paradoxical, but the paradox dissolves on careful scrutiny. To claim rights for ourselves and to insist that those rights be extended universally is to impose on ourselves the correlative duty to respect the rights of others. Insofar as we affirm that these rights are to be given practical reality, we impose on ourselves the further duty to support the political and legal institutions whose existence is necessary to secure the conditions under which those rights may be exercised.

The greater the scope of the freedoms we claim for ourselves as universal entitlements, the more onerous the duties we impose on ourselves and the wider the range of civic obligations we undertake to perform. Respect for the rights of others requires that we refrain from injuring others, either deliberately or negligently, in their persons and in their properties. Respect for the rights of others to speak and worship as they wish may necessitate that we tolerate speech and conduct that is vulgar, blasphemous, and downright offensive. Respect for the rights of others also demands that we take affirmative steps in addition to the forbearances already mentioned. We must pay taxes to support a variety of public services, including the provision of financial support to the poor and elderly; we may be compelled to give evidence in a court of law; and, in time of war, we may be conscripted to service in the nation's armed forces.

To all of these obligatory activities of citizenship there correspond certain virtues. This is so as a matter of definition: to any given activity or function there corresponds a virtue—the state of being able to perform the activity well.[4] As Berkowitz has rightly emphasized, this conception of the virtues as functional excellences does not entail the belief that human beings have a final end or that one can speak intelligibly about the virtue of a human being. One can, for example, identify the knowledge, skills, and affective dispositions required of a great tennis player—the virtue, in short, of a tennis player—without reaching any judgment about the nature of an excellent human being. Where the activity in question is complex, requiring the coordination of a number of simpler actions, the virtue corresponding to the comprehensive activity will be correspondingly complex. The excellent tennis player, for example, must master a variety of distinct skills (serving, volleying, judging the trajectory of the ball, and so on), and integrate them into a larger, complex performance. To be sure, being a good citizen in a liberal republic is a far more complex activity than being a good tennis player, but that implies only that the virtue corresponding to liberal

4. Ibid., 7–10.

citizenship is substantially more complex than the virtue of an excellent tennis player. Just as particular virtues correspond to the variety of specific activities required of citizens, so too there may be said to be a comprehensive civic virtue, which is the state of being able effectively to integrate the various, minor civic virtues into an excellent overall performance of one's duties as a citizen.

As Aristotle long ago observed, to possess civic virtue and to be an excellent citizen is not necessarily to possess human virtue or to be an excellent human being.[5] In fact, Aristotle supposed that in most regimes, and for most citizens in those regimes, the demands of human virtue and those of civic virtue would diverge. In such regimes, the tragic necessity may arise of choosing between being an excellent human being and an excellent citizen. Whatever their other differences, those liberals who affirm the existence of universal, human rights—John Locke and Immanuel Kant among them—aspire to obviate the need for citizens to make that choice. In their view, citizenship demands of us that we respect in our fellow citizens the basic moral rights that all human beings possess in virtue of our common humanity. Liberals need not, and Locke and Kant do not, deny that human virtue can be more demanding than the civic virtue corresponding to citizenship in a liberal state, but universal rights liberals are committed to the view that human virtue can demand no less of us than does the civic virtue corresponding to liberal citizenship.

To say that liberal citizenship requires the virtue of respecting the rights of humanity in one's fellow citizens is not to illuminate in any significant way either the nature or the content of this civic virtue, however. To define the *content* of this liberal virtue we require an account of the rights of humanity; we need an answer to this first question: What do we owe to one another? To define the *nature* of this liberal virtue we require an account of the human soul; we need an answer to this second question: What are the basic principles or motives that move us to act? The answers to these two questions are necessarily interrelated. No reasonable political doctrine can require us to do the impossible. It may be that our nature is such that we need only to know what our duties are in order to be motivated to fulfill them, in which case the nature of human virtue would in no way limit its content. This seems to have been Socrates' view. It may be, however, that our natures are not so fortuitously constituted as Socrates had supposed. If, for example, our natures are found to contain an ineliminable core of selfishness, as so many modern philosophers believe, then it follows that a limit exists to what we can responsibly demand of one another as human beings and citizens.

5. Aristotle, *Politics*, 1276b15–1277b30.

Contemporary political philosophy has addressed the first of those two questions—that regarding the content of our duties—with an extraordinary profusion of insightful scholarship. The second question—about the nature of the human soul—has been substantially left to scholars working in the history of political thought to address, as if it were a question of no more than antiquarian interest. This tendency can be seen with particular clarity in the work of John Rawls, whose work is the font from which flows one of the broadest and deepest currents in recent political philosophy. In this respect, as in so many others, Rawls's view merits particular attention because he articulates clearly a position the essentials of which are widely shared today, but which few others have explored with equal penetration. For Rawls, the central question of political philosophy is the first of the two questions identified in the previous paragraph; he asks: *What does justice require?*[6] Roughly speaking, he answers that the extent of our just obligations to one another can be determined by looking to see what duties rational and reasonable persons would agree to accept, if they were to begin their deliberations from an appropriately fair initial position of choice.

Rawls suggests, however, that he need not answer the second question, about the nature of the basic motives that operate in the human heart or soul. Although he does not make any sustained inquiry into human nature, he nevertheless makes some confident assertions about what it is like. He writes optimistically that "human nature and its natural psychology are *permissive*"; at worst, he concedes, these "*may* limit" the range of ideals human beings can in practice realize.[7] He rightly scorns the suggestion that something in the human heart precludes the possibility of our acquiring any "principle-dependent" motives—desires to act in accordance with certain moral or political norms we have, with sufficient reason, adopted.[8] But to say that it is not impossible for such motives to arise is a far cry from showing that they will necessarily or are even likely to arise when they will actually be needed.

Rawls's refusal to inquire into the nature of the human soul is not as modest as it may at first appear. We have seen that Rawls's account of what we owe to one another begins from the premise that the parties to his hypothetical contract are rational and reasonable. As he uses the terms, rationality and reasonableness denote two "virtues of persons," corresponding to two distinct ways of reasoning well about action.[9] To say that the parties to a deliberation are *rational* is to say that they have a conception of

---

6. John Rawls, *A Theory of Justice* (Cambridge: Harvard University Press, Belknap Press, 1971).

7. John Rawls, *Political Liberalism* (New York: Columbia University Press, 1993), 87.

8. Ibid., 85.

9. Ibid., 48.

their own welfare and intelligently pursue it. To say that they are *reasonable* is to say that they are disposed to treat others fairly, to cooperate with others who show themselves to be similarly disposed.[10]

Insofar as Rawls's hypothetical social contract serves only as a "device of representation," designed to elucidate the logical entailments of a set of premises about the nature of citizens and their society, there can be nothing objectionable about supposing that the parties to the contract possess in sufficient measure the two virtues of rationality and reasonableness.[11] That is not the case, however, when we consider whether the political principles thus derived are normatively binding for any empirically existing human beings. To answer that question, we must know whether the parties to the hypothetical contract sufficiently resemble the empirical human beings whose interests they purportedly represent and whose moral powers their hypothetical situation of choice aims to model. Rawls does not ask whether, or under what conditions, human beings are disposed to act fairly; he simply assumes that we possess in sufficient measure the virtue of reasonableness. In *A Theory of Justice*, Rawls seems to have embraced a version of the Enlightenment idea that human beings are naturally social, assuming that human nature spontaneously supports the demands of reason and justice.[12] In *Political Liberalism*, by contrast, Rawls aims to avoid the problem of nature entirely. He does so by grounding his political conception of justice on a normative model of the person derived from the public political culture and then assuming that, as a contingent and empirical matter, we are in fact close enough to what our ideals imply we ought to be for his theory to apply to us. This move does not solve the problem, however; it only sidesteps it.

Once we assume away the possibility of refractory motives, political philosophy risks becoming emptily utopian, prescribing duties so stringent that none can hope to fulfill them. To preach a strenuous morality to individuals, as Kant did, may or may not be an effective strategy for bringing about moral improvement, but at least it is not likely to cause anyone harm. At worst, the stern moralist is likely to end up being ignored. In the political sphere, however, the consequences of miscalculation are inevi-

---

10. Ibid., 49–50.
11. Ibid., 24–27.
12. See Rawls, *Theory* §§ 69–72. Rawls cites Rousseau's *Emile* for the proposition that "moral learning is not so much a matter of supplying missing motives as one of the free development of our innate intellectual and emotional capacities according to their natural bent" (*Theory*, 459). The present work argues, against Rawls's optimistic reading of Rousseau, that moral learning is *both* a matter of developing our innate intellectual and emotional capacities according to their natural bent *and* a matter of supplying the motives that remain missing when we find that, though we have developed our own talents to their fullest extent, we nevertheless still fall short of Socrates' wisdom and moral excellence.

tably higher. In his *Reflections on the Revolution in France*, Edmund Burke presciently observed the despotic potential implicit in the revolutionaries' dogmatic faith in abstract principles of justice and their sublime indifference to the mores of those whose lives they aimed to improve. To be sure, Rawls is no Robespierre, and his academic disciples are no revolutionaries. But it should not be forgotten that Rawls's austere principles of justice ask far more of us than the laws of any existing state now require, and some of Rawls's followers demand social transformations that are greater still than anything Rawls has envisioned. A worrisome tendency also exists among academic political moralists to display considerable impatience toward those unenlightened souls who do not accept their understanding of what justice demands. To say that the unreasonable claims of one's fellow citizens are categorically to be accorded "no weight,"[13] particularly when a great many of our fellow citizens make such claims, is either to invite undemocratic action to impose duties whose force they do not recognize on a populace unwilling to fulfill them or to encourage an unreasonable cynicism, which infers from the impossibility of perfection the futility of melioration.

Given that the practice of liberal citizenship requires the exercise of certain virtues, it remains to be seen whether today we possess the requisite virtues in sufficient measure and whether we have any clear idea of how to cultivate them effectively. Rawls allows himself to hope that the "institutions of a well-ordered society" and the exercise of public reason will be "mutually sustaining," but given the nature of his intellectual project, this can be no more than a hope.[14] Much evidence, alas, suggests that the cultivation and exercise of reason does not by itself generate the disposition to be reasonable. If it did, one would expect our society to be quite different than it is. Indeed, one would expect that our society would today substantially resemble Rawls's vision of the society that is well ordered in accordance with the principles of justice as fairness.

In fact, the virtue of reasonableness is remarkable for its rarity. Everywhere we see instead the complementary Rawlsian virtue—or is it vice?—of economic rationality. The fully reasonable citizen would not resent the obligations civic life imposes on us but would, rather, embrace them. Thus, for example, the reasonable citizen should look forward to paying his taxes, rejoicing on April 15th that he is able to support those institutions which do so much to advance our common good. Reasonable business owners and reasonable consumers should embrace new environmental and other regulations as the just requirements of protecting our nation's

13. Rawls, *Political Liberalism*, 209.
14. Ibid., 252.

well-being. But, in all seriousness, how many people feel this way? Do not the vast majority of us regard paying our taxes as a burden? Do not businesspeople revile government regulations? Do not consumers resist new environmental regulations just as avidly? If, as Rawls maintains, citizenship in a liberal republic requires that citizens possess some master virtue, such as the virtue of reasonableness, which inclines us to respect the rights of others and bear the just burdens of membership in a community of free and equal citizens, then it would appear that we still have much to learn about how to teach this virtue. It would appear, therefore, that we still have much to learn about the nature of the human soul.

It may seem willfully perverse to suggest that modern liberals should turn for guidance on these matters to that notorious critic of both liberalism and modernity, Jean-Jacques Rousseau. The suggestion may seem less perverse when we recall the powerful impact that Kant—whose influence can be seen throughout the work of Rawls and other contemporary liberals—felt on reading Rousseau's *Emile*: he wrote that that work taught him to "honor mankind" and moved him to turn his philosophical attention to "what really matters": the problem of "restoring the rights of mankind."[15] In all of the works comprising his "system" but above all in *Emile*, Rousseau confronts directly the questions our contemporaries decline to ask: he seeks the nature of the human soul in order to discover a practical, efficacious means of teaching virtue, which he understands as the strength of soul or will required to faithfully carry out one's duties to others. What Rousseau presents in *Emile* as human virtue is in fact the most important virtue required of citizens in liberal regimes: the Rousseauian man of virtue steadfastly respects the rights of others, even at great cost to himself.[16] At the emotional climax of the narrative, the novel's eponymous hero pro-

15. Quoted in Susan Meld Shell, *The Rights of Reason: A Study of Kant's Philosophy and Politics* (Toronto: University of Toronto Press, 1980), 21.

16. The male pronoun is used here (and throughout this work) in order to draw attention to a problematic aspect of Rousseau's thought. As every reader of his works must know, Rousseau insists that the biological differences between men and women generate certain limited, but nevertheless significant, differences in the moral psychologies of men and women in society. Rousseau's account of the nature of women and his corresponding treatment of the appropriate education for girls (E 357–406) are probably impossible to defend in their entirety, and even a minimally adequate discussion of these issues and the vast literature they have generated proved to be outside the scope of the present work. Nevertheless, it must be noted that, despite his "sexism," Rousseau consistently maintains that virtue—the strength of character to rule over one's passions, so that one can make oneself do what one knows one ought to do—is limited neither to men nor to women. Rousseau's heroine Julie comes to possess virtue quite as completely as does his hero, Emile, and the *Moral Letters*, addressed to Sophie d'Houdetot contain fundamentally the same teaching as the Profession of Faith of the Savoyard Vicar, which is addressed to a young man. My own view is that Rousseau's account of virtue does indeed apply equally to men and to women, but because I cannot claim to have demonstrated that proposition here, it would be presumptuous to adopt a gender neutral usage that would imply otherwise.

claims to his beloved that nothing—not even her love for him—is dearer to him than "the rights of humanity" (E 441).

The suggestion that Emile's virtue amounts to the virtue of liberal citizenship may seem contradicted by the suggestion, often imputed to Rousseau,[17] that one must choose between being a man and being a citizen.[18] But that is not exactly what he says. He does not say that one cannot *be* both man and citizen; he says that "one must choose between *making* a man or a citizen, for *one cannot make both at the same time*" (E 39, emphasis added). The argument of *Emile* holds out the possibility that a man "educated uniquely for himself" will also, as a consequence of his education, be good for others (E 41). Such a man could be a citizen anywhere, in any regime— even in a modern, commercial republic. Rousseau indicates as much in the choice of the name he gives his novel's hero: Emile. Allan Bloom plausibly suggests that Rousseau derives the name from Aemilius, the name of an illustrious patrician family in ancient Rome (E 31 n. 1). It is possible that Rousseau had Plutarch's Aemilius Paulus in mind when he named his protagonist, as Bloom seems inclined to believe. But the evidence for that attribution is scant, and other, more suggestive, possibilities exist: a Quintus Aemilius was co-consul with the Fabricius whom Rousseau imagines denouncing the vices of the imperial Romans in the *First Discourse*;[19] and Tacitus, describing the collapse of morals in Rome under the emperor Tiberius, remarks an exception to the general decline: "the Aemilii have always produced good citizens," he observes.[20] Rousseau's Emile is fit to be a "good citizen" in whatever place or time he finds himself.

JEAN-JACQUES ROUSSEAU: A FRIEND OF VIRTUE

Like today's political theorists, Rousseau fiercely condemned the injustices he perceived everywhere around him. Rousseau is certainly more strident than today's canons of academic propriety would allow, but the substance of Rousseau's complaints reveals a positive vision of society that in many important respects resembles Rawls's conception of a society well-ordered in accordance with the principles of justice as fairness. Like Rawls, Rousseau insists that the basic right of all individuals to security in their per-

---

17. For example, by Judith N. Shklar's extraordinary work *Men and Citizens: A Study of Rousseau's Social Theory* (Cambridge: Cambridge University Press, 1985).

18. Tracy B. Strong also rejects this view, but for a different reason: he suggests that Emile *"requires and will generate, come what may, a political society." Jean-Jacques Rousseau: The Politics of the Ordinary* (Thousand Oaks, Calif.: Sage, 1994), 138.

19. Plutarch, "Life of Pyrrhus," in *The Lives of the Noble Grecians and Romans*, trans. by John Dryden, edited and revised by Arthur Hugh Clough. 2 vols. (New York: Modern Library, 1992), 1:536.

20. "Aemilium genus fecundum bonorum civium." Tacitus, *Annals* VI 27.

sons and property must be respected; like Rawls, he insists that public of-
fices and stations of private responsibility should be filled in accordance
with genuine merit; and like Rawls, he insists that none should abound in
superfluities while others lack for necessities.[21]

Rousseau's critique of injustice diverges from Rawls's, however, at two
points. The first divergence is substantive, the second, structural. Substan-
tively, Rousseau's account of the nature of virtue does not support the
Rawlsian demand that government strive for neutrality in its treatment of
different conceptions of the good life. Structurally, whereas Rawls and his
followers focus primarily on the justice and injustice *of institutions*, Rousseau attends principally to the virtue and corruption *of the people* who animate those institutions. Rousseau's two departures from the orthodoxy of
contemporary liberalism are linked. He attends to the virtues of individual
human beings because institutions have no existence apart from the dispositions of the men and women who constitute them. If the people desire
injustice strongly enough, they will find a way to circumvent even the best-
designed institutions in order to accomplish their malevolent ends. It follows that only a society that reliably cultivates virtue in its citizens can
effectively protect the basic rights of all its citizens or assure a just distri-
bution of property.

Throughout his oeuvre, Rousseau advances one consistent, critical
theme: he complains that his contemporaries lack virtue. By this he means
that they lack the basic orientation of heart and mind that is essential to
morality. They are not disposed to do what is right for its own sake, and
though they may profess rigorous principles of justice, they lack the
strength of character to practice what they profess. Instead, they are moved
to act by consideration of their own advantage. To use the modern terms
introduced earlier, Rousseau objects that his contemporaries are *rational*
but *unreasonable*. Worse still, he maintains that modern, commercial society is constituted so that the rational and the reasonable are systematically
at odds with each another (PN 100–101). "What will become of virtue," he
asks, "when one has to get rich at all cost?" (D1 18). That question may
seem like nothing but an intellectual's *bon mot*, but Rousseau asks it in
earnest. Rephrased, it is the question Rawls should ask but does not: *What
will become of the virtue of reasonableness, when we perceive no rational advantage in it?*

Virtue is also the central lesson of Rousseau's constructive works; it is
the link that connects the "individualistic" teachings of *Emile* and *Julie* with
the "collectivistic" doctrines of *On the Social Contract* and the *Discourse on
Political Economy*. Although Julie always professes to love virtue, she does

---

21. Compare Rawls, *Political Liberalism*, 5–6, and D2 188.

not initially live up to the ideals she professes; she experiences a dramatic conversion on her wedding day, however, and cleaves steadfastly to virtue thereafter. Virtue is also the culminating lesson of Emile's education. In the course of the young man's upbringing, Jean-Jacques gives only one simple but comprehensive moral precept to his protégé: "Be a man" (*sois homme*). In context, it is clear that this means: "be virtuous" (E 445). Finally, virtue is central to Rousseau's account of politics. The *Social Contract* teaches that the only legitimate regime is one where the government is bound by constitutional laws that are willed by the sovereign people to reflect its general will (SC 66–68; cf. E 462–463). In the *Discourse on Political Economy* we find that, if citizens are to will the general will, virtue must reign in the hearts of the people and their magistrates (see PE 13, 15, and SC 112).[22]

Rousseau's account of virtue, however, has received only a small fraction of the scholarly attention devoted to other central Rousseauian concepts, such as freedom, nature, and the general will. Of the two most influential accounts of Rousseauian virtue, one finds his view to be repulsively narcissistic; the other sees it as deplorably insensitive to the full range of genuine human perfections. Carol Blum charges that, for Rousseau, virtue was not part of "an ethical system in any usual sense," but "rather a state of being that could be entered by the willing disciple." Central to this state of being was a "feeling of righteousness" that Rousseau himself possessed and that could be shared by his disciples, if only they would merge their wills and fuse their very identities with his.[23] In contrast, Arthur Melzer does perceive in Rousseau's works a consistent account of ethics and of virtue, but he charges that Rousseau so radically alters traditional ideas that his teaching amounts to a "moral revolution."[24] In Melzer's judgment, Rousseau teaches that "the final end of life and the root of all happiness" is to be found in a distinctive feeling—the "sentiment of existence," the feeling of being most truly alive.[25] Because he finds that this distinctive sentiment arises when our hearts are not torn by contradictory desires, Melzer's Rousseau teaches that "'unity of soul,' as a purely formal condition" is "the sole determinant of existence and thus the

---

22. In his *Considerations on the Government of Poland* and *Constitutional Project for Corsica*, Rousseau advises aspiring founders of republican regimes to craft elaborate institutional mechanisms for cultivating virtue in the hearts of ordinary citizens and magistrates (see e.g., GP 189–193, 239–248; CP 933–937).

23. Carol Blum, *Rousseau and the Republic of Virtue: The Language of Politics in the French Revolution* (Ithaca, N.Y.: Cornell University Press, 1986), 37, 72. For similar views, see H. Gaston Hall, "The Concept of Virtue in *La Nouvelle Héloïse*," *Yale French Studies* 28 (1961): 20–33; and Jeanne Thomas Fuchs, *The Pursuit of Virtue: A Study of Order in La Nouvelle Héloïse* (New York: Peter Lang, 1993).

24. Arthur M. Melzer, The *Natural Goodness of Man: On the System of Rousseau's Thought* (Chicago: University of Chicago Press, 1990), 103.

25. Ibid., 41, 104.

primary good."[26] Whereas Aristotle recognized a variety of different and possibly incompatible human excellences, Melzer holds that Rousseau reduces virtue to a single attribute: "self-forced obedience to law as such."[27] According to this understanding of virtue, all that matters is that the soul be unified; thus it does not matter "*what* a man is so long as he is it wholly and consistently."[28]

Blum and Melzer both misapprehend Rousseau's teachings about virtue, however, because they do not sufficiently attend to the aims of Rousseau's intellectual project. Blum rightly perceives the centrality of virtue to Rousseau's thought, but the primary goal of her work is to make sense of the French Revolutionaries' appropriation of Rousseau's idea of virtue, rather than to offer a coherent reconstruction of Rousseau's own view. In contrast, Melzer aims to understand Rousseau's thought on its own terms, working from the premise that his works form a coherent intellectual system—just as Rousseau himself constantly insisted (PB 108; LB 928; LM 575–576; D 687, 829, 932–933; C 309).[29] In his view, however, Rousseau's system is nothing less than a comprehensive "philosophy of morals and of politics."[30] Melzer seeks to discover in Rousseau's works an account of the rational foundations of morality, as if he, like Kant in the *Groundwork of the Metaphysics of Morals,* had sought "to seek out and establish *the supreme principle of morality.*"[31]

Unlike Kant, however, Rousseau does not claim to have discovered any "ultimate norm of moral judgment."[32] Nowhere, for example, does he offer a definition of justice more specific than his statement in *Emile* that "the love of justice" is "nothing other" than "the love of mankind" (E 252). Although he acknowledges that a moral "law of reason" exists (GM 155), Rousseau says nothing about the rational foundations of morality except that "all justice comes from God" (SC 66). Nor does Rousseau advance any particularly innovative moral doctrines. Throughout his moral and political works, Rousseau draws on a substantially conventional moral vocabulary that he assumes the reader will already know and accept.[33] He praises the traditional virtues of justice, temperance, courage, and wisdom, and he

---

26. Ibid., 65.
27. Ibid., 103.
28. Ibid., 65.
29. Ibid., 4–9.
30. Ibid., 13.
31. Immanuel Kant, *Groundwork of the Metaphysics of Morals,* translated by H. J. Paton (New York: Harper and Row, 1948), 60.
32. Ibid., 57.
33. Rousseau's discussion, in the Fourth Walk (RW 43–59), of the ethics of truth telling and lying has attracted so much scholarly attention because it is one of the few such discussions in the whole Rousseauian oeuvre.

condemns such vices as licentiousness, gluttony, irascibility, envy, avarice, and dominating ambition.

What Rousseau does claim, repeatedly and insistently, is that he judges his books to be uniquely *useful*. He makes this claim, not only about his polemical interventions into Genevan politics, where they might be expected, but also about his discourses and novels, where they may seem out of place.[34] Throughout the *First Discourse,* however, Rousseau criticizes other writers for having done nothing to promote "genuine felicity" (D1 26) and asserts repeatedly that what he has to say will help us, his readers, to be both happy and worthy of happiness. The *Discourse on Inequality* purports to address "the most useful and least advanced" branch of human knowledge; Rousseau adds that the "political and moral investigations occasioned by" the question it raises are "in every way useful" (D2 124, 128). In the preface to *Emile* Rousseau tells us that "the maxims concerning which [he is] of an opinion different from that of others . . . are among those whose truth or falsehood is important to know and which make the happiness or unhappiness of mankind" (E 34; see also E 112n, 416). Even the apparently frivolous novel, *Julie,* is said to be genuinely, practically useful (J 3, 12–18). These claims are reaffirmed frequently in Rousseau's autobiographical writings as well (see, e.g., C 338, 343, 349, 366, 472–473, 480–481).

It is important to be reminded how frequently and how directly Rousseau insisted on the usefulness of his works because that claim strikes so many readers of Rousseau today as altogether incredible. Of what use to us, such readers may ask, can be Rousseau's fanciful visions of a lost golden age and his enthusiasm for austere Sparta? We certainly cannot go back to the pre-political condition of our "savage" ancestors, which represented for Rousseau man's golden age (D2 166–167, OL 268).[35] Just as surely would it be madness to re-create Sparta in the modern world. Rousseau himself says as much, which means that we must seek the utility of his visions elsewhere. Judith Shklar has rightly stressed that Rousseau's "great claim was that he alone had been 'the painter of nature and the historian of the human heart.'"[36] Rousseau's vivid portrayals of radical human possibilities enable him to uncover useful truths about the na-

---

34. On the relationship of Rousseau to the political situation in Geneva, see Helena Rosenblatt, *Rousseau and Geneva: From the First Discourse to the Social Contract, 1749–1762* (Cambridge: Cambridge University Press, 1997).

35. It should be noted that the English word, "savage" ordinarily carries strongly negative connotations that its French equivalent (*sauvage*) does not. To Rousseau, the savage state represents the condition of human life prior to the establishment of political societies; many of the indigenous peoples of Africa and the New World were still, in Rousseau's day, savage in this sense (D2 164–167). Whenever the word savage and its cognates appear in the text, it this technical, Rousseauian usage that is intended.

36. Shklar, *Men and Citizens,* 1. The internal quotation refers to D 52 (Shklar's translation).

ture of the basic passions that move the human heart, which in turn enables him to discover the nature of virtue. Thus, rather than devote his works to answering the philosopher's questions, What ought I to do? and What does justice require? Rousseau answers the moralist's questions, How can I make myself do what I know ought to be done? and How can one order a society so that the people will be motivated to respect the rights of others?[37] What is novel about Rousseau is not his substantive account of morality, but rather his moral psychology—his understanding of the passions that move the human heart. And that knowledge, rather than what the philosophers would teach us, is indeed most useful for living a life that is happy and worthy of being so.

"THE PRINCIPLES OF THE PASSIONS"

Rousseau sought so avidly to understand the human heart because he perceived that "passions are the motive of all action" (D 9). Although he senses that reason is "free in its essence" (OC 4:1024), Rousseau observes that the rational awareness that we ought to do something—"cold reason"—supplies only the weakest *motive* to do it (J 405; E 321). To be sure, Rousseau recognizes that certain extraordinary individuals, such as Socrates, find little difficulty in following the dictates of reason. Most of us, however, lack Socrates' temperance and wisdom, and nowhere can a nation of people like him be found. The rest of us are ruled by our passions. Tempted by evils that we recognize but whose allure we find so hard to resist, too often we succumb. What would be really useful to us is a means of imposing order on our passions, so that we are reliably motivated to do only what reason tells us we may rightly do (E 80, 219). What we need for that task is an understanding of the human passions and a way to predict and direct their movements—a physics of the soul. That is what Rousseau provides.

He was hardly the first to have put an account of the passions at the center of his reflections about politics and ethics. Thomas Hobbes begins from the premise that human beings are moved by their passions (he calls them "appetites" and "aversions"), and he constructs his political science on that foundation, notoriously insisting that to motivate men to keep their covenants, "the passion to be reckoned upon is fear."[38] It was Montesquieu's great insight in *The Spirit of the Laws* to perceive that each regime has its own distinctive "principle," by which he meant the "human passions that set it in motion."[39] Thus he argued that the principle of democracy is

37. Victor Gourevitch makes this point in his "Introduction" to LPW, xiii. See also Charles W. Hendel, *Jean-Jacques Rousseau: Moralist*, 2d ed. (Indianapolis: Bobbs-Merrill, 1964).

38. Thomas Hobbes, *Leviathan*, edited by Edwin Curley (Indianapolis: Hackett, 1994), 88.

39. Charles de Secondat, baron de Montesquieu, *The Spirit of the Laws*, trans. and ed.

virtue,[40] which he understood as the "love of the laws and the home-land."[41] He defined honor as the principle of monarchy,[42] and saw that the principle of despotism is fear.[43] Although he understood human nature to be everywhere the same, he saw that both political and natural causes combined to produce the diversity of different peoples recorded by travelers and historians.

Rousseau agrees with Montesquieu that the diversity of dominant passions is both the cause and consequence of different political regimes, but he takes Montesquieu's analysis one step further. Montesquieu's political science is primarily descriptive of more or less *static* states of affairs: it explains the distinctive passions that make each regime what it is, but has little to say about the genesis of those passions and the changes they are likely to undergo as the circumstances that produced them vary. Rousseau, however, aims to formulate a *dynamic* and predictive understanding of politics and peoples: he seeks to understand why one people is moved by virtue, another by ambition or avarice, and yet another by the love of freedom—and to discover what causes a people's dominant passion to change. In a manuscript fragment, he describes the kind of knowledge required to construct such an account: "In order to judge well of the formation of peoples and of their revolutions, it is necessary to trace them back to the principles of the passions of men, to the general causes which make them act" (OC 3:529). A truly dynamic understanding of politics requires more than just a taxonomy of the different passions that move human beings, such as Hobbes supplies in *Leviathan*. It demands knowledge of the *principles of the passions*, an account of the causes that, by making individuals experience this or that passion, explain why they are disposed to act as they do.

Rousseau's account of the principles of the passions embodies two fundamental conceptual innovations. First, as previously noted, Rousseau views human nature as *dynamic* rather than static. Although our biological nature is fixed, that nature includes principles that account both for the development and changes in the passions individuals experience over the course of their lives and for the changes in the ruling passions of peoples over time. Thus, Rousseau's model of the soul explains why "each age [of life] has its own springs that make it move" (E 431) and why "the Mankind of one age is not the Mankind of another age" (D2 186). The second major conceptual innovation in Rousseau's account of human nature is this: his

Anne M. Cohler, Basia Carolyn Miller, and Harold Samuel Stone (Cambridge: Cambridge University Press, 1989), 21.

40. Ibid., 22–24.
41. Ibid., 36, 42–43.
42. Ibid., 26–27.
43. Ibid., 28–29.

account of the principles of the passions is *dialogical* rather than monistic, recognizing that fully human souls are not isolated monads, but are, rather, constituted in part by their relations with other persons.[44]

Rousseau's model of human nature is like a physics of the soul in that it seeks to explain the genesis of all the passions in terms of a few fundamental principles, which are set in motion by external stimuli. The most basic such principles are *self-love*, which inclines us to seek our own well-being, *perfectibility*, which accounts for the power of the human mind to develop itself, and *sensitivity* (which in the *Discourse on Inequality* is glossed as pity).[45] Two of the complex passions are particularly important in Rousseau's system. The foremost of these is *amour-propre*, which is a reflexive form of self-love that inclines us to seek the esteem of others.[46] The other is *conscience*, which inclines us to feel pleased with ourselves when we have done what we judge to have been reasonable and good and dissatisfied when we have done what we judge to have been unreasonable and wicked. In order to understand the problem of virtue as Rousseau conceives it, it will be helpful to look briefly at each of these five principles.

Self-love, Perfectibility, and Sensitivity

The most fundamental principle in the human soul, and indeed in the soul of every sentient creature, is self-love: "The source of our passions, the origin and principle of all the others, the only one born with man and which never leaves him so long as he lives is self-love—a primitive, innate passion, which is anterior to every other, and of which all the others are in a sense only modifications" (E 212–213; see also E 92, LB 935). That self-love is the most fundamental principle in the soul implies that an ineradicable part of our being constantly longs for our own, personal happiness. Rousseau consistently maintains that happiness is the sole end imposed on us by our nature, putting the point most forcefully in a speech delivered by Jean-Jacques to his younger friend: "You must be happy, dear Emile. That is the goal of every being with senses [*être sensible*]. It is the first desire which nature has impressed on us, and it is the only one which never leaves us" (E 442). The existence of this core of selfishness within the hu-

---

44. I borrow the expression "dialogical" from Charles Taylor, *The Ethics of Authenticity* (Cambridge: Harvard University Press, 1991), 33–35.

45. Note that these three basic principles in Rousseau's model of the soul roughly correspond to the three capacities that Aristotle perceives in the soul: self-love (desire, *orexis*), perfectibility (understanding, *nous*), sensitivity (perception, *aisthesis*). Aristotle, *Nicomachean Ethics*, translated by Terence Irwin (Indianapolis: Hackett, 1985), 1139a20.

46. In order to preserve the distinction between the two forms of self-love that Rousseau discusses, I will always leave the phrase "*amour-propre*" in the original French. Whenever the phrase "self-love" appears in a quotation from Rousseau, the original is *amour de soi*. Note that to achieve this consistency I have occasionally departed from the published translations.

man heart considerably complicates efforts to teach human beings to be good to others. Given that we generally do what our strongest passion inclines us to do, we rarely prefer the interest of another to self-interest, unless we are either "denatured" like the ancient Spartans, or unless we come to feel that attention to the welfare of others is a necessary condition of the enjoyment of any kind of personal happiness. The latter, of course, is the aim of Emile's education (E 41).

Rousseau calls the unlimited capacity human beings possess to develop their minds the faculty of *perfectibility*; this faculty is what distinguishes man from the other animals (D2 141, 207–208). Perfectibility, rather than reason, is our distinctive attribute because what we possess by nature is the ability to learn, the capacity to become rational and reasonable, and the capacity to develop an active and creative imagination, not the developed powers of reason itself. Perfectibility is also the primary principle that accounts for the distinctively malleable or dynamic nature of the human character: all of the other passions can be explained in terms of the interaction between self-love and reason, either conscious or unconscious. Although he insists that we do not naturally desire to know, Rousseau claims that the human mind nevertheless develops according to a regular pattern; as we become capable of more sophisticated ways of thinking, we learn to conceive our own well-being in new ways, and the original passion of self-love begins to manifest itself in more complex forms:

> As soon as we have, so to speak, consciousness of our sensations, we are disposed to seek or avoid the objects which produce them, at first according to whether they are pleasant or unpleasant to us, then according to the conformity or lack of it that we find between ourselves and these objects, and finally according to the judgments that we make about them on the basis of the idea of happiness or of perfection given us by reason. These dispositions are extended and strengthened as we become more capable of using our senses and more enlightened: but constrained by our habits, they are more or less corrupted by our opinions. Before this corruption they are what I call in us *nature*. (E 39)

When the only good we know is physical pleasure, self-love moves us to seek pleasure and to avoid pain. At this stage, what pains and pleases us is determined by our biological instincts: we experience our natural needs as pains (such as hunger, thirst, the soreness of injury, the pain of excessive heat or cold), and we experience the satisfaction of those needs as pleasurable. In the state of nature, the primitive human who pursues what is pleasant and avoids what is painful is guided reliably toward his preservation.

With further intellectual development, we learn to distinguish between what is pleasant and what conforms to our needs (i.e., what is useful); Emile discovers the idea of utility when he is about thirteen years old (E 177–178). At this stage, our interest in our own welfare inclines us to prefer what is useful to what is merely pleasant when they conflict (for example, we would eagerly swallow the bitter medicine in order to cure a fatal disease). With still further intellectual development, we come to form ideas about what it means to be a happy and good human being and act based on those ideas. This level of intellectual development is attained by all normal adults in any society, even the savage protosociety of the golden age; Emile reaches this stage when he is about sixteen.

To say that we are *sensitive* is simply to say that we are capable of *feeling*; that is, we are so constituted that we respond to external stimuli. Rousseau states that we possess a purely "passive and organic sensitivity" as one of the basic elements of our biological makeup. This organic sensitivity is nothing other than our capacity to receive information about the world around us by means of our sense organs (D 112).[47] As our minds and our bodies develop, however, human beings acquire an "active and moral sensitivity" (D 112). This moral sensitivity is a complex principle, produced in a mature body by the interaction between a developed intelligence and the principle of self-love, and it enables us to attach "our affections to beings who are foreign to us" (D 112). Rousseau maintains that this moral sensitivity is the source of all of the distinctively human passions, both the benign ones—pity, compassion, benevolence, affection, and the rest—and the vicious ones—envy, hatred, resentment, avarice, and so on.[48]

47. In order to attend carefully to the ways in which Rousseau deploys the concept of *sensibilité*, that French term has consistently been translated in the present work as "sensitivity," though the English word "sensibility" could also be used. Likewise, the adjective *sensible* has consistently been translated as "sensitive," though "sensible" is also possible. Note that to achieve this consistency, I have occasionally departed from the published translations. It has, unfortunately, proved impossible to be equally faithful in English to the linkages between these concepts and the related verb *sentir* (to sense or to feel) and the noun *sentiment* (sentiment or feeling). The reader should bear in mind that the English terms related to both sensing and feeling refer to a single family of etymologically related French terms.

48. In the *Discourse on Inequality*, which he wrote before *Emile* or *Rousseau Judge of Jean-Jacques: Dialogues* (hereafter referred to as the *Dialogues*), Rousseau ascribed the origin of all the benign passions not to sensitivity, but to pity (D2 153–154), which he describes as one of the "two principles prior to reason" that operates in the human soul (D2 127). As Roger Masters has demonstrated, however, the evidence Rousseau cites in the *Discourse on Inequality* is inadequate to support his claim that pity is a truly fundamental element in the soul. See Roger D. Masters, *The Political Philosophy of Rousseau* (Princeton: Princeton University Press, 1968), 139–141. In fact, Rousseau offers a few hints in the *Discourse on Inequality* itself to suggest that he was offering in that work a simplified account he knew to be less than fully correct (see, e.g., D2 153, 163). For the purpose of his argument about the foundations of society, all that matters is that pity be "prior" only to the development of reason that "engenders *amour-propre*" (D2 153–154), and that is precisely what Rousseau claims in *Emile*, where he maintains that pity is "the first relative sentiment which touches the human heart according to the order of nature" (E 222).

Rousseau suggests, however, that our "nascent sensitivity" has a "natural inclination," an innate tendency to develop in a certain direction (E 223). We are naturally inclined to extend our being to others, to identify ourselves with those around us, and to feel "goodness, humanity, commiseration, beneficence, and all the attractive and sweet passions naturally pleasing to men" (E 223). Rousseau calls this inclination "natural" because it is "directly derived from self-love" (D 9, 112). As these sweet passions are pleasurable, our interest in happiness gives us motive to seek them out. In contrast, the hostile passions (resentment, envy, anger, etc.) are *unnatural*, according to Rousseau, because they are "at odds with their own principle" (E 213). Although these passions, like the others, have their roots in our moral sensitivity (an aspect of our biological nature), Rousseau insists that the hostile passions are unnatural because they make it harder for us to attain our only natural end, happiness. In order to see how we come to feel such hostile passions, we must understand the most important principle in Rousseau's model of human nature, *amour-propre*.

Amour-propre, Conscience, and the Problem of Nature

At the most primitive stage of human development, self-love moves us only to seek our own, absolute well-being. But with the birth of moral sensitivity, we begin to feel that there are other beings like ourselves, whose relationship to us matters profoundly to our own well-being. At first, we take only pleasure in the company of others. Soon, however, we begin actively to compare ourselves to others ("reflecting," in Rousseau's terminology) (D 112; D2 153). Comparing ourselves to others, we naturally desire "to be in the first position;" this is when "self-love turns into *amour-propre*" (E 235). Reason is "the guide of *amour-propre*" because we may seek to determine how we measure up against others according to a variety of different yardsticks: Am I a faster runner than he? More musical? More skillful? More powerful? (E 92). The effects of *amour-propre* depend on the quality for which we seek to be esteemed, on what we care most about—in short, on what we love. This in turn often depends on the preferences of those people on whom we depend, either for the satisfaction of our material needs or simply because we believe that their love or esteem is necessary for our happiness (see, e.g., E 330–331).

In one who desires the love of a particular beloved, *amour-propre* manifests itself as desire and jealously. In one who desires wealth, *amour-propre* takes the form of avarice and envy; in one who desires power, it becomes ambition and resentment. Although *amour-propre* lies at the root of every vice, it can also inspire virtuous action. In one who lives for country, *amour-propre* appears as patriotism. In one who seeks the esteem only of those who are wise, *amour-propre* manifests itself as virtue. This point is essential to a proper understanding of Rousseau's social theory, and it has been in-

sufficiently appreciated by many commentators: *amour-propre* is not necessarily bad for us, and it does not necessarily incline us to do evil. *Amour-
propre* is only bad for us when it is inflamed into the desire to be richest or
most powerful or indeed to achieve any distinction that entails the subjection of others. But *amour-propre* need not always be thus inflamed. Indeed,
that is why it can be "a useful . . . instrument," albeit a "dangerous" one (E
244). Rousseau suggests that we transform *amour-propre* "into a virtue" by
extending it to others (E 243, 338), and this transformation represents the
culminating achievement of Emile's education.[49]

Conscience, according to Rousseau, is the faculty that inclines us to delight in what we judge to be good and to be distressed by what we deem
to be evil. In this way, it serves as the bridge between practical reason and
action, connecting knowledge of right and wrong with the passions that
motivate action. Every normal adult has a conscience (D 242), but not every
conscience is equally well formed: vicious people brazenly commit wrongs
that would pain the more sensitive consciences of the virtuous.[50] Reason
alone makes moral judgments, which is why Rousseau insists that the conscience "cannot be developed without it" (E 67; LB 936). Although conscience cannot act in a soul without reason, Rousseau nevertheless also
maintains that the operation of conscience is "independent of reason" (E
67). This observation has the air of paradox about it, but Rousseau's point
has a straightforward explanation: conscience operates independently of
our *active and conscious* power of reason, acting instead, like love, in the *unconscious* operation of our minds. This distinction between the active
power of reason and the conscience explains how it is possible to convince
oneself on the basis of bad but plausible reasons that an action is morally
innocent and then, having done the action, to feel guilty about it later.

In Rousseau's model of the soul, the conscience is an outgrowth of our
natural self-love as that principle interacts with our developing intelligence. At the first two stages of intellectual development, we regard ourselves solely as sensitive creatures—beings who feel. At each of these
developmental stages, self-love issues a single command. At first it is *seek
what is pleasant*; then it is *seek what is useful* (E 39). At the highest stage, how-

49. N. J. H. Dent, *Rousseau: An Introduction to his Psychological, Social and Political Theory*
(New York: Basil Blackwell, 1988), chap. 2.
50. A number of scholars have concluded otherwise, holding that the Rousseauian conscience is in effect an innate moral compass, itself distinguishing right from wrong (see, e.g.,
Judith N. Shklar, *Men and Citizens: A Study of Rousseau's Social Theory* [Cambridge: Cambridge
University Press, 1985], 64). It is true that the Savoyard Vicar and Rousseau's own *Moral Letters* to Sophie d'Houdetot suggest as much, but both of these sources contain a number of doctrines that, though they do not comport with the more sophisticated account of the soul
developed in the body of *Emile*, would be useful for their addressees to believe. Belief in the
infallibility of conscience is one such edifying, but false, doctrine.

ever, self-love mediated by reason leads us to see ourselves in a double light. We come to see ourselves not only as *sensitive* creatures, but also as *intelligent* ones—beings who think and who willingly act based on those deliberations. At this stage, self-love issues two commands, corresponding to the two aspects of our dual nature: *seek happiness* (that is, seek the good of a sensitive being), and *seek perfection* (that is, seek the good of an intelligent and moral being) (E 39). Mediated by our intelligence, the single end we have from nature becomes doubled: we long both to be happy *and* to be worthy of being so. Rousseau's account of human nature implies that no person of developed intelligence can achieve a lasting state of well-being without both. The fact that the demands of happiness and moral perfection do not always coincide is the permanent aspect of the human problem as Rousseau understands it.

Rousseau's dynamic model of human nature explains how and why human nature can seem to change over time, even though our genetic inheritance remains essentially constant. The dynamic aspect of human nature, however, considerably complicates the effort to distinguish what is natural from what is not, as Rousseau knew perfectly well. His contemporaries, the *philosophes*, maintained that nature is nothing but habit, that no permanent motives or principles occur in the human soul, only habits that have been acquired and could in principle be entirely replaced by other habits (E 39). Rousseau agrees that external influences can induce people to adopt almost any habit, but he notes that many habits do not endure once their external supports have been removed. The difference between those that endure and those that pass away is this: some harmonize with the basic motives in our souls, whereas others oppose them; the first are "conformable to nature," and the others are not (E 39). Thus Rousseau himself implicitly distinguishes between what is "conformable to nature" or natural relative to some condition and what is simply or unconditionally natural (because it is a constitutive and permanent component of human nature). Late in *Emile*, for example, he warns his readers against conflating "what is natural in the savage state" with "what is natural in the civil state" (E 406). In that passage, he notes explicitly the condition under which some attributes can be understood as natural. Unfortunately, Rousseau is not always so explicit, and in order to present a clear account of his thought it will be helpful to distinguish between what is *conditionally* natural from what is *unconditionally* (or *absolutely*) natural.

Rousseau supposes that the human mind develops according to a regular pattern, just as the body does. As our bodies and minds mature, our innate self-love manifests itself in progressively more complex forms, but it continues to direct us to one constant end: namely, our own well-being. Emile is the "man of nature" (E 205, 255) because he is educated so that his natural disposition to seek his own welfare is "strengthened and extended as [he] become[s] more capable of using [his] senses and more enlightened" (E 39). These strengthened and extended dispositions are "what [Rousseau] call[s] in us *nature*" (E 39). Emile is moved, first to seek what is pleasant, then what is useful, and finally he will come to understand that seeking his own welfare requires him to pursue both his own happiness and his moral perfection. At each stage, his dispositions are conditionally natural—natural relative to the circumstances in which he finds himself. Rousseau designs Emile's education so that he will not be moved by any passions that tend contrary to the end indicated by the principle of self-love: he will not have any of the vicious and self-destructive (hence, in Rousseau's view, *unnatural*) passions associated with inflamed *amour-propre*.

FRIENDSHIP AND EDUCATION TO VIRTUE

Rousseau's practical, and *useful*, response to the political and moral condition of his age is that of the citizen in the passage from the second preface to *Julie* quoted at the beginning of this chapter. Rousseau does not merely tell his readers to be good and wise so that we will be happy: more knowledge is not what we need to solve our problems. We need to change the objects of our love and thus the orientation of our *amour-propre*. Rather than seek esteem based on wealth, influence, or any other good whose pursuit characteristically puts us at odds with others, we must seek esteem on the basis of some genuinely common good, such as our devotion to the good of our community or our attachment to the moral law of reason. To make us love the state of virtue that alone can enable us to be happy, Rousseau composed his enchanting romances, *Emile* and *Julie*, which depict for us in the most attractive light possible the life of an ordinary man and an ordinary woman whose lives are only made extraordinary by the self-commanding virtue both come to possess. These are truly Rousseau's exemplary lives.[51]

It is not so easy for an ordinary man, reared in the conventional manner, to emulate Emile; it is no easier for a woman, reared in the ordinary manner, to emulate Julie. (Julie's lot is in fact far harder than Emile's.) Certain of the external features of their lives are, of course, easily enough adopted. It is possible to live in the country rather than in the city; it is possible to find a career such as Emile's that offers maximum independence from any

---

51. In contrast, Christopher Kelly argues that Rousseau depicts himself in his *Confessions* as the exemplary man. *Rousseau's Exemplary Life: The "Confessions" as Political Philosophy* (Ithaca, N.Y.: Cornell University Press, 1987), 69, 75. I think Kelly's view cannot be sustained because Rousseau insists so strenuously on his own uniqueness. See, e.g., C 5, 52.

particular employer's will. It is possible for a mother to breast-feed her children and to care for them herself (E 45–46). It is also possible for both men and women to devote a portion of their time to caring for some of their neighbors who are in need (E 435–436, 439–442; J 96–100, 436–439; ML 1117–1118). These "externals" are important because they help us transform our hearts, reorienting our lives away from the pursuit of goods such as money and status that typically set us at odds with one another and toward the pursuit of goods that can genuinely be shared such as love and friendship.

These "moral strategies" are an important part of the psychic transformation Rousseau means to encourage, but they do not suffice to accomplish it. To adopt a morally healthy way of life, such that our interests do not set us at odds with our fellows, is not yet to love virtue. The virtuous man lives in an imperfect regime as though he lives in a model state: he respects the law, does the good, and treats his neighbors as equals and friends. These are precisely the lessons that Emile ultimately learns from his tutor. Such virtue is rare because it requires an extraordinary degree of wisdom to consistently resist the seductions of the imagination and to distinguish real goods from merely apparent ones. The virtuous man must constantly resist the temptation to see himself as the many would see him, judging him according to his wealth or influence. He must see himself as a wise man would see him, judging him according to his character. Only the exceptional few—and Rousseau tells us that he personally was *not* among them—have the capacity thus to rule themselves unaided (see D 158). We ordinary people require an authority to rectify our judgment and to strengthen our will, a figure through whose eyes we are enabled to see ourselves correctly. Even the product of Rousseau's ideal education, Emile, continues to require his tutor's guidance once he has become a man. It follows *a fortiori* that those of us who have not received Emile's education will require the guidance of a wise figure of authority if we are to stop loving false goods and are to learn to love what is truly good.

If we need to be guided to virtue by the influence of a wise figure of authority, to whom should we turn? Rousseau consistently maintained that the inequality that authority presupposes generally reduces to servility or inspires resentment among those who would be improved by it, and he was personally well acquainted with the failures common to actual figures of authority.[52] For authority to be genuinely palliative, Rousseau saw that it would have to be democratic—that is, compatible with equality; and he knew of only one relationship of equality, namely friendship. Friendship in its best form is a freely chosen state of reciprocal affection and mutual

---

52. Shklar, *Men and Citizens*, chap. 4, esp. 162–163.

influence, according to Rousseau: where friendship exists, the barriers erected by *amour-propre* are temporarily breached. Paradoxically, only a friend can exercise influence or authority without provoking rebellion or creating dependence. That is why all the authority figures Rousseau describes in any detail accomplish their educative work by befriending their pupils.[53]

In both his novels, Rousseau makes himself present to the reader through the force of his unprecedentedly personal writing,[54] and he invites his readers to befriend the authorial Jean-Jacques they perceive in his writings. Indeed, Rousseau consistently describes the ideal relation of author to reader as one of friendship (J 14–17; D 53, 244–245; RW 7). To the readers who see themselves as aspiring Emiles and Julies, Rousseau represents himself as their personal tutor and friend, Jean-Jacques. Just as the tutor introduces Emile to the ideals of love and virtue that he comes to accept, so also does Rousseau introduce those ideals to his readers. In *Emile*, Rousseau presents the tutor's mediating friendship as the harmonizing influence that stabilizes Emile and Sophie's love for each other, enabling them to find happiness in their virtue. Likewise, when Rousseau directs his readers to imitate his happy and virtuous couple, he seeks to inspire his readers to share Jean-Jacques' lofty ideal of love and the family.

In writing didactic and hortatory novels, Rousseau adopts a political stance akin to that of the Great Legislator he describes in the *Social Contract*.[55] The Legislator invokes divine authority in order to transform a people of self-interested individuals into a body of citizens united by a general will (SC 68–72). The Legislator must rectify the moral perceptions of "the people," that "wills the good, but by itself does not always see it"; he must enable the people to see the good and then to act accordingly (SC 68). In other words, Rousseau writes, private individuals "must be obligated to conform their wills to their reason" (SC 68). By dint of his extraordinary authority, the Legislator inspires a people to affirm the law he has crafted for them; if he has proposed good laws, the operation of those laws over time will tend to produce the right kind of citizen.

Similarly, Rousseau strives to tame his readers' selfish *amour-propre* so

---

53. The tutor, Jean-Jacques, makes Emile his friend; the Savoyard Vicar makes the young Rousseau his friend; and M. de Wolmar makes Saint-Preux into his friend.

54. Strong, *Rousseau*, 8–12.

55. Thus I agree with Shklar that Rousseau cannot be seen as an actual Legislator for real bodies politic—even for Poland and Corsica. He clearly acknowledges that he lacks the specific information a real political founder would require. (On his lack of knowledge about Corsica, see C 543–546. On Poland, see GP 177–178). Similarly, I must disagree with Hilail Gildin, who maintains that Rousseau acts as a philosophical legislator in the *Social Contract* because he tells legislators what they must do. Hilail Gildin, *Rousseau's "Social Contract": The Design of the Argument* (Chicago: University of Chicago Press, 1983), 24, 78, 82–83, 89.

that they will be able to perceive the goodness of a universal justice and to will accordingly. As with the Legislator, Rousseau has only the authority and the force of his personality at his disposal to persuade his subjects to adopt the reforms he proposes: according to the *Social Contract*, "the great soul of the Lawgiver is the true miracle which must prove his mission" (SC 71). For this reason, Rousseau had to make his soul publicly known through autobiography and defend his public persona against the attacks of both the authorities and the *philosophes*.[56] Of course, Rousseau is not literally a legislator because he does not establish new political institutions and because he seeks primarily to transform *individual* readers with his novels. But in attempting to create motives for individuals to act with the justice appropriate to a universal republic, Rousseau's novels lay the foundation for a better political order where the effects of disordered *amour-propre* will be less apparent.

In the *Republic*, Plato's Socrates educates the group of friends with whom he is conversing even as he describes in his speeches the educational institutions of his Kallipolis. Lacking the wisdom imputed to the philosopher-kings, Socrates' young friends must aspire to a lesser, but still worthy ideal. Their personal encounter with Socrates teaches them to aspire to be worthy of living in the beautiful city he has described for them in speech, whose institutions will serve for them as a model of right conduct and a standard against which to judge the regimes they will construct in their own souls. "In heaven," Socrates tells them, "perhaps, a pattern is laid up for the man who wants to see and found a city within himself on the basis of what he sees. It doesn't make a difference whether it is or will be somewhere. For he would mind the things of this city alone, and of no other."[57] Socrates gave his friends an image of the sublime principles of justice he alone could see and thus enabled them to love it.

As with the *Republic*, to which it is Rousseau's "democratic" reply, the *Emile* proceeds on more than one level.[58] Just as Plato's Socrates teaches his young friends to love justice by describing for them the more perfect educational institutions of the beautiful city in speech, so also does Rousseau's idealized Jean-Jacques educate us, the readers of *Emile*, by describing for us the perfect domestic education that exists only in Rousseau's text. Rousseau sees that life in modern regimes requires of us a hard virtue: we must be disposed to respect the rights of others. Little in our societies as they are tends to inspire us with this disposition, however. To the contrary,

---

56. For an excellent account of the *philosophes'* hostility to Rousseau, see Mark Hulliung, *The Autocritique of Enlightenment: Rousseau and the Philosophes* (Cambridge: Harvard University Press, 1994), chap. 6.

57. Plato, *Republic*, trans. by Allan Bloom (New York: Basic Books, 1968), 529b.

58. Bloom, "Introduction" to *Emile*, 4.

we are constantly tempted to see ourselves as others do, judging ourselves by their unwise standards. To secure him against this temptation, Emile is introduced by his teacher and friend to the pattern of a regime and a new basis for judging himself. Jean-Jacques teaches his pupil and friend that "[T]he eternal laws of nature and order do exist. For the wise man, they take the place of positive law. They are written in the depth of his heart by conscience and reason. It is to these that he ought to enslave himself in order to be free" (E 473). In thus addressing Emile, Jean-Jacques speaks also to us, the readers. For us, however, it is Emile himself who serves as a pattern. We come to Rousseau's text imperfectly educated ("sick with ills that can be cured" according to *Emile*'s epigraph), unable to act on the "eternal laws of nature and order" that the disorder of our lives has done much to obscure. By showing us the soul of Emile, Jean-Jacques gives us a glimpse of the sublime virtue that Rousseau alone can see and thus enables us to love it. Rousseau's procedure is ultimately more democratic than Plato's because the form in which he presents his teaching makes it accessible to a wider audience: unlike the Platonic dialogues, which make the greatest demands upon the understanding, Rousseau's romances speak directly to the heart.

AN OUTLINE OF THE ARGUMENT

The argument of this book divides into two parts. The first half examines Rousseau's diagnosis of our ills and introduces the model of human nature in terms of which he formulates it. The second examines the solutions he proposes in order to make us happier and better. The present chapter has introduced the basic elements of Rousseau's model of the human soul and has shown, in outline, how a small number of fundamental principles interact to produce the complex passions that move the hearts of civilized human beings. Chapters 2 and 3 examine the evidence and arguments Rousseau uses to demonstrate the validity of that model; the first of the two chapters examines the *political argument* he advances in support of his model, and the second evaluates the *ethical argument*. Both chapters and both arguments share a similar structure: each begins by identifying certain human phenomena for which no adequate explanation can be formulated if one assumes that human beings are basically moved by some combination of self-love and reason alone; each then proceeds to show how Rousseau's model of the soul, which places *amour-propre* at its center, can make sense of the otherwise inexplicable phenomena.

Chapter 4 links the two parts of the book, showing that Rousseau's model of human nature can indeed account for the reality of friendship and love. The model's ability to explain the sharp differences between erotic love and friendship also proves the superiority of Rousseau's conception of human nature to Aristotle's model of the soul, which treats erotic love as a species of friendship. Chapter 5 explains why Rousseau's model of the human soul leads him to the conclusion that virtue is a necessary condition of happiness for civilized human beings. In chapter 6, the course of Emile's education is examined to discover the principles of moral education, as Rousseau understands them. Chapter 7 examines the novels *Emile* and *Julie* as didactic novels, which contain an education on virtue designed specifically for us, the readers. The book concludes with some Rousseauian reflections on the relationship between virtue and contemporary liberal politics.

2 The Political Argument

UNLESS ROUSSEAU'S ACCOUNT of human nature can be shown to be true, or at least substantially so, we have scant reason to accept his moral and political teachings. Rousseau himself plainly aspired to do more than design a provocative but fanciful portrait of the human soul, claiming to have based his account on what he had observed "in Nature, which never lies" (D2 133). He advances three lines of argument to support his model of human nature: political, ethical, and autobiographical. The first two of these arguments share the same structure. Each begins by identifying certain aspects of human behavior for which it is impossible to account if we assume, as did the *philosophes*, that human beings are moved by reason and self-interest tempered by a principle of natural sociability. The political argument, developed in the *Discourse on Inequality*, claims that only Rousseau's account of human nature can explain the true foundations of political society. This argument is examined at length in the present chapter. The ethical argument, developed primarily in *Emile*, claims that only Rousseau's model of human nature can adequately explain the causes of human unhappiness and evil. That argument is examined in chapter 3.

Rousseau's autobiographies contain a third, distinctive line of argument in support of his model of human nature. In those works, Rousseau presents a detailed account of himself and claims that he is himself "the man of nature." If this assessment were altogether correct (which is doubtful), Rousseau's autobiographies would present a more direct route to understanding human nature. This autobiographical argument, however, is parasitic on the other two: absent independent evidence that Rousseau rightly regards himself as "the man of nature," insufficient reason exists for us, as readers, to base our understanding of human nature on the results of Rousseau's introspection. Used judiciously, however, the autobiographical writings can help to explicate Rousseau's model of human nature. Insofar as he sought to make sense of his actions and feelings in the terms outlined in his own model of human nature, we may reasonably rely on the autobiographical writings to clarify the *content* of Rousseau's views.[1] But in order to judge whether to accept those views as true, we must examine the

---

1. Kelly, *Rousseau's Exemplary Life*, 47.

arguments Rousseau formulated on the basis of evidence to which we have independent access—the political argument of the *Discourse on Inequality* and the ethical argument of the *Emile*.

THE PUZZLE OF POLITICAL RIGHT

Rousseau composed the *Discourse on Inequality* to compete for the prize offered by the Dijon Academy in 1754, but by the time he was finished with it, Rousseau was certain that his submission would not be honored with the prize (C 326). His judgment was entirely correct. The Academy had solicited essays on the topic, What is the origin of inequality among men, and is it authorized by natural law? Rousseau's *Discourse on Inequality* answers both questions (see D2 159, 188) and also explains why those two questions have rather less to do with each another than their authors evidently supposed. It was the question of the origin of inequality that most interested Rousseau, and he perceived directly that no normative account of natural law could explain what motivated our most distant ancestors to establish the first inequalities of wealth, power, and status.[2] To answer that question would require knowledge of the principles of the human passions, and the *Discourse on Inequality* contains Rousseau's first effort to formulate such an account as well as his first systematic attempt at a demonstration of its truth—the political argument mentioned previously.[3] Rousseau makes clear the structure of his proof by stating precisely what he expects a sound theory of the soul to accomplish: it makes available "the solution to an infinite number of problems of ethics and of Politics" that had previously been unsolvable (D2 186, 128). In the *Discourse on Inequality*, however, Rousseau focuses his attention largely on solving one specific, but complex problem: identifying what he calls "the real foundations of human society" (D2 125). Stated somewhat differently, Rousseau seeks to discover the moment when "Right replacing violence, Nature was subjected to Law" (D2 131).[4]

It turns out that the search for the foundations of political society requires knowledge of the prepolitical, "savage" societies civilization sup-

2. As Rousseau observes in a related context, "moral proofs are without great force in matters of physics" (D2 213): that an outcome is rationally justified is no guarantee that anyone will be motivated to bring that outcome about.

3. What Rousseau explicitly claims to have proved in the *Discourse on Inequality* is that "man is naturally good" (D2 186–187, 197). But since Rousseau's proof of that claim presupposes the truth of his conception of human nature, I take him to be claiming to have established its truth as well.

4. That moment is, of course, the transaction described in the opening sentence of part 2: "The first man who, having enclosed a piece of ground, to whom it occurred to say 'this is mine' and found people sufficiently simple to believe him, was the true founder of civil society" (D2 161).

planted. As we shall see, Rousseau maintains that the structure of these savage societies is conditionally natural, and he calls its foundation *natural right* (*droit naturel*). The savages did not require formal constitutions and written laws; their social orders were created and sustained by the passions that were spontaneously generated in their hearts. In contrast, Rousseau holds that the structure of civil society is conventional; he calls its foundation *civil* or *political right* (*droit civil, droit politique*). It has not, as yet, been sufficiently appreciated that Rousseau's terms *droit naturel* and *droit politique* carry a range of meanings not conveyed by their obvious English equivalents, natural right and political right. The problem inheres in the word "*droit*," which carries a much wider range of meanings than does "right." Specifically, Rousseau's terms do not refer to Hobbesian liberties "to do or forbear" from doing certain things.[5] Rather, he uses the terms *natural right* and *civil right* to denote the different configurations of the passions that motivate people to fulfill their roles in the two different kinds of human social order.

It was not obvious to Rousseau's contemporaries, religious and secular, that the establishment and continuance of political society particularly required explanation. To the religious, it was evident that God had made man sociable, and that, but for original sin, humanity would have lived in a perfect state of harmony. After the Fall, however, the disordered passions of our sinful nature required restraint by the yoke of law, the sanction of force, and the establishment of inequality. Having become necessary, this inequality was understood by the religious to have been authorized by the law of nature and sanctioned by God in the Sacred Scriptures.[6] Nor did *philosophes* such as Voltaire and Buffon find the existence of political society in any way puzzling since they maintained that human beings are naturally social.[7] A bit more skeptical than his successors, Locke did not exactly claim that man is naturally social, although he did assert that a law of nature directs all human beings to preserve themselves as commodiously as possible and, insofar as is compatible with self-preservation, to refrain from harming others as well.[8] In his view, the establishment of civil society is sufficiently explained by reference to the numerous advantages of life in society over the state of nature—advantages that would be evident, he thought, to any rational person.

    5. Hobbes, *Leviathan*, 79–80.
    6. These, indeed, were the very doctrines advanced by the Abbé Talbert, in the discourse that won the prize awarded by the Dijon Academy in 1754. Roger Tisserand, ed., *Les concurrents de J.-J. Rousseau à l'Académie de Dijon pour le prix de 1754* (Paris: Boivin & Cie., 1936), 22.
    7. Mark Hulliung, *The Autocritique of Enlightenment: Rousseau and the Philosophes* (Cambridge: Harvard University Press, 1994), 61.
    8. John Locke, *Two Treatises of Government*, edited by Peter Laslett (Cambridge: Cambridge University Press, 1988), 270–271 (*Second Treatise*, §6). Further references to the *Second Treatise* use the abbreviation ST and a reference to the numbered sections in Locke's text.

To make sense of Rousseau's argument in the *Discourse on Inequality*, we must appreciate how completely he rejected these views and understand why he did so. In contrast to his contemporaries, who believed in the natural sociability of humanity, Rousseau regarded the very existence of political society as a puzzle requiring explanation. Few intellectuals today will find fault with him for "setting aside all the facts" about the early condition of humanity contained in the Bible (D2 132). Rousseau rejects Locke's account of the "rise of government" and the "original of political power," however, for essentially the same reason: he finds that the historical evidence contradicts it.[9] Locke suggests that civil society was born when people, recognizing the duties imposed upon them by the law of nature, consented to form a commonwealth in order to secure their natural rights more effectively. Insisting on the great advantages to be derived from civilization and on the considerable inconveniences of the state of nature, Locke concludes that people would be "quickly driven into society."[10] Rousseau, however, disagrees, pointing to the example of the savages— the indigenous peoples of the New World encountered by the European explorers. *They* lived in the state of nature, apparently quite contentedly, fiercely resisting all efforts to civilize them.

The frontispiece to the *Discourse on Inequality* vividly illustrates this resistance. That engraving depicts a man, discarding his European garb and abandoning a European settlement, apparently to go live among the savages. Actually, the engraving does not just illustrate the general failure of the colonial powers to civilize the natives; it illustrates a specific and well-documented episode that Rousseau judged to be of supreme importance (D2 219–221). The Governor of the Dutch colony at the Cape of Good Hope had reared from infancy a child taken from among the natives. The youth had received a fine education and had sufficiently impressed his patron that he was sent to work in a position of some responsibility. Having chanced to visit some of his native relatives, however, the young man abandoned his civilized existence, choosing instead to live among the savages. To Rousseau, the importance of this incident lay in this: the Europeanized savage was in the rare position of being able to appreciate the advantages of both ways of life, and, from this epistemically privileged position, he rejected civilization. Here, then, is the crux of the first problem that his account of human nature aimed to solve: How can political society have first come into being, given that those people who were in a position to choose intelligently between them (in the seventeenth and eighteenth centuries, at least), preferred the savage life to civilization?

In the preface to the *Discourse on Inequality*, Rousseau draws attention to

9. Ibid., ST § 1.
10. Ibid., ST § 127.

a second aspect of political society that those inclined to regard man as naturally rational and social had overlooked. He writes that:

> Human society viewed with a calm and disinterested gaze seems at first to exhibit only the violence of powerful men and the oppression of the weak; the mind rebels at the harshness of the first; one is inclined to deplore the blindness of the others; and since nothing is less stable among men than those external relationships that are more often the product of chance than of wisdom, and that are called weakness or power, wealth or poverty, human establishments seem at first to be founded on piles of quicksand. (D2 128)

Looking at the horrific inequalities he could see all around him in Paris, Rousseau was both appalled and mystified. His disgust is easily understood: it *is* revolting that "a handful of people abound in superfluities while the starving multitude lacks in necessities" (D2 188). One requires no elaborate moral theory to see the injustice of that state of affairs; it is *"manifestly against the law of nature, however defined"* (D2 188, emphasis added). What is mysterious is the fact that the people of Paris, and indeed the peoples of virtually every nation known to Rousseau, generally put up with such oppressive inequalities, in effect acquiescing in their own subjection. Here is the second puzzle requiring a solution: Why does the "multitude" everywhere put up with being oppressed by "a handful of people"?

ROUSSEAU'S STATE OF NATURE: PSYCHOLOGICAL NOT PHILOSOPHICAL

In the first part of the *Discourse on Inequality*, Rousseau puts a new slant on what was, by the middle of the eighteenth century, a familiar philosophical device: namely, to envision the state of nature, which had been understood since Hobbes as "the state of men without civil society."[11] What is most novel about Rousseau's approach to the idea of the state of nature is what he hopes to learn from the thought experiment. In his hands, it is an exercise not in philosophy, but in psychology, which is what he needs to know in order to identify the real, historical foundations of political society. Although both Hobbes and Locke suggest that something akin to their states of nature may once have existed in the historical past or even in some places during their own times,[12] their main purpose in seeking the state of nature is neither historical nor psychological but philosophical. In their hands, the state of nature is what John Rawls terms a "device of representation,"[13] a theoretical construct used to illustrate the consequences of their

---

11. Thomas Hobbes, *De Cive*, translated by Thomas Hobbes, in *Man and Citizen*, ed. Bernard Gert (Indianapolis: Hackett, 1991), 109.
12. Hobbes, *Leviathan*, 77; Locke, ST §§ 101–108.
13. Rawls, *Political Liberalism*, 24.

conceptions of the natural freedom and equality of human beings and thus to discover the ends that political society is established to accomplish.

Rousseau's account of "man's natural state" scarcely resembles the states of nature presented by Hobbes and Locke (D2 134). That divergence is hardly surprising, since the question Rousseau introduces it to answer and the method he uses to develop it differ from his predecessors' accounts. Since Rousseau aims to show how the simplest passions found in the human heart are combined and modified under the influence of our developing reason to produce the more complex passions that account for the establishment of political society and for the changes that we perceive within those societies, he begins by imagining human beings without any intellectual development of any kind (D2 134). Rousseau's method is, at first, analytic: he examines the developed abilities and passions of modern human beings, discerns what must be attributed to reason, and concludes that what remains must be attributed to instinct—that is, to nature. But there are also two somewhat more empirical dimensions to his search for the innate passions and powers of human beings. First, he supposes that human beings without developed powers of abstract reasoning must be in some ways similar to the animals, that also lack them. Second, he supposes that, since the savages are closer to nature than are the civilized people known to us, the most natural human beings must resemble the savages more closely than they resemble us. All of this is to say, however, that Rousseau's account of nascent man's way of life is necessarily hypothetical.[14]

Rousseau's account of the state of nature begins with a description of the most primitive man's physical existence.[15] This is plainly the most speculative part of his argument, but, fortunately, little or nothing in his larger argument depends upon its being true. Because he does not know whether human beings had undergone far-reaching physical changes in the most distant past, Rousseau assumes that human beings have always been physically constituted as we are today (D2 134). Comparing the strength and vigor of wild animals to the weakness and servility of their domesticated counterparts, Rousseau concludes that nascent man must have been stronger and more vigorous than civilized men and women (D2 138–139). Extrapolating from the physical strength and self-sufficiency of the savages, Rousseau concludes that nascent man must have been even stronger, less intelligent, less sociable, and even more at home in the wil-

14. Victor Gourevitch, "Rousseau's 'Pure' State of Nature," *Interpretation* 16 (1988), 33–34.

15. All references in the text to "primitives" refer to the inhabitants of the most ancient period of Rousseau's state of nature, described at D2 157; following Rousseau's usage (see D2 161), the term "nascent man" is sometimes also used to describe these primitives. Both nascent man and the primitive are to be distinguished from the "savage," who inhabits the second period of Rousseau's state of nature (and possesses a greater degree of intellectual and "moral" development than they do).

derness than the savages encountered by the Europeans had been seen to be (D2 136–140).

Far more important is Rousseau's account of the soul of nascent man, since this is his account of the basic capacities and motives—the principles of soul—in terms of which he explains the origins and foundations of political society. In this section of the argument, Rousseau's claims rest on more secure epistemological foundations because he can here proceed, as he could not before, by analyzing the attributes of the men and women known to his experience. He perceives in the human soul two principles "prior to reason"—*self-love* and *pity* (D2 127). (It should be remembered that the account of the soul Rousseau develops in the *Discourse on Inequality* is subsequently revised in *Emile*, where pity is presented no longer as a basic passion in the human soul but as a manifestation of our natural sensitivity interacting with our developing reason). Rousseau holds, further, that human beings naturally possess the capacity to become rational and reasonable. This capacity he calls *perfectibility* (D2 159).

The most controversial aspect of Rousseau's account of human nature is what it omits: any reference to a natural principle of sociability. Rousseau declines to posit the existence of any such principle because he perceives that to say that human beings form societies because they are naturally sociable does not actually *explain* anything, but merely states a tautology. If human beings invariably formed the same social orders in every place and at all times, as ants and bees form identical colonies, then it would be plausible to suppose that a single, constant instinct was the cause. But human societies are notable for their diversity; not only are different sorts of political and communal structures formed, even the structure of the family varies from time to time and from place to place. By declining to posit a principle of natural sociability in the human soul, Rousseau allows himself to seek more profoundly for the true causes that explain why we form different kinds of social orders.

The resultant portrait of man's natural state typically shocks readers. Rousseau's natural primitive wanders alone in the forests "without industry, without speech, without settled abode, without war, and without tie, without any need of others of his kind and without any desire to harm them, perhaps even without ever recognizing any one of them individually" (D2 157). The primitive is able to live on his own thus isolated because, moved more by instinct than by intelligence, "he sensed only his true needs" and was able to satisfy them by his own efforts (D2 157). All of these consequences must follow, however, if we undertake the thought experiment Rousseau prescribes: to imagine what human beings would be like if deprived of all of the developed faculties whose exercise depends on the cultivation of reason. Rousseau's portrait of this primitive man has been harshly criticized for its historical implausibility.[16] Modern anthropology tells us that human beings never lived in the solitary, silent, wandering style of the Rousseauian primitive.

This anthropological evidence does not necessarily invalidate Rousseau's argument about human nature, however. Recall that, lacking knowledge of the physical evolution of the human race, Rousseau conceived the pure state of nature as a time when human beings, although physically constituted as we are, lived wholly without benefit of any developed culture or power of abstract reasoning. If it is true that human beings, constituted as we are, did not exist in the most primitive state Rousseau envisions, that would show only that the creatures from which Homo sapiens evolved must have already possessed the first rudiments of culture, so that the first human beings were reared within some kind of cultural framework from the start. It does not matter whether human beings ever lived in Rousseau's pure state of nature because the point of the thought experiment in the first part of the *Discourse on Inequality* is not to discover the truth about the biological origins of the human species. (Had that been his aim, he would have had to pursue the suggestion he raises at the outset (D2 134) that our most distant ancestors did not always possess the same bodily form as we now enjoy). His aim, rather, is to establish the groundwork for the argument of the second part of the *Discourse on Inequality* by disclosing the principles and capacities that are natural to mankind, that is, are innate aspects of our biological makeup.

Rousseau announces two noteworthy conclusions at the end of the first part of the *Discourse on Inequality*: namely, that human beings in the pure state of nature would be happy and that neither subordination nor oppression would occur among them. Neither conclusion is of much substantive importance, since both descriptions are of a purely hypothetical state of affairs, which in all likelihood never existed.[17] Both conclusions are, however, illustrative of important formal consequences of the model of human nature that Rousseau articulates in the *Discourse on Inequality*. Rousseau supposes that the primitive humans of the pure state of nature would have generally lived contentedly because their instincts would have reliably identified their true needs and their powers would generally have sufficed to enable them to satisfy those needs (D2 142–143, 149–150). Having neither natural motive nor need to harm others, and a weak motive dis-

16. Masters, *Rousseau*, 431.

17. Rousseau seems to have believed that the state of nature might have existed as he conceives it; he concedes only that it "perhaps never did exist" at D2 125 and draws on the best biological and anthropological evidence available to him to show that it might well have existed as he envisions it. Nevertheless, this concession indicates that Rousseau himself did not believe that the large, "moral" argument of the *Discourse on Inequality* depended for its validity upon the historical accuracy of his claims about the pure state of nature.

posing him not to harm them (pity), the most primitive human would have lived in a state of natural peace. Rousseau's portrait of the contented human primitive, living ignorantly in the pure state of nature is simply a striking illustration of the formal principle that one is happy when one has no unsatisfiable desires, i.e., when one's powers are perfectly proportioned to one's desires (see E 80–81).

Rousseau argues that despite the range of physical inequalities that would necessarily be present in any population of human beings, neither mastery nor servitude, nor indeed any "moral" inequality of any kind would occur in the pure state of nature. Once again, this argument is important, not for what it shows about Rousseau's hypothetical state of nature, but for the vivid fashion in which it illustrates the conditions required for inequality and oppression to arise:

> I constantly hear it repeated that the stronger will oppress the weak; but explain to me what the word oppression here means... A man might seize the fruits another has picked, the game he has killed, the lair he used for shelter; but how will he ever succeed in getting himself obeyed by him? If I am tormented in one place, who will keep me from going somewhere else? Is there a man so superior to me in strength, and who, in addition, is so depraved, so lazy, and so ferocious as to force me to provide for his subsistence while he remains idle? . . . If his vigilance relaxes for a moment, I take twenty steps into the forest, my chains are broken, and he never sees me again in his life. (D2 158)

Breaking off this illustration, Rousseau states plainly the lesson he learns from these reflections: "Since ties of servitude are formed solely by men's mutual dependence and the reciprocal needs that unite them, it is impossible to subjugate a man without first having placed him in the position of being unable to do without another" (D2 159).

THE "TRUE FOUNDATIONS OF THE BODY POLITIC"

By the end of the first part of the *Discourse on Inequality*, Rousseau has introduced a simple model of human nature. By nature, human beings are ignorant, but perfectible: capable of acquiring language and of learning to reason abstractly. We are also sensitive beings, that is to say, we get information from our senses and respond emotionally (this is only implicit in the *Discourse on Inequality* account). As sensitive creatures, the most fundamental principle of our actions (our most basic motive) is self-love, the desire for our own welfare. At first, lacking any developed intelligence, we pursue our own welfare by seeking what pleases us and by avoiding what pains us; insofar as we live an existence close to that of the animals, our instinctive desires and aversions lead us more or less reliably to preserve ourselves, just as their instincts suffice to preserve the other animals as well. The behavior of human beings in the pure state of nature can be wholly explained in terms of this one principle. A second basic, albeit not absolutely fundamental, principle of our action is pity: the aversion to witness the suffering of others like ourselves.

In the second part of the *Discourse on Inequality*, Rousseau proposes to show the "origin and progress" of moral inequality "through the successive developments of the human mind" (D2 159). In other words, he aims to show how these two principles (self-love and pity) come to manifest themselves differently according to the developments of the human mind and the influence of the external environment, first accounting for the foundation of savage society and later for the foundation of political society. The first developments of the human heart, leading to the emergence of love and jealousy, account for the establishment and stability of the savage societies characteristic of the golden age, thus solving the first of the two mysteries to which he promises an answer. The most important psychic change, however, is the doubling of self-love into *amour-propre*, a transformation that takes place after human beings have begun to live together in communities and so have developed the ability to compare themselves to others and to conceive the desire for the esteem of others. Having shown how and why this new principle of human action arises in the savage state and is subsequently transformed, Rousseau uses it to explain the origins and foundations of political society, solving the other great mystery he had identified in the preface to the *Discourse on Inequality*. If his solution to both difficulties is sound, then he will indeed have vindicated the model of human nature in terms of which that solution is constructed.

Although the historical development Rousseau describes in the second part of the *Discourse on Inequality* contains many conjectural elements (and Rousseau explicitly calls it a "hypothetical history" at D2 128), he insists that the "consequences" he draws from that history will *not* be mere hypotheses, but truths (D2 159–160). In this section of the argument, Rousseau has two significant points of data with which to work. First, the existence of the savages, who were nearly all found living in prepolitical societies, in which they generally preferred to remain than to become civilized (D2 166–167, 177); and second, the existence of the oppressively inegalitarian, yet generally stable political societies of eighteenth-century Europe. These are two, real facts; where history does not record the actual transition from the savage state to the political state, Rousseau sees that "it is up to Philosophy to ascertain similar facts that might connect them" (D2

160).[18] Here is where knowledge of the principles of the passions proves its utility. Rousseau's conjectural history reveals the truth about the foundations of political society because "on the principles . . . established [in part one of the *Discourse on Inequality*], no other system could be formed that would not give . . . the same results and from which [one] could not draw the same conclusions" (D2 159). Although the particular events recounted in Rousseau's hypothetical history may be no more than conjectures, what matters is whether his dynamic model of the soul in fact explains what it purports to explain: the genesis and subsequent alteration of the different configurations of the human passions that constitute the basis of the prepolitical order of the savages (natural right) and that constitute the basis of civil society (civil right). Although one can tell different stories that correspond to the terms of Rousseau's model, that model of the soul does in fact account for everything it is required to explain.

"The happiest and most lasting epoch"

Rousseau begins his account by explaining how the savage societies discovered by the European explorers could have come into being, given that human beings do not naturally possess language or any social instinct (D2 161–164). The gist of his account is simple enough: human beings must have begun to develop their innate capacity to reason abstractly and to use language in response to external necessities. In the struggle to survive in hostile environments, human beings first learned to think abstractly, to speak in languages, to use tools, to cooperate with others, and so on. These first developments of the mind in turn led to the emergence of the configuration of reason-dependent passions that moved the savage peoples to live as they did. Rousseau emphasizes that even the most savage peoples known to anthropology owe much more to culture (and much less to nature) than any of his predecessors had realized. Having attributed the emergence of the first savage societies to the first developments of reason prompted by the operation of natural self-love, Rousseau proceeds to illustrate in detail the ways in which his model of human nature also explains the most distinctive features of those prepolitical societies. Above all, it explains why those societies were so resilient that very few natives were willing to become civilized when the European colonists proposed to teach them their way of life.

Although the savage peoples encountered by the European explorers were closer to nature than their civilized cousins, Rousseau insists that their way of life was not unconditionally natural (D2 166). The savages

18. My interpretation of this passage follows Gourevitch, "Rousseau's 'Pure' State," 36; for a different view, see Hulliung, *Autocritique*, 69–70 and the works cited by Gourevitch, in "Rousseau's 'Pure' State," 35 n.19.

were moved by a variety of acquired, reason-dependent passions not part of the innate constitution of man, including pity and a variety of manifestations of *amour-propre*, including love, jealousy, and the desire for public esteem. Life in primitive society caused the constitution of humans to change in other ways also. Insofar as the sexes come to lead different ways of life, they begin to become dependent on each another for more than the satisfaction of natural lusts. Inventing new "conveniences," such as tools and homes, the savages gradually become dependent on these things—finding it difficult (or impossible) to survive without them (D2 164).

This is an important point that demands further examination. Put in its strongest form, Rousseau's thesis holds that technological developments necessarily make human beings worse off. Although Rousseau sometimes seems to embrace this strong and obviously false thesis, his argument in the *Discourse on Inequality* requires only a weaker and much more plausible claim: that technological developments generally make little net contribution to the well-being of those who take advantage of them. Consider what happens when a new invention is introduced. At first, we must suppose, it improves the lives of those who make use of it—otherwise, it would not be adopted. However, a substantial cost results from reliance on tools or machines: the more our powers are enhanced artificially, the less we are compelled to exert ourselves; the less we exert ourselves, the weaker we become as individuals, and the more dependent we become on the help of others. Rousseau supposes that this dynamic must have begun when our most distant ancestors discovered the use of the first tools and built the first huts, and we can observe this same process happening today. We are no longer in a position to take any genuine delight in electric lighting or central heating because we have never had to live without them. These technological wonders add little to our subjective sense of well-being because we have been habituated to them; we feel that they are part of the baseline against which we judge ourselves to be better or worse off. Being dependent on them, we are vulnerable to new forms of vexation and irritation: before the widespread use of electricity, our ancestors did not lament its absence, but in today's world, an extended power outage causes untold grief and frustration.

Returning to the argument of the *Discourse on Inequality*, we find that Rousseau traces not only the direct effects of these first technological developments but also their indirect influences on the souls of the people who begin to use them. He perceives that, as men and women began living together, a number of important psychic developments spontaneously ("naturally") occurred, drawing them together to form the first (prepolitical) societies. "The habit of living together gave rise to the sweetest sentiments known to man, conjugal love, and Paternal love" (D2 164). As men and women found it pleasant to live together and to form families, and as those families grew into large extended clans, further developments followed:

> As the mind and the heart grow active, mankind continues to grow tame, contacts expand and [social] bonds tighten. It became customary to gather in front of the huts or around a large tree: song and dance, true children of love and leisure, became the amusement or rather the occupation of idle men and women gathered together. Everyone began to look at everyone else and to wish to be looked at himself; and public esteem acquired a price. The one who sang or danced best; the handsomest, the strongest, the most skillful, or the most eloquent came to be the most highly regarded. (D2 166)

Rousseau supposes that when adult human beings of a certain level of mental complexity live together, *amour-propre* naturally emerges. In this passage quoted from the *Discourse on Inequality*, he presents that observation in a historical form. The key question, however, is whether the emergence of *amour-propre* (given the general conditions of the savage societies) can account for the most important features of those societies. The savage societies present a paradoxical aspect. On the one hand, the resilience of those societies suggests that the peoples who lived in them must have been fundamentally happy or at least content with their lot; if they were miserable or perceived that a different way of life promised a better life, surely they would have grasped at it (which, as we know, they did not). On the other hand, the savages could be "bloodthirsty and cruel" at times (D2 166). Nevertheless, such outbursts of violence were relatively rare, and on the whole, the savages lived in a relatively peaceful and contented state without the need for laws or permanently constituted governments to enforce them (D2 167).

Generally, *amour-propre* is the desire to be esteemed by others in the same way and for the same reasons that one esteems oneself. It is the desire to have a certain standing in the moral world constituted by the opinions of the others among whom one lives, and it operates with greater intensity as we become more dependent for our well-being on the opinions of others. As the systematic division of productive labor was unknown among the savages, every normal adult was largely self-sufficient and so not dependent on his fellows for physical survival. This material independence protected them from the worst manifestations of *amour-propre*. Moreover, because they all lived more or less the same way of life, with few arenas of competition and few goods to be awarded on the basis of opinion. Even so, every adult demanded a certain consideration or esteem from others. From this new awareness of and concern for the regard of others, writes Rousseau, "arose the first duties of civility even among Savages"

(D2 166). Each person, believing himself or herself to merit the regard of others, takes affront if injured by another; when injured, the response is not to the material injury suffered, but rather to the supposed contempt that the injury signifies. That is why "vengeances became terrible," but it is also why they were rare: for among those who are materially self-sufficient and therefore roughly equal, no motives to desire anything occur other than to be esteemed as an equal. Moreover, since no unusual talents or skills were required to be a fully participating member of society, this desire for regard could more or less be satisfied for every normal adult (PN 101n).

The emergence of romantic love complicates this equation, but only a little. We have already seen that Rousseau surmises that, along with the development of reason arises the idea of love for a specific beloved (not just for "one who happens to be my mate"). Unfortunately, "jealousy awakens together with love" (D2 165). A man who feels that his happiness depends on winning the love of a particular woman becomes for the first time dependent on the opinion of another and for the first time acquires a motive to willingly harm those who do (or might) prevent the winning of that affection. Nevertheless, Rousseau sees that the competition for mates cannot cause more than occasional, private quarrels. The roughly equal numbers of men and women all but guarantee that every person will find some other person willing to offer love—especially since the differences among members of each sex remain relatively small as long as they all continue to secure their sustenance in the same way.

We are now in a position to see how the first "developments of the human mind" in fact make sense of everything that was heretofore puzzling about the golden age. Rousseau sees this era as "the happiest and . . . best for man" (D2 167) because the new pleasures of conjugal love, parental love, and pity add a sweetness to human life that can be tasted by nearly all members of society and that are offset by only a few new sources of evil. It is true that the ideas of love and regard give birth to the vices of jealousy and arrogance and the evils that follow in their train. There are, however, good reasons to suppose that, in a state of rough equality and independence, these vices will arise only rarely and with limited ill effects. Rousseau perceives that the men and women in the savage state will not always be able to do as they please, lest they give offense to a neighbor and risk provoking his vengeance. Nevertheless, he sees that the simplicity and equality of the savage way of life guarantee that the savages will have very few motives to harm one another and relatively strong motives of commiseration, inclining them to live together in harmony or at least without open hostility (D2 167). With no properties or positions to fight over and where individuals are equally self-sufficient, how many motives for quarrel can arise? Lacking both foresight and avarice, who would be motivated to seek more goods than necessary to satisfy daily needs? Where everyone is equally free, where no laws exist, no rulers, and no onerous employments required to acquire one's subsistence, when one can at every moment do virtually anything that pleases him, what advantages might one expect from some other way of life?

In sum, Rousseau suggests that the savage societies exist in a kind of spontaneous equilibrium; their social order arises without the need for any convention or artifice. Most important, Rousseau's account explains how these primitive social orders could have arisen among men whose minds had remained very largely uncultivated. The savage way of life is thus conditionally natural. That is why this primitive social order is rightly given the name of *natural right*. The passions that "naturally" (regularly) arise in the hearts of people who live in the savage state dispose them to live more or less contentedly and at peace with one another. Those passions are two: pity, which disinclines us to injure others, and the desire to be esteemed as an equal (which is one of the first, and most benign, manifestations of *amour-propre*). A kind of natural reciprocity is built into the structure of both. We pity others who suffer because we ourselves suffer; we desire public esteem only insofar as we deem the judging public to be estimable. That natural reciprocity explains why this spontaneous social order is so robust, which in turn also explains why no need arises for the establishment of government or laws in this state.

"The origin of society and of laws"

As discussed earlier in this chapter, Rousseau aims to demonstrate the superiority of his physics of the soul to the conventional eighteenth-century account of man as moved by a combination of self-love and reason, by showing that his model of human nature can make sense of two political phenomena that remain puzzling if we accept the conventional account. We have already seen how his account solves the first puzzle by explaining the natural genesis of the prepolitical societies of the savages. It is now time to consider Rousseau's explanation of the second puzzle: that human beings, who had previously been perfectly contented with their savage existence (who indeed, when given the choice, *preferred* a life of savage independence to becoming civilized) somehow came to find the civil way of life desirable and even necessary.

Rousseau attributes the destabilization of the savage equilibrium to a "fatal accident." "The more one reflects on it, the more one finds that this state was the least subject to revolutions, the best for man, and that he must have left it only by some fatal accident, which, for the sake of the common utility, should never have occurred" (D2 167). We do not need to search too keenly for the specific sequence of events that caused the disruption of the savage equilibrium because we know for certain that the savage way of life gave way to political societies. What Rousseau must—and can—explain, however, is *how* the constitution of man must have changed in order for the golden age to have ended and how man's new constitution made the establishment of political societies necessary. The structure of Rousseau's account of the state of nature is deceptively familiar, but we must take care lest similarities obscure the distinctiveness of his argument. Like Locke, Rousseau supposes that the first state of nature is peaceful, but that men's passions eventually lead them to war with one another. Like Hobbes, he supposes that the state of war, when it comes, pits all against all. Like both Locke and Hobbes, he supposes that the state of war ends with the establishment of political societies by consent. What is distinct about Rousseau's account is that he is not so much interested in the *reasons* that justify the establishment of civil society as in the *motives* that led to its establishment (and that continue to sustain political societies into the present). As we shall see, the key to that account is the passion of *amour-propre*.

Rousseau makes very clear that the most important structural feature of the savage equilibrium is self-sufficiency, which by preserving the independence of all, prevents the worst manifestations of *amour-propre* from making themselves felt. "So long as they applied themselves only to tasks a single individual could perform, and to arts that did not require the collaboration of several hands, they lived free, healthy, good, and happy as far as they could by their Nature be, and continued to enjoy the gentleness of independent dealings with one another" (D2 167).

In Rousseau's view, four major developments mark the end of the savage equilibrium. Although his account takes the form of a historical narrative, it is important not to inquire too closely into the accuracy of all the "historical" details. For the purpose of his argument about the origins of political society, it is enough that he offer a schematic account of the major cultural developments that is accurate in its broad outlines.

The first major development is the introduction of specialized labor, epitomized in Rousseau's account by the division of men into agriculturists and metalworkers (D2 142–144). Once labor has thus become specialized, human adults for the first time become dependent on the labor of others for their physical survival. The artisans require food, which they no longer have the skill (or land) to grow; the farmers require tools and other goods they cannot produce for themselves. To survive, economic exchanges become necessary for them; this is the second development. Money is presumably introduced at this point to facilitate exchange, although Rousseau does not attribute much importance to the invention of money. Whereas Locke had explained the failure of some peoples to become civilized by the absence of materials suitable for use as money,

Rousseau focuses instead on more pedestrian resources. He suggests that "perhaps" the abundance of iron in Europe and its fertility in wheat may explain why that continent experienced "political order, if not earlier then at least more continuously and better than other parts of the world" (D2 168).[19]

The changes wrought by the introduction of agriculture and metallurgy do not stop there. The introduction of agriculture leads to the third development: the invention of property. Among the savages, a primitive form of property had surely been known: individuals and families presumably "owned" their huts and perhaps a few small items, but their holdings would have been secured by constant possession. The security of the savage's holdings is guaranteed by a combination of pity and fear: his fellows would be disinclined to cause suffering for no reason, and, having to use force to take an item held by another, the savages would rarely find it worth the trouble. The farmer, however, is in a very different position and finds himself making the novel claim that his right over a piece of land should persist even during his absence, even during the time when it is fallow. He claims to impose on others the *obligation* not to disturb his property, even (or especially) when it would be easy for them to trespass. These claims of right soon lead to the further idea that an individual has the right to grant or to exchange the land in which one has previously acquired a property by labor. With the idea of property is born that of justice; at this stage, they are basically the same idea, namely: that we ought to render unto each what is his own (D2 169). With the rise of property and commerce is born the distinction between rich and poor. This is the final development. Those who produce more efficiently or anticipate the demands of the market will gain riches and power, while the others lose on both counts (D2 169–170). Having become part of an economy based on the division of labor and having as a consequence lost the ability to provide for their own needs, those who lose out in these exchanges are trapped. Lacking the strength and skill they would need to survive without the help of others in society, they cannot simply abandon their quasi-civilized life and "return to their equals" like the civilized savage in the frontispiece to the *Discourse on Inequality*. They must accept their poverty and do what they can to improve their lot within a more or less social order.

With these four pieces in place—the division of labor, economic exchange, ideas of property and justice, and the emergence of wealth and

19. A view that is, to some extent, corroborated by Jared M. Diamond, *Guns, Germs, and Steel: The Fates of Human Societies* (New York: W. W. Norton, 1997), the central thesis of which is that variations in natural resources available for the use of human populations (especially the number of plant and animal species suitable for domestication) account for the different levels of civilization reached in different parts of the world.

poverty—Rousseau telescopes his historical narrative, moving at once to describe the far-reaching consequences of these four developments. "Here, then, are all our faculties developed, memory and imagination brought into play, *amour-propre* interested, reason become active, and the mind almost at the limit of the perfection of which it is capable" (D2 170). Now, although we do not naturally possess either foresight or unlimited desire, the changes in our environment just noted give us new motives to plan ahead, seeking ways of becoming wealthier (or avoiding poverty) by any means necessary. Once each person is dependent for his survival on the labor of others and has recognized his position, he "must constantly try to interest them in his fate and to make them really or apparently find their own profit in working for his" (D2 170). The consequence of this development is to reinforce the power of *amour-propre* in the soul of each individual. Requiring the cooperation of others, everyone has a strong interest in attending to the way in which he is seen by others and a powerful motive for trying to appear to be what others want him to be, regardless of what he truly is. Now that individual welfare depends on making profitable exchanges with others, a man has new motives to lie and to cheat others and to seek his own advantage in causing harm to others.[20]

As Hobbes long ago perceived, foresight and imagination only make matters worse for us, as long as we remain in the state of nature.[21] Recognizing that we should wish to secure our position, not for the present only, but for the indefinite future as well, our desires and ambitions grow larger. Recognizing that others face the same incentives, we perceive that we can only secure ourselves if we acquire *more* than others, and our ambitions grow limitless. This concern for wealth and status—for bettering our position relative to others in society—has a way of becoming disconnected from our interest in securing our own happiness or well-being. Significantly, Hobbes observes this development as well, including among the causes of war not only motives arising out of self-interest but also the desire for glory, a passion virtually identical to Rousseau's *amour-propre*. Writes Hobbes: "every man looketh that his companion should value him at the same rate he sets upon himself, and upon all signs of contempt, or undervaluing, naturally endeavors . . . to extort a greater value from his contemners, by damage, and from others, by the example."[22]

Rousseau's account of the resulting psychologies of rich and poor also owes much to Niccolò Machiavelli. He observes that "the rich . . . had scarcely become acquainted with the pleasure of dominating than they disdained all other pleasures" (D2 171). Self-love ceases to be the primary

20. This issue will be discussed further in chapter 3.
21. Hobbes, *Leviathan*, 75–76.
22. Ibid., 74–75.

principle of their action, supplemented by a particularly malign form of *amour-propre*: the desire to have more money and power than others; the desire, that is, to oppress. The poor, having no hope of oppressing others, seek only not to be oppressed. Their dependence for their survival on the products of other hands, however, limits their options. They cannot abandon their quasi-social way of life based on the division of labor. No more than the rich are they still moved primarily by self-love and the concern for their own absolute well-being. The same malignant growth of *amour-propre* has gripped their souls as well. Made desperate by the precariousness of their situation, they wish only to avoid losing what little they have—a wish that will lead some to become servile and others rebellious and violent (D2 171).

It is now evident why Rousseau disagrees with Locke about the importance of the invention of money. In Locke's account, the desire to accumulate property without limit is naturally checked by the absence of money: as he sees it, it is pointless to acquire a vast hoard of perishable goods, only to see them spoil. The moral precept of the law of nature, which forbids us from acquiring goods only to waste them, is thus naturally self-enforcing. Only with consent to the use of money does it become possible to accumulate limitlessly without wasting any of the perishable products of the earth; at that juncture, it also becomes permissible. Locke implicitly supposes that the desire for property is related to concern for one's own absolute well-being because the desire to acquire expands only after we have found a way (with the invention of money) to assure that an increased fortune can still be *useful* to us. Only with the invention of money are we able to secure our well-being into the indefinite future, and it is only then (in Locke's view) that we attempt it. Rousseau, however, treats the desire for property as basically the same as the desire for power: both amount to the desire to be acknowledged by others as superior, and both operate independently of concern for one's absolute well-being. In Rousseau's vision, the desire for limitless power does not wait for the invention of money to arise. It arises once those who possess goods on which others depend for their survival first taste "the pleasure of dominating." This feeling of inflamed *amour-propre* not only drives the powerful; it affects the poor and powerless too: seeing how they are oppressed, they predictably come to seek their own welfare in the accumulation of wealth and power. Even if they could hope to attain self-sufficiency and independence, the poor do not seek it any more than the rich. They hope only to become rich and powerful themselves.

With the introduction of property, the birth of inequality, and its attendant inflammation of *amour-propre*, the stage is set for Rousseau's account of the degeneration of the peaceful state of nature into a state of war and the genesis of the political state. He sees that the circumstances in which the rich and poor find themselves drive them into conflict with one another and indeed set every individual at odds with every other individual.

> As the most powerful or the most miserable claimed on the basis of their strength or of their needs, a kind of right to property, equivalent, according to them, to the right of property, the breakdown of equality was followed by the most frightful disorder: thus the usurpations of the rich, the Banditry of the Poor, the unbridled passions of all, stifling natural pity and the still weak voice of justice, make men greedy, ambitious, and wicked. . . . [Thus] nascent society gave way to the most horrible state of war. (D2 171–172)

The problem is not just that different people want the same *things* for themselves; they are making incompatible claims on one another's *wills*. That is what it means for them to be making moral claims—claims of right—on one another. When the poor claim a right to their rich neighbor's goods in virtue of their need and the rich claim a right to property in the possessions that their strength or skill has enabled them to acquire, the conflict is not about the particular items claimed by both, nor is it a philosophical disagreement about the rational adequacy of competing theories of justice. In fact, Rousseau makes clear that no claims to own property are valid in the state of nature, which is still ordered according to natural right (D2 169, 172). The property claims of the rich and poor are, at bottom, about status: the rich are demanding that the poor willingly acknowledge the mastery of the wealthy; the poor make the contradictory demand that they be acknowledged as possessing the same right to make valid claims on others as the rich exercise for themselves (D2 171).

Rousseau insists that the state of war ends, not with the discovery of a reasonable accommodation of the parties' material interests, but when the parties agree on a solution all of them are *motivated* to accept. Only one possible solution to the problem exists: the parties must form a community in which all agree to protect the lives and properties of each (D2 173; SC 49–51; PE 7, 9–10). In the *Discourse on Inequality*, he dramatically illustrates this solution, even presenting the very speech he imagines the first father of civil society might have used to make the proposal to his neighbors. It does not matter whether anyone actually delivered the speech; what matters is the *content* of the proposal and the motives of those who make it and of those who willingly accept it. The arrangement gives both the rich and poor the bulk of what they want, satisfying their most pressing needs: everyone's interest in self-preservation dictates the formation of civil society. Rousseau puts the point starkly in the *Social Contract*, where he assumes that society arises when "humankind would perish if it did not change its way of being" (SC 49).

Self-love is not the only principle of soul motivating the parties to accept the proposed social contract. Both rich and poor are also moved by inflamed *amour-propre,* keenly concerned about their status relative to others,
and wanting *acknowledgment* as rightful owners of property and bearers of
rights in their persons. That is what the social compact provides. To reach
this arrangement, however, all must alienate a portion of their liberty to the
community that makes and enforces laws, which alone give practical effect
to the various claims of right. The parties do so willingly, sacrificing "one
part of their freedom" in order to preserve the rest, "as a wounded man has
his arm cut off to save the rest of his Body" (D2 173). Rousseau says that
only "the wise" see the formation of the social compact in such stark terms;
everyone else makes the transaction eagerly, not to say blindly. The rich
hope to take advantage of the new state of affairs to find a more secure
means of exercising dominion over others than had been possible in the
state of nature (D2 173), and the poor hope to become rich and to dominate
others in turn.

Actually, the image of a contract as the foundation of society is mis-
leading. To speak of a contract is to suggest that a particular moment in
time occurred when services or promises of service were exchanged: I will
do this (now or in the future) in exchange for some consideration you give
me now or promise to transfer to me in the future. Hobbes saw very clearly
the difficulty of conceiving the act of founding a society as a contract by
which one promises to forbear from injuring others in exchange for a like
promise from them. The problem is to understand what could motivate
me, after I have received the benefit of others' forbearance, to keep my
promise not to harm them if it should subsequently prove advantageous
to me to do so. His answer, of course, is fear—fear of what the sovereign
will do to me if I am caught breaking my promise. Locke also supposes that
one becomes a member of a political community by giving consent, although he is less interested in finding out what motivates consenters to
keep their promises of obedience than he is in discovering how those who
have not expressly given consent may still be seen to have, in some way,
agreed to the rule of those who govern them. Dramatizing the foundation
of civil society in the *Discourse on Inequality,* Rousseau also presents the
founding act as an exchange of promises. What he sees is that the same interests and passions that lead us initially to make the contract continue
thereafter to bind us to it. We do not simply promise in one moment and
then wonder at our leisure later why we should keep it. The very structure
of our needs and deepest desires—epitomized by our desire to own property—binds us into ongoing relationships with others.

The political theory Rousseau develops based on this account is examined in chapter 5. For now, we examine the conclusions Rousseau announces at the end of his account of the foundation of society:

> Such was, or must have been, the origin of Society and of Laws, which gave the weak new fetters and the rich new forces, . . . irreversibly destroyed natural freedom, forever fixed the law of property and inequality, transformed a skillful usurpation into an irrevocable right, and . . . henceforth subjugated the whole of Mankind to labor, servitude, and misery . . . .
>
> I know that some have attributed other origins to Political Societies, such as conquest by the more powerful, or the union of the weak; and the choice between these causes does not make a difference to what I want to establish. (D2 173–174)

Rousseau's claims in these two passages are bold but fully justified. In the second quoted paragraph, he correctly insists that it does not matter whether the idea for the first society was really proposed by a clever rich man seeking to dupe his neighbors into leaving him free to enjoy his wealth. What he is trying to find out is not so much *who* established the first societies as *why* they came into being: why did people come to want to live in a world structured by property relations (that is to say, a world ordered by political right) when their ancestors had found property unnecessary? Only when we recognize that Rousseau's account focuses on motives rather than reasons, can we understand why he concludes that the social compact creates "an irrevocable right" to property, even though he admits that, by its terms, the compact basically amounts to a fraud perpetrated by the rich on the poor. The issue that interests him is not whether the contract is reasonably accepted; the issue is why people become motivated to accept it. The answer, as we can now see, is that political societies become necessary when human beings cease to be self-sufficient, instead becoming dependent for their survival on the willingness of others to cooperate with them. Under those conditions, self-love interacts with the developing mind to manifest itself as *amour-propre*, the passion that interests us in our standing relative to others. In Rousseau's account, the passion of *amour-propre* is the true foundation of civil society. We see that the goodness or badness of any particular regime is largely determined by the particular form of *amour-propre* that lies at its foundation.

It is essential to a sound understanding of Rousseau's political theory that we recognize that this claim is descriptive, not normative. Every political society is constituted by the wills of those who comprise it—the settled dispositions of those who comprise it to regard its institutions and laws as legitimate, as a source of valid obligations. This is as true of very oppressive societies as it is of the most egalitarian—as true of ancien régime France as it is of Rousseau's idealized image of Geneva. The alternative to a political relationship is a despotic relationship: the Helots were no part of the community of the Spartans; they were not parties to the social compact and had no standing in the moral world of the Spartiates. They were held down solely by force. In other words, the essence of despotism is the denial of reciprocity: the slave is he who can make no claim at all on the master. This is why one cannot really consent to be a slave: it is physically impossible to alienate one's will, the part of oneself that makes choices and presses claims upon others. If it were possible, to do so would be to become something less than human—an automaton, a tool moved only by the will of another.[23] That is why Rousseau concludes that: "to renounce one's freedom is to renounce one's quality as a man, the rights of humanity, and even its duties" (SC 45). One can choose, of course, to acquiesce in one's servitude for reasons of prudence, but a slave cannot have any valid moral duty to obey his master.

"An assemblage of artificial men"

Rousseau's political argument in support of his conception of human nature concludes by showing that his account of the origins of political society also enables us to understand the *stability* of existing political societies, which would otherwise remain puzzling. He asks, in effect: Why do the poor put up with being thus oppressed? Why do they feel any sort of allegiance to their rulers and acknowledge the legitimacy of those who purport to rule them? Do they not have more than adequate motive (arising from their concern for their own welfare) to do something about it? Plainly, Rousseau's contemporaries in France and across the European continent generally accepted the legitimacy of their rulers. Had they not done so, there would have been frequent rebellions or coups d'état (D2 186). But rebellions of any kind are quite rare; there must therefore be some other explanation than the superior force of the rulers. "Since nothing is less stable among men than those external relationships that are more often the product of chance than of wisdom and that are called weakness or power, wealth or poverty, human establishments seem at first glance to be founded on piles of Quicksand" (D2 128).

Locke posits something like a principle of inertia to explain why revolutions so rarely occur: "People are not so apt to get out of their old forms, as some are apt to suggest;" he adds that there is a "slowness and aversion in the people to quit their old constitutions."[24] As claims about the British people in the last quarter of the seventeenth century, Locke's observations

---

23. Compare Aristotle, *Politics*, 1253b23–1255b15.
24. Locke, ST § 223.

are unobjectionable. Rousseau, however, wants to be able to answer deeper questions than Locke's argument compels him to ask. Rousseau wonders: What makes people so disposed to put up with bad governments? What would make them more inclined to civil strife? What can be done to shape the character of the people so as to make it more or less disposed to violence? Hobbes in effect accounts for the inertia Locke observes by noting that the horrors of civil war are so great that any rational person would be better off putting up with just about anything than fight a civil war to change the government. In practice, Rousseau's horror of civil war was equal to Hobbes's, and he did everything he could to prevent the protests of the Genevan bourgeoisie from causing civil war. Once more, however, Rousseau pursues a deeper question, not asked by his predecessors: What makes people willing to fight civil wars? Why has it been so depressingly easy for tyrants to find so many willing servants?

Once again, these phenomena cannot be adequately explained if we assume that human beings are essentially moved by a combination of reason and concern for their own well-being. It might seem that rational self-interest alone explains the acquiescence of the many in oppressive forms of social order. What could any individual Paris slum-dweller hope to do against all the forces at the disposal of Louis XIV? Basically, nothing at all: self-interest counsels patience and obedience, in this case. The further question that must be asked, however, is why the oppressed subject finds such a potent constellation of forces arrayed against him. Can rational self-interest explain the willingness of peasants to become soldiers and the willingness of soldiers to obey their officers? That willingness, as Rousseau knew, could extend very far indeed: "A time would come when [the defenders of the Fatherland] would be heard to say to their Country's oppressor: *If you order me to plunge the sword into my brother's breast, or my father's throat, or even my pregnant wife's womb, I shall do so, though my right arm be unwilling*" (D2 185).

Only by positing the existence of a passion such as *amour-propre* can such conduct be made comprehensible. Where great inequalities of wealth and status occur (as in the monarchies of the ancien régime), we are constantly reminded that others measure our worth by our wealth. As a consequence, we find it hard not to judge ourselves by the same measure. If, as is likely under such conditions, one cares profoundly about where one stands within the social hierarchy, one will have the motivation to do whatever is necessary to raise one's relative standing, even if doing so tends to run against the conditions of one's own happiness. The eighteenth-century peasant's son could, perhaps, have led a perfectly decent life on his father's provincial farm, but he would have suffered from the awareness of his poverty and of the disregard with which his betters would have treated

him. His *amour-propre* would constantly have been dissatisfied. But to en-
list as a soldier offered the opportunity for money and position he could
not otherwise have enjoyed; once in the service, the path to further rewards
(such as it was) lay open to those who would serve most willingly. This
same dynamic, extended across the whole society, explains how people
come not only to accept, but even to embrace inequality, and it explains
why people come to accept unjust governments: "Citizens let themselves
be oppressed only so far as they are swept up by blind ambition and, looking down below more than above themselves, come to hold Domination
dearer than independence, and consent to bear chains so that they might
impose chains [on others] in turn" (D2 183).

CONCLUSION

Rousseau's model of the soul, with *amour-propre* at its center, enables him
to make sense of political phenomena that must remain puzzling on any
other account. He can explain the nature and resilience of the protosoci-
eties of the savages; he can explain the first foundations of political society, and by reference to *amour-propre* he can explain why those foundations
are so solid. To see how well Rousseau's account of human nature makes
sense of the passions in the individual human heart is the task of the next
chapter.

3 The Ethical Argument

ROUSSEAU'S POLITICAL ARGUMENT demonstrates the existence of *amour-propre* in the soul by showing that it is the previously unrecognized "true foundation" of political society. Although it provides strong reasons for accepting Rousseau's model of human nature, that argument cannot, by itself, suffice to establish the adequacy of that model. It must also be shown that his account of human nature can make sense of what is observed directly in the behavior and character of individuals; this further demonstration is called here the ethical argument. As with its political counterpart, the ethical argument seeks to vindicate Rousseau's conception of human nature by showing that it has more explanatory power than competing accounts. It does so by identifying certain aspects of human behavior for which no adequate explanation had as yet been given and then showing that Rousseau's model of human nature makes available a solution to the theretofore unsolved mysteries.

The first line of *Emile* introduces the problematic state of affairs for which the whole work aims, if possible, to find a remedy: "Everything"—including man himself—"is good as it leaves the hands of the Author of things; everything degenerates in the hands of man" (E 37). Rousseau begins that work by drawing a kind of composite portrait of a representative man of society, the "bourgeois," based on his own observations of "these men of our days" (E 40). Rousseau does not claim that all of his contemporaries shared all the traits he assigned to the bourgeois, nor does he deny that some can be found who are in every respect unlike the bourgeois. Nevertheless, Rousseau knew plenty of men who fit the portrait perfectly, as a reading of the *Confessions* makes plain. Moreover, he had every reason to suppose his portrait of the bourgeois to be a fair likeness of a great many men in his own time, and it is clearly a good representation of a certain type of person we can see around us today, perhaps even when we look in the mirror.

The details of that portrait will be examined shortly. For now, it suffices to observe that Rousseau draws particular attention to a pair of features he takes to be characteristic of the bourgeois, which together constitute the puzzle his model of human nature is introduced to unravel: the bourgeois is "good neither for himself nor for others" (E 40, 41). Unlike the savage, who lives for himself, the bourgeois who follows "the sentiments of nature" is not led reliably to happiness: he is not good for himself. Unlike the virtuous citizen, he does not manage to subordinate his desire for private well-being to the interests of any community, to the demands of justice: he is not good for others. "Neither man nor citizen," neither happy nor just, the bourgeois is, in Rousseau's harsh judgment, "nothing" (E 40). Confident that human beings are good by nature, Rousseau finds the sad state of his contemporaries' souls as perplexing as it is depressing. Thus he is led to ask two simple but powerful questions: *Why are we not happy?* and *Why are we unjust?*

WHAT AILS US?

No one who reads Rousseau's *Discourse on Inequality* can fail to perceive, however dimly, that its author regarded the vast political, economic, and social inequalities he described as highly unjust. In contrast, many readers have found themselves puzzled by what he has to say in *Emile*, the *Discourses*, and *Julie* about the character of his bourgeois contemporaries. Much of the problem is that the obvious reading of the remark in *Emile* that they are "good neither for themselves nor for others" generates the bold and disturbing claim that a sizeable number—perhaps most—of his fellows in society possess neither happiness nor that commitment to justice characteristic of virtue. That was a very hard claim for his contemporaries to accept because it contradicted so much of what they wanted to believe about themselves and their society, and it is no less difficult to accept today. Of course, it must be conceded that *some* people in any society are unhappy and that *some* are unjust, but Rousseau is claiming more than this. He means that unhappiness and injustice are *characteristic features* of a type of person commonly found in certain kinds of political societies, and he aims to make us see the unpleasant truth about our condition, observing bluntly that we have: "honor without virtue, reason without wisdom, and pleasure without happiness" (D2 187).

"Honor without virtue"

At first sight, most of what Rousseau has to say about his contemporaries may seem to have nothing to do with either justice or happiness. He calls them hypocrites and conformists, who do not so much live their own lives as play the role of what is expected of them in the great theater of society. That complaint figures prominently in the *First Discourse*: "all minds seem to have been cast in the same mold: constantly politeness demands, propriety commands: constantly one follows custom, never one's own genius" (D1 8). This complaint recurs in the *Discourse on Inequality*: "everything being reduced to appearances, everything becomes factitious and play-acting" (D2 187). Rousseau returns to the theme in *Julie* as well, where Saint-Preux describes the fashionable people of Paris as "so many marionettes . . . pulled by the same string" (J 205). Such remarks have led many readers of Rousseau to conclude that he is fundamentally repelled by his fellows' *inauthenticity*, by the disjunction between the appearances they strive to project and the reality of what transpires in their hearts. He is repelled by this aspect of their behavior, but it is not the principal target of his ire. His contemporaries' hypocrisy and inauthenticity are only the most visible symptoms of a deeper and more serious problem: their "souls have become corrupted" by a host of vices (D1 9). Rousseau's point is not that his fellows are constantly committing acts of injustice; that claim would plainly be false. He insists, rather, that his contemporaries' souls are corrupted *insofar as they lack the basic orientation of heart and mind that is essential to true morality or to virtue*, namely: the desire to do what is right because it is right and the strength of will to carry out one's duty, regardless of the consequences.

There are two reasons why Rousseau cannot be understood as objecting fundamentally to the inauthenticity or insincerity of the bourgeois. First, if he objected primarily to the fact that the bourgeois seem to be other than they are (rather than to the fact that they are, in truth, vicious), he would have no reason for criticizing those who both appear to be, and are, vicious. Arthur Melzer, who views him as a critic of inauthenticity, draws precisely this conclusion; in his view, Rousseau teaches that: "it no longer matters what a man is, so long as he is it wholly and consistently."[1] Rousseau seems not to have adopted this radical moral doctrine, however. He very clearly insists that the vicious are *never* to be emulated, whether, like the urban cosmopolites, they cover their "black morals" with a "seductive veneer" or, like the vicious among the peasantry, they display their vices "unadorned and in all their coarseness" (E 95).

Second, Rousseau's repeated praise of the Spartans would make no sense if he were particularly troubled by his contemporaries' lack of authenticity.[2] The Spartan citizen, whom he invites his readers to emulate at the end of the *First Discourse*, certainly "follows custom," not his "own genius." When Rousseau calls the Spartan citizen "denatured" (E 40), he means precisely that his education and training had all but eradicated his natural inclination to seek happiness by radically subordinating his natural self-love to a powerful manifestation of *amour-propre* that impelled him to excel in his devotion to the city. What the Spartan does that is worth

---

1. Melzer, *Natural Goodness*, 65.
2. Ruth W. Grant, *Hypocrisy and Integrity: Machiavelli, Rousseau, and the Ethics of Politics* (Chicago: University of Chicago Press, 1997), 60.

emulating is simply this: he "acts well," which, as is clear from the context, means that he embodies virtue (D1 28; E 39–40). It is clear why virtue and vice, rather than authenticity and hypocrisy, should be Rousseau's central preoccupation in the *First Discourse*: the very question it was written to address is a question about moral character: *Whether the restoration of the Sciences and Arts has led to the purification of morals?* Rousseau, notoriously, answers in the negative, and he insists over and over in the body of the *Discourse* that his contemporaries, like other, similar peoples, lack virtue.

It must be emphasized that Rousseau's understanding of the virtues and the vices is substantially quite traditional. That should not be surprising: Rousseau consistently presents himself as a defender of traditional morality against the innovations of a corrupt present (see, e.g., D1 17, 24–25, 27–28). From the publication of the *First Discourse*, the first-published work in his system, Rousseau writes disapprovingly of the same vices condemned since before the time of Aristotle and praises equally traditional virtues (D1 16, 23). This is the position to which he clings in *Emile*: by the time he reaches manhood, Emile is described in terms that suggest he possesses (perhaps imperfectly) all of the Aristotelian virtues of character except for magnanimity and magnificence, which, being essentially aristocratic virtues, are inappropriate to his station in life.[3]

Rousseau draws so much attention in the works comprising his system to his fellows' concern with appearances because he knows that no readers would immediately accept the provocative claim he is trying to establish—that they, his readers, have hearts corrupted by vice. To get his readers to accept this conclusion, Rousseau proceeds by indirection. He begins his portrait of their souls by drawing attention to aspects of their character and behavior he expects them to find attractive; only later does he try

---

3. Bravery (E 78, 111, 208). Temperance (E 208). Generosity (E 103–104, 435–436). The nameless virtue concerning small honors (E 339). Mildness ("the mean concerned with anger" [*Nicomachean Ethics*, 1125b27]; E 251), Friendliness in social intercourse (the man possessing this virtue will "choose in itself . . . to share pleasure and avoid causing pain. But he will be guided by consequences—i.e., by what is fine and what is expedient—if they are greater; and, moreover, to secure great pleasure in the future he will cause slight pain" [*Nicomachean Ethics*, 1127a4–8]; E 230), Truthfulness ("someone who is truthful both in what he says and how he lives, when nothing about justice is at stake, simply because that is the state of his character" [*Nicomachean Ethics*, 1127b1–3]; E 207, 250). Wit ("Those who joke in appropriate ways are called witty" [*Nicomachean Ethics*, 1128a10]; it is not clear that Emile will be witty, but Rousseau's account of his reception in society at E 338–339 suggests that he must possess to a sufficient degree the appropriate social graces, which may well include an appropriately moderate degree of wit), and Justice (E 250–252). Emile's chosen station in life precludes him from exercising magnanimity, but in other works Rousseau praises men such as Fabricius, Cato, and Francis Bacon, who seem to exemplify Aristotelian magnanimity. See D 13, 27, and PE 16. Only magnificence seems nowhere to be praised by Rousseau, although it may perhaps be considered one of the virtues specific to the aristocratic regime to which he alludes at SC 94.

to show that those superficially pleasing attributes are inconsistent with the attachment to justice for its own sake that is definitive of virtue. Rousseau's early remarks in the *First Discourse*, we must recall, include at least a hint of praise—praise that would be wholly out of place were it his aim to mount a critique of insincerity: he praises their urbanity, their intellectual achievements, and even their manners (D1 7). Rousseau also professes admiration for the external appearances his contemporaries seek to present, admitting that it would be most "sweet . . . to live among us if the outward countenance were always the image of the heart's dispositions" (D1 7–9). None of these observations was particularly new; Montesquieu, for example, had already described the Parisians similarly in his *Persian Letters*.[4] But their familiarity is vital to Rousseau's rhetorical strategy: his argument only succeeds to the extent that we find his portrait of the bourgeois to be immediately recognizable.

The next step in his argument is to show that the traits his contemporaries regard as virtues are, at best, alien to and, at worst, inimical to true virtue (see LSR 65). To reach this issue, Rousseau calls into question the intentions and motives that govern the actions of people in society. If they were virtuous, the good maxims that they profess would be the rules that actually govern their action, but, Rousseau insists, those maxims are regularly belied by the reality of their conduct (D1 7–9; see also E 116). Part of the problem is that so many people so casually wrong one another. But there is also a deeper problem with our concern with appearances. In society, he complains, people do what "politeness demands" and what "propriety commands." But, to do something—even if it be to respect the rights of another—because it is what one is expected to do is not really to act morally. A world of difference exists between refraining from vicious actions because they are held in dishonor or are ridiculed and refraining from them *because they are vicious* (J 203). Only the latter is characteristic of virtue; the former is a merely a "refinement of intemperance" (D1 8).

In fact, this refined intemperance is what motivates both our professions of virtue and our less than virtuous deeds. We profess high-minded moral principles because we are expected to do so; he who would openly disparage justice and virtue would find himself opposed at every turn. Similarly, our intemperance—our desire to succeed, to win fame, power, money, or some other distinction—is what generally gives us reason to conform outwardly to the requirements of virtue, even as it gives us reason to wrong others, when we can get away with it. But the desire to succeed does not generate the moral imperative, *do what is right, regardless of the consequences*

---

4. See, for example, Montesquieu, *Persian Letters*, trans. C. J. Betts (Harmondsworth: Penguin Books, 1973), esp. letters 28, 36, 54, 87.

to oneself; instead, it generates the instrumental imperative, *conform to the demands of justice as far as is necessary, but be ready to wrong others when it can be done to advantage.* Thus they find themselves, when the occasion permits, doing wrong to others, and even when they are not doing wrong, they carry evil intentions in their hearts (PN 101).

We can understand the phenomenon Rousseau describes as follows. This refined intemperance (we will see later that this passion is a disordered manifestation of *amour-propre*) alters the descriptions under which we view others, so we see them primarily in terms of how they are related to ourselves: master or servant, the competition or someone not to be worried about, a person useful to know or a parasite best avoided. Observing the same people, the man of virtue views them under descriptions without reference to himself or to their position: he sees them first and foremost as *human beings*—who, to be sure, each possess different talents and each have different needs. An example may help illustrate the point. On their way to reach the home of Emile's beloved Sophie, Jean-Jacques and Emile hear the cries of an injured man, lying some distance from the road, calling for help. Like the priest and the Levite in the parable of the Good Samaritan (Luke 10:29–37), which this episode echoes, they could easily have continued on their journey without stopping. Presumably, the priest and the Levite kept walking because they saw no reason to help: they saw only the inconvenience to themselves involved in giving aid. Perhaps they justified their indifference by viewing the man with scorn or contempt: no need to help him—he is just a drunk, or a beggar, or maybe a thief. Like the Samaritan, however, Emile and Jean-Jacques see nothing more and nothing less than *a man who needs their help.* And so help they do, without pausing to calculate the cost to themselves of doing so (E 439–440). Justifying himself the next day to Sophie, who is angry because she has been distressed by worry since her suitor failed to arrive at the appointed time, Emile tells her firmly that "the rights of humanity . . . are more sacred to me than yours" (E 441). In the heart of a just and virtuous man, the particular claims of a lover are subordinate to the claims of a human being in dire need of aid.

The figure in Rousseau's portrait of the bourgeois is immediately recognizable, as he expected it would be. What is remarkable about it, however, is the dark coloration Rousseau gives it. Most of us wearily take it for granted that people are basically self-interested, without any profound commitment to the welfare of others beyond their immediate connections. We admit as much every time we remark on the rarity of true virtue. Rousseau, however, views this state of affairs as a scandal and a mystery. We are not born evil; we have no innate desire to harm others. There have been societies in which one did not have to be a moral prodigy to conceive a genuine attachment to justice. Yet, we bourgeois become vicious, if not in our actions, then in our hearts. How this terrible transformation happens is the first of the ethical puzzles to which Rousseau's model of human nature provides a satisfactory solution.

"Pleasure without happiness"

We have seen that when Rousseau complains that we are not good for others, he means not that we are conspicuously wicked but that we have lost sight of true virtue, mistaking a false appearance of justice for the real thing. So too, when he claims that we are not good for ourselves, he does not mean that we are all consistently miserable and wretched, but that we have lost sight of true happiness, mistaking a false appearance of happiness for the real thing. To be sure, genuine suffering is prevalent in society, particularly among the poor and oppressed. Much as Rousseau sympathized with their plight, however, they are not the primary subjects of his inquiry in *Emile* because the nature of their unhappiness is readily perceived: they are wretched because their basic needs are unmet and their every desire is thwarted by circumstances. Harder to understand is the unhappiness of one whose desires are satisfied, who gets all or much of what he wants (see E 242–243). That is the case of the bourgeois, whose soul Rousseau particularly seeks to understand. Rousseau claims that we, who typically deem ourselves happy, have nevertheless somehow lost sight of the true sources of happiness, mistaking apparent goods for real ones.

Can it be true that many of us who are outwardly successful are less than happy, as Rousseau claims? On its face, this claim seems extremely presumptuous. In fact, however, this proposition is closely related to the claim, already established, that the bourgeois does not possess virtue, and Rousseau supports this claim in much the same way as he supported the first. He presents portraits of men as he sees them and invites us to consider whether we see the same evidence and reach the same conclusions he does. Once again, Rousseau proceeds indirectly, by drawing his readers' attention to certain behavioral phenomena he expects them to recognize in themselves and then showing that those behaviors are in fact symptoms of the underlying malady we have heretofore refused to see. To sharpen the contrast between our condition and true happiness, Rousseau also offers vivid portraits of truly happy souls, both in the *Discourse on Inequality* and *Emile*.

Let us first consider Rousseau's images of happiness. In the *Discourse on Inequality*, he claims that the savage state—the "golden age," as he sometimes calls it—was the "happiest . . . epoch" and the "best for man" (D2 167). For the present argument, it does not matter whether the savage state was as happy as the picture Rousseau creates; what matters is why he judged the savages to be happy. It is easy to see what Rousseau finds so attractive. His savages live in idleness and freedom (D2 166, 187); he imagines them spending their hours of leisure in spontaneous festivals of song and dance or delighting in the company of their wives and children (D2 166). No one commands, and no one is compelled to serve anyone else. Having limited desires, ample strength, and the freedom to do as they please, savages are substantially able to satisfy their every desire. With little imagination and less foresight, they live in the present, not worrying about the future. If they are subject to physical ills, at least they do not aggravate them with fears and cares.

Emile is Rousseau's other great image of happiness, and, as Rousseau frequently points out, he bears more than a passing resemblance to the savages (E 205, 243, 255, 474). During his childhood and youth, Emile lives much as they do, spending his time in freedom and leisure, and, like them, he lives happily. With all the energy of childhood, he is not idle as they are, but he does not toil, either. Whatever he chooses to do, he does wholeheartedly, eagerly, intently. When it ceases to please him, he does something else. He is not troubled by restless desires or made uncomfortable by solitude. Wherever he finds himself, he is content. It may be that no young person could ever be as continually contented as Rousseau supposes his Emile to be, but we have all seen the unselfconscious joy of children absorbed in their play. That, in short, is Rousseau's image of happiness.

It is clear that we adults do not much resemble happy children, a reason why we look back nostalgically at childhood. We are, as Rousseau sees, restless, constantly busy, and nearly always at work, eyes focused not on the present but on the future (D1 17; D2 187, 197). Those who have leisure, Rousseau suggests, fare little better than those who toil: they find themselves restless, bored, and vaguely discontented; as a result, they find themselves searching for an indefinite something that they lack but cannot name (ES 886; J 209–210). It has rightly been pointed out that the feelings Rousseau does attribute to the bourgeois, especially the sense that he is "floating" or "drifting" between various divergent courses of action, are not actually painful.[5] That is true, but those feelings are nevertheless signs that all is not right in their hearts. Neither he who finds himself bored and restless in leisure nor he who finds himself driven to a feverish intensity of work possesses the radiant happiness seen in a child at play.

What is surprising in Rousseau's account is not that he perceives this difference, but that he finds it so puzzling and problematic. A substantial literature documents that many modern Westerners feel the sorts of vague discontent, unease, and dissatisfaction with their lives that Rousseau saw

5. Melzer, *Natural Goodness*, 64–65.

as characteristic of the bourgeois.[6] But we do not usually regard this state as mysterious or problematic because we take it to be normal: of course children are happy, we say to ourselves, but then they are only children. They do not have the serious cares of adults. Rousseau reminds us, however, that mere life is pleasant for those who have not forgotten how to sense it. Children delight in the sheer joy of being alive, in the feeling of their own existence; so do the animals. We, generally, do not. This is the second great mystery Rousseau aimed to solve: *How have we lost sight of happiness?*

"IT IS NOT NECESSARY TO SUPPOSE THAT MAN IS EVIL BY HIS NATURE"

Where does *evil* come from? Prior to Rousseau, evil was almost universally regarded as a natural feature of the human condition. It may be supposed that this view of evil as natural reflects a praiseworthy "tough-mindedness," but that is not so. To attribute man's evil to his nature or to the effects of an original sin is not so much to explain human wickedness as it is to declare in advance that our wickedness *requires no explanation*. Rousseau, however, insists that "it is not necessary to suppose that man is evil by his nature, since one can make out the origin and progress of his wickedness" (LB 967). He proposes, in short, to explain the genesis of evil in natures that are originally good. In doing so, he does not challenge the conventional view that evil actions represent a failure to conform our actions to the requirements of practical reason (the "eternal laws of justice and order" [E 473]). Rather than viewing evil as a predictable matter of failing to accomplish the difficult task of restraining our evil impulses, he offers an account of why we have evil impulses in the first place.

Rousseau's answer to the question, *Where does evil come from?* proceeds in two steps. In the first, he examines why human beings, alone on earth, are capable of doing what is morally evil. In the second step, he asks the further question: once we are moral beings, free to choose good or evil, why do we so often choose evil, when it is also in our power to choose good?

"We enter the moral order"
In order to uncover the genesis of evil, Rousseau begins with a conception of man as a mere animal, who, moved solely by pleasure and pain, remains perfectly subject to the natural laws according to which the whole of physical nature is ordered. He supposes that this most primitive man,

6. See, for example, Robert N. Bellah et al., *Habits of the Heart: Individualism and Commitment in American Life* (Berkeley: University of California Press, 1985). Robert E. Lane, *The Loss of Happiness in Market Democracies* (New Haven: Yale University Press, 2000).

like everything else in nature, is good, at least in that he is not actively evil (E 37). A primitive man has no instinctive desire to harm any of his kind; if anything, he is weakly disinclined to harm others who resemble himself. At some point in our development as a species, however, something happened that made it possible for us to become moral beings, capable of doing moral good or moral evil. And something else happened that made it not only possible, but *likely* that we would choose to do evil, or at least to harbor evil intentions in our hearts. The same developments can be seen in the lives of individuals. Children are not born capable of either moral good or moral evil, but something happens between birth and adulthood that ushers them into the moral world, and in bourgeois societies such as ours, something happens that makes them more likely to become evil than good.

Part of what happens to make us moral agents is the birth of reason that awakens us to a consciousness of our freedom (D2 141). Rousseau is emphatically not making any sort of metaphysical claim about the extent of our freedom or the degree of our subjection to the physical laws of nature: he does not know whether physical causes can explain the movement of the will, but he does not think it matters. What matters is that, subjectively, when we experience a pain or desire, we feel that we are free to act or not to act accordingly: we cannot help but regard ourselves as the authors of our own actions. If we were not thus free, we would not be capable of morality at all (SC 45–46; E 280–281). That is so because what makes an action morally good or morally bad is the purpose or intention behind it, not merely the consequences of the action (E 93). If the injurious consequences of an action were sufficient to deem it good or evil, it would be wrong for us not to regard children (and animals) as moral actors, because they are quite capable of doing a great deal of damage to anything they get their curious little hands on. We do, and in Rousseau's view, rightly, regard the actions of children as neither morally good nor morally evil because they are incapable of formulating the requisite intention. Their incapacity in this regard cannot be attributed precisely to the undeveloped state of their minds. It is of course true that very small children cannot foresee all the consequences likely to follow from their actions, but though an average ten-year-old knows perfectly well that playing with matches can cause a dangerous house fire, we do not usually prosecute ten-year-olds for arson.

According to Rousseau, moral evil cannot be rightly imputed to any being whose soul is constituted only by self-love and reason. This is so because morality only exists in the *relationships between or among persons*, others who can make claims on us and on whom we in turn can make claims.[7] Nothing moral exists in our relationship to the world of things;

---

7. It seems to me that Rousseau's understanding of morality is similar to (albeit far less

writes Rousseau: "dependence on things . . . has no morality, is in no way detrimental to freedom, and engenders no vices" (E 85). A solitary man on a desert island who cuts down a tree does not wrong the tree any more than a beaver or tornado would do by felling it. The tree is only an object, a thing existing in a web of physical relationships (it requires water, sunlight, and carbon dioxide to live; it releases oxygen as a byproduct of photosynthesis; etc.). By itself, reason only perceives already existing relationships: when we reason about the natural world, reason (theoretical reason) discerns the ordered relations among objects, and after we have entered the moral world, reason (practical reason) discerns moral relationships, distinguishing good from evil (E 67, 214). Many particular physical relationships (e.g., that this tree depends on the water of that stream to survive) exist independently of human action, and the general relationships we call laws of nature (e.g., the law of gravity) cannot be altered by human action.

All particular moral relations, however, are brought into being by choices, by acts of conscious willing (e.g., a promise) or by unconscious and internal judgments (e.g., the experience of falling in love). As with the physical laws of nature, the general moral relations that Rousseau calls the "eternal laws of justice and order" exist independently of deliberation and choice. The principle of self-love, which interests us in our own welfare, cannot not move us to create such moral relationships until *after* we have become sensitive to the difference between persons and things. That is why Rousseau insists that "the child reared according to his age is alone. . . . He loves his sister as his watch, and his friend as his dog" (E 208, 219): the child does not yet sense or feel the difference between persons and things. He is intelligent, he is moved by self-love, but some further aspect of his character must be awakened for him to join the adults in the moral world.

That further motive arises out of our moral sensitivity, which causes us to react differently to pains we believe to have been caused by brute nature and those we believe to have been willingly inflicted on us. It can readily be observed that some such sensitivity is an innate aspect of our nature. Even the smallest child reacts differently to a painful bump on the head than to a slight, glancing blow delivered with the "manifest intention of offending him" (E 66). Rousseau tells us that he had once observed a nurse strike an infant with the aim of making him stop crying. Choked with rage, the infant was momentarily silenced; when he caught his breath, however, he screamed out with all the signs of "resentment, fury, and despair" in his voice (E 66). Rousseau observes that, had he ever thought to doubt it, this one example "would have convinced" him that "the sentiment of the just

---

carefully worked out than) the roughly Kantian views recently articulated by Christine M. Korsgaard. See Korsgaard, *The Sources of Normativity* (Cambridge: Cambridge University Press, 1996).

and the unjust [are] innate in the heart of man" (E 66). What we possess by nature (or, more precisely, what we naturally acquire as soon as nascent reason produces in us a first sentiment of our freedom) is more or less a sense—a feeling—of our own importance, of our own standing in the world. As soon as we are at all aware of our surroundings, we begin to feel that we can make things happen in our environment; with an act of will, I can make my body respond, and with my body, I can move objects in the world. In an infant, of course, this feeling is inchoate and ill-defined, but there nonetheless. Although the infant is generally insensitive to the wills of those around him, he can sense when his own agency, his own power over himself, is attacked. Because it is an assault on his *will* and only incidentally an attack on his body, the baby feels the nurse's assault as an *injury*—a wrong; we know this because we can see that he does not merely feel pain: he responds with anger. This sentiment of our freedom, our sense that we alone have rightful control over ourselves, is the natural source of our capacity for morality; this is what Rousseau means when he writes that the "sentiment of the just and unjust" are "innate in the heart of man" (E 66).

Even though the smallest child reacts with anger when his will is deliberately thwarted by another's will, the child is not properly regarded as a full participant in the moral world because he only senses the wills of others when his own will is directly attacked. Otherwise, the opinions of others and their judgments do not matter at all for him. For the most part, he lives in a world of things in which he alone possesses a will, in which he alone is important. For that reason, Rousseau concludes that "as long as children find resistance only in things and never in wills, they will become neither rebellious nor irascible" (E 66, 97). Adults can shatter a child's self-absorption, however, either (as we have already seen) by opposing their will to the child's or by making themselves into servants of the child's will. In either case, the willful adults introduce the child prematurely to relationships of domination and servility (E 67–68, 91–92). It must be stressed that these relationships are not exactly moral relationships because the child does not yet sense that others view themselves as having the same sort of standing in the world as he claims for himself. The rebellious child is in no position to understand whether the claims one makes on him are morally valid; he treats them all as assaults, and responds accordingly. Nor is the bossy child yet really wicked, though he treats everyone around him as a thing existing solely for his benefit. He may be irascible, temperamental, and manipulative, but he is in no position to sense that he should act differently. He does not (yet) cry with the intention to hurt his parents, to make them suffer. It is simply what he needs to do to make them serve his will—like raising his hand in class to be recognized to speak.

We begin to enter the moral world only after we recognize and feel that we make claims on others who in turn make claims on us. Rousseau is very clear about this: in *Emile*, the first step into "the moral world" is an exchange of promises (E 101). When Emile is still a boy, Robert the gardener promises to respect Emile's rights over a small piece of land in exchange for Emile's promise to respect Robert's rights over his land. With that act, each recognizes the other as a valid source of claims against himself. This exchange of promises is only a *first* step to morality. Emile is induced to make the promise, not because he yet recognizes that he owes anything to others, but as an effort to protect his rights over a piece of property he claims for his own. Thus for the child, as for the infant, "the first sentiment of justice" relates to what we feel others owe to us (E 97). Moreover, Emile keeps the promise, not because he senses that it is right to keep a promise, but because he feels it is useful for him to do so. As long as he wants to see his plants mature and as long as he knows that Robert will uproot his plants if he should disturb Robert's, he is amply motivated to respect Robert's property. He has no more abstract feeling that he should generally keep his promises, however. That is why Rousseau insists that his pupil must, at this age, only make commitments that he will have "a present and palpable interest in fulfilling" (E 102). Since he believes that no child can feel the full force of an obligation to respect the rights of others when it is not in his interest to do so, Rousseau observes that "there is no true property of any kind at that age [childhood]" (E 106).

We truly enter the moral world, however, when a permanent feeling arises in us that we live in a world with other persons, not merely in a world of things. "So long as [a child's] sensitivity remains limited to his own individuality," writes Rousseau, "there is nothing moral in his actions" (E 219). When we begin to feel that the judgments of others can matter to us, when we constantly feel the weight of their eyes on us, and begin to think about how we must appear to them, at that moment, we *truly* enter the moral world (E 235). As Rousseau astutely observes, this development happens for most of us during puberty: we awaken to self-consciousness and become acutely, and usually painfully, aware of how we must appear to others. Once we sense that the judgments others make about us matter to us, our natural self-love, which inclines us to seek our own well-being, now also inclines us to seek to be first in the esteem of others (E 235). This new, complex inclination, arising out of the interaction among self-love, reason, and sensitivity, Rousseau calls *amour-propre*. When *amour-propre* arises in the soul, writes Rousseau, we are truly "born to life" and "nothing human is foreign to" us (E 212). Only when we perceive the web of human relationships that constitute the moral world and realize that we are capable of forming such relationships ourselves is it possible for us to formulate truly moral or immoral intentions. In striking an adult, the child attacks an inconvenient object; in assaulting the same adult, the adolescent intends harm to another person.

It should be stressed that it is not precisely *amour-propre* itself that causes us to enter the moral world. It is true that *amour-propre* usually emerges at the same time as we become aware of our moral relations with others (E 214–215), but in fact both the birth of *amour-propre* and the emergence of our capacity for moral action stem from the same underlying cause—the emergence of that active and moral sensitivity that makes us feel our relations with others. That is why Rousseau supposes that "the first sentiment of which a carefully raised young man is capable is not love; it is friendship" (E 220). Emile's emerging friendship for his tutor is a consequence of their similarity; Emile senses how much he has in common with his tutor and he senses the latter's attachment for him. Indeed, Jean-Jacques takes care to direct Emile's nascent moral sensitivity so that the young man senses only his similarities with others. Only subsequently does he perceive men's differences, and only then does *amour-propre* make its presence felt in his soul (E 235). Although reason is not exactly what causes us to enter the moral world, reason does help us navigate within it. That is why Rousseau insists that "when [Emile] begins to sense his moral being, he ought to study himself in his relations with men" (E 214). It is by means of such study that "reason teaches us to know good and bad" (E 67).

It should now be clear that Rousseau's belief in man's natural goodness in no way implies a naïve ignorance of our capacity for evil. It is true that he holds that there is nothing evil about our biological nature and no evil instinct or principle in our psychological makeup. But Rousseau also maintains that the *capacity* for good and evil is part of what makes us, not merely animals, but recognizably human. Although Rousseau never calls the capacity for evil a part of our nature, his account of human nature implies that the capacity for morality (which includes the possibility of choosing evil) is conditionally natural for human beings.[8] Thus Rousseau largely agrees with the substance of his predecessors' views of human evil as an ineradicable aspect of our nature as social beings, but with one important difference: unlike his predecessors, Rousseau explains how we have come to find ourselves in this predicament.

The Positive Source of Evil

The preceding account of why it is possible for us to choose evil does not yet fully answer the question with which this chapter began: Why are we unjust? As discussed previously, Rousseau insists that his contempo-

8. The Savoyard Vicar, however, does affirm the existence of an evil principle in the soul (E 278). The Vicar's view is best understood as a simplified application of Rousseau's more sophisticated (and general) theory to the particular case of imperfectly educated persons in imperfect, modern societies.

raries exhibit a characteristic corruption of soul or pattern of vices: although they may outwardly appear to do what justice requires and to affirm virtuous maxims, inwardly, their hearts are corrupted. However the bourgeois *declares* his motives, he generally acts well only when disadvantageous for him to do otherwise, and in his heart he cares more about keeping up appearances and getting ahead in the world than in conforming his actions and desires to the requirements of justice. In short, he is vicious, that is, having the nature or quality of vice or immorality, in that he lacks the commitment to justice for its own sake that is definitive of virtue; his apparent commitment to morality is just one of the many tools he wields in his struggle to acquire those things—whether it be wealth, status, power, fame, or whatever—that he believes will bring him happiness.

Rousseau suggests that something about the structure of the social order in his time especially fosters this particular deformation of soul. If human evil were caused by our nature, then there should be no reason why men at one time and place should be any better or worse than the men of another time or place. Observation reveals, however, that this is not the case: although the indigenous peoples of the New World were capable of brutal violence, at least they did not exhibit the same settled dispositions to falsehood and vice characteristic of the bourgeois. Similarly, the historians of classical antiquity show us that in some political societies, such as the Rome of the early republic and Sparta for much of its existence, vice was rare and virtue common. What, then, is it about the bourgeois social order that fosters the spread of vice?

Rousseau seems to give two different answers. In book I of *Emile*, he writes that "all wickedness comes from weakness" (E 67), and in book II, he claims that "dependence on men engenders all the vices" (E 85). Properly understood, the two answers do not contradict each another. The first statement articulates a necessary condition for the emergence of an evil will; the second states a sufficient condition for the emergence of every vice. Although all wickedness comes from weakness, not all weakness leads to wickedness: for example, a child is weak, but not wicked. If it is true, as Rousseau supposes, that "no one does the bad for the sake of the bad" (E 243),[9] then it follows that if we do evil, we do it in order to attain some good we cannot otherwise attain. Even when I seem to be acting out of pure hatred or spite, it may still be said that in injuring my enemy I get a kind of gratification I could not have secured in any other way (see E 244). Weakness is, as Rousseau observes, a relative condition: one is weak "whose strength surpasses his needs," and the inability to be happy independently is, after all, a kind of weakness (E 81).

Nevertheless, the kind of weakness Rousseau calls "dependence on

9. Compare Aristotle, *Nicomachean Ethics*, 1094a1, 1097a16.

men" does indeed cause men to do evil; more than this, it causes men to acquire the habit of doing (or wishing to do) evil, which is to say, it "engenders all the vices." Savages rarely do evil because they rarely find themselves in a condition of weakness, and they do not become vicious because they never find themselves in a condition of ongoing dependence on any other individual's will (see PN 101n). Physically strong and materially self-sufficient, they do not depend on the cooperation of others to assure their physical survival. They do need others in another sense, however: they feel the regard of others and feel the need of their fellows' esteem, and they form particular attachments that make them even more needy. Love, after all, is a kind of weakness: the lover needs something he cannot himself supply, namely the affection of his beloved (E 221). These two weaknesses lie at the root of the two kinds of crimes the savages commit—crimes of violence, motivated by the desire to avenge real or perceived slights to their honor (D2 166), and crimes of passion, motivated by jealousy (D2 165). Among the savages, however, the causes of crime are particular and arise only intermittently. Since no permanent inequalities of status or permanent relationships of needy dependence exist, no permanent relationships of domination can provoke the kind of seething resentment and settled disposition to assert oneself at any cost that one sees among "civilized" men.

Unlike the savage, however, the bourgeois lives in conditions of radical and permanent "dependence on men," and this state is what causes the specific deformations of character that distinguish him from other human types. Unlike the self-sufficiency characteristic of the savage way of life, a modern society is marked by a complex division of labor that makes each individual dependent for his physical survival on the labor of many hands. Rousseau cannot be understood to blame the distinctive vices of the bourgeois entirely on the division of labor, however, for the simple reason that Rome and Sparta—societies in which virtue flourished—were also based on a division of labor. To understand the why the division of labor produced different effects in the ancient republics than it does in modern, commercial societies, we must examine more closely Rousseau's account of the different sorts of dependence:

> There are two sorts of dependence: dependence on things, which is from nature; dependence on men, which is from society. Dependence on things, since it has no morality, is in no way detrimental to freedom and engenders no vices. Dependence on men, since it is without order, engenders all the vices, and by it, master and slave are mutually corrupted. If there is any means of remedying this ill in society, it is to substitute law for man and to arm the general wills with a real strength superior to the action of every particular will. If the laws of nations could, like those of nature, have an inflexibility that no human force could ever conquer, dependence on men

would become dependence on things again; in the republic all of the advantages of the natural state would be united with those of the civil state, and freedom which keeps man exempt from vices would be joined to morality which raises him to virtue. (E 85)

What distinguishes us moderns from the citizens of the ancient republics is that, unlike them, we are dependent for our survival on the "particular will" of many others. As Rousseau explains in the *Social Contract*, a man's particular will is oriented toward his own well-being, *as he understands it*; in other words, it is oriented by his self-interest. What is distinctive about bourgeois, commercial societies such as ours is that their organizing principle is a particular conception of self-interest. What the bourgeois most cares about is preserving or enhancing his status relative to others; his interest, as he conceives it through the lenses of inflamed *amour-propre*, necessarily includes the subordination of others. When two men, each of whom longs to be superior to others, seek to undertake a task together, each one serves the interests of the other only because (and only insofar as) he judges it to be in his own, exclusive interest for him to do so. The temporary community they create is riven by conflict because the partners do not have necessarily shared interests; each seeks to use the other in order to advance his own, exclusive well-being.

Setting himself boldly against the conventional wisdom of his age (and of ours), Rousseau attributes his contemporaries' characteristic vices to the fact that they characteristically relate to one another in terms of self-interest. Rousseau's reference to *vices* here is significant: his point is not just that the bourgeois occasionally acts badly, but that the bourgeois character is marked by morally corrupt habits. This systematic corruption arises in the bourgeois and not the savage because the bourgeois, unlike the savage, finds himself in *ongoing relationships* of weakness and dependence. Rousseau adds that the "dependence on men" typical of a society based on self-interest "engenders all the vices" because "it is without order" (E 85). In a footnote, he explains this puzzling remark by observing that he had shown in the *Social Contract* "that no particular will can be ordered to the social system" (E 85n). What he means is that no individual's well-being corresponds on all points with the good of the community. Moreover, when all conceive it to be in their interest to be superior to others, the pursuit of self-interest necessarily disregards what is good for others (SC 57).

In light of this, Rousseau's observation that "master and slave are mutually corrupted" by "dependence on men" takes on new significance. It is true that he judged the most profoundly corrupting relationships to be those of personal dependence—relationships in which one party depends for his whole livelihood on the good will of another, as a valet depends on his master. Those relationships corrupt for two reasons. First, because master and valet typically have different and often have diametrically opposed material interests. The master wants his servant to do his bidding, to run his errands, to advance his interests. The servant, conversely, wants to be free to do his own will. Dependent for his very survival on the good opinion of his master, however, the servant can only advance his material interests by acting strategically, manipulating his patron as best he can to get as much benefit for himself at as low a cost as possible. A master who recognizes these dispositions in his valet has every reason to act strategically in turn—devoting his energies to figure out how best to induce the valet to do his bidding. Because both master and servant adopt an essentially manipulative relationship to each other, less difference exists between them than it appears. Thus Rousseau observes that "even domination is servile when it is connected with opinion, for you depend on the prejudices of those you govern by prejudices. . . . They have only to change their way of thinking, and you must perforce change your way of acting" (E 83). Relationships of personal dependence are corrupting for a second reason: master and servant have necessarily opposed moral interests as well as accidentally opposed material interests. That is the natural effect of *amour-propre*. A master looks down on his servants as his inferiors, taking a kind of satisfaction in the contemplation of his own superiority of status. Recognizing the signs of their master's disdain, the servants naturally (predictably) seek to assert their superiority over him in the only ways available: by tricking, deceiving, and perhaps by stealing from him. He may legally be the master, but as long as he is their dupe, a servant can meet the master's disdain for his status with his contempt for the master's stupidity.

Corrupting as these relationships of personal dependence may be, they are not the focus of Rousseau's critique because they are not the whole story behind the vices of the bourgeois. Even in eighteenth-century Paris, a man's character was formed by more than just his relationships with his servants. In any case, were these relationships the whole source of the moral corruption Rousseau observes in his contemporaries, there would be no reason to expect that we, today, in the United States would find much to recognize in Rousseau's portrait of the bourgeois. Yet, it cannot be denied that the bourgeois, as Rousseau describes him, is a common figure in modern American life. That is because *all relationships grounded in the narrowly economic self-interest of the parties share some of the character of relationships of personal dependence*. The mutual corruption of master and slave is only a particularly clear case that vividly displays the traits common to all such relationships, namely that they are at some level manipulative, and the parties to them at least to some extent recognize it and act accordingly.

That is why Rousseau never limits his critique to relationships of personal dependence, and in fact, boasts of his iconoclastic critique of the politics of self-interest:

> Of all the truths I submitted to the judgment of the wise, this is the most arresting and the most cruel. All our writers regard the crowning achievement of our century's politics to be the sciences, the arts, luxury, commerce, laws, and all the other bonds which, by tightening the social ties among men through self-interest, place them all in a position of mutual dependence, impose on them mutual needs and common interests, and oblige everyone to contribute to everyone else's happiness in order to secure his own. . . . What a wonderful thing, then, to have put men in a position where they can live only by obstructing, supplanting, deceiving, betraying, destroying one another! From now on we must take care never to be let ourselves be seen as we are: because for every two men whose interests coincide, perhaps a hundred thousand oppose them, and the only way to succeed is either to deceive or to ruin all those people. (PN 100; see also D2 197–198)

Is this account valid? On first inspection, Rousseau's critique of self-interest seems overstated. Surely not every servant aims to deceive and defraud his master: the portrait of the faithful butler Stevens in Kazuo Ishiguro's *The Remains of the Day* is also a recognizable human type, and it is possible that the noble servant of a better master than Lord Darlington would not have found himself forced to sacrifice his own conscience in the service of his master's vicious anti-Semitism. And, surely not every exchange of goods or services in a market economy is marred by the parties' overt will to manipulate one another. These objections are all sound, but they do not contradict Rousseau's analysis. His account does not purport to predict or explain the behavior of every individual; he aims, rather, to identify certain broad patterns or regularities in the conduct and character of men living in certain kinds of social settings. In particular, he alleges that living in a society based on self-interest produces a strong tendency to deprave our morals, causing the distinctive sort of corruption described earlier in this chapter. We come to view the demands of morality—the claims of others on us—as an arbitrary limitation on our freedom to pursue our own interest; resentful of the abridgement of our freedom it demands, we adopt an instrumental attitude to morality.

Where we openly acknowledge self-interest as a legitimate principle of action, we tend to conceive our interest narrowly—in terms of our wealth and power—thus increasing the likelihood that our interest will put us at odds with others. We tend also to cultivate our instrumental rationality: we think about the variety of things we would like to acquire, and we think about how we can most effectively manipulate the things in the world around us to accomplish that desired task. Unfortunately, when viewed from the perspective of instrumental reason, the demands of morality appear only as arbitrary limitations on our freedom. To the question, *Why should I not lie?* instrumental reason answers only: *Because it would be bad to be caught lying.* To the question, *Why should I not lie if I will not be caught?* there is no answer (see E 90).[10] The more we think about the goods we hope to acquire, the more vividly our imagination presents to us the delights we expect to enjoy when we do acquire them. We count as ours what we only hope to get, and so we view as enemies and even thieves—robbers of what is rightfully ours—those who stand between us and what we hope to acquire (see, e.g., C 69). In a society organized by self-interest, we often find that we stand to benefit from events that will necessarily mean harm to others. Although most of us feel that we can readily resist a single temptation to do wrong, things are much more difficult when we find ourselves in a *lasting situation* where our interest and our duty are opposed. We can be weakened without even being aware of the change in ourselves, and though we remain convinced of our own virtue, in our hearts we wish evil to befall another that would bring benefit to ourselves. That malevolent wish is the natural effect of our own self-love, as one can readily observe (see, e.g., C 46–47). Inflamed *amour-propre* only exacerbates this effect by filling our hearts with passions that are necessarily inimical to the welfare of others. He who seeks wealth for the status its possession confers finds himself necessarily at odds with vast numbers of people, since *amour-propre* views the prosperity of others as an affront to his own (LB 937).

UNHAPPINESS

Does Rousseau's model of human nature enable him to solve the second of the two puzzles at the heart of his ethical argument—the mystery of the unhappiness of the bourgeois? The mystery is this: Rousseau's bourgeois is a man who gets what he wants, who often has every reason to expect that he will continue to get what he wants, and who nevertheless fails to find the true happiness that comes so easily and so naturally to us as children. Rousseau perceptively observes that his problem is a kind of moral blindness: the bourgeois looks for happiness in the wrong places, and he keeps looking in those same wrong places because he believes, and persists in believing, that where he is looking is correct. That is the only possible explanation: no one in his right mind prefers the worse to the better, misery to

10. This is, in effect, the question asked by the "fool" (in *Leviathan*, 90–91), which Hobbes struggles—unsuccessfully, in my view—to answer (*Leviathan*, 91–93).

happiness. The question, of course, is: How it is possible for anyone to be thus deceived about what goods are genuinely productive of happiness?

Reason, or more precisely, the active imagination and foresight to which it gives rise, are clearly a part of the problem. Neither animals nor children are deceived about what conduces to their happiness because neither animals nor children possess much in the way of reason. We bourgeois add to the physical ills, inseparable from the lot of any sensitive being, other ills of our own making—above all, the fear of death. Animals and children do not fear death because they do not know what it is. We do not know what death brings either, but we fear it because of what we imagine it to be (E 82). In addition, we multiply pains for ourselves in other ways: making plans for the future and, envisioning in our imagination the success we expect, we become attached to goods that we only hope to acquire. This process of attachment involves not only the operation of our self-love and reason (that together incline us to seek our own well-being) but also our active sensitivity (that lies at the root of our ability to bestow meaning on things so that we feel them to be almost an aspect of our own well-being). We come to regard our plans and hopes as extensions of ourselves, and we suffer the disappointment of our expectations as if it were the loss of what we already possess.

Although the faculties of imagination and sensitivity may explain why we are so much more vulnerable to suffering than the animals, they cannot account for the bourgeois' characteristic and curious blindness to his own real welfare. In his inability to recognize that the goods he pursues are more apparent than real, he resembles those in the grip of the vices. The greedy man, for example, finds no lasting satisfaction in his money; however much money he has, he always wants more. The seducer finds no lasting happiness in his last conquest; like Don Juan, he moves restlessly on from one affair to the next. The ambitious man finds no lasting happiness in his power; like Caesar Augustus lamenting the destruction of his legions by Varrus, he suffers more from his impotence than he relishes the taste of his power (see E 242–243). Moreover, those in the grip of vice characteristically have trouble perceiving these effects. Thus the greedy man attributes his restlessness not to his immoderate love of money, but to the smallness of his fortune; the seducer blames the failure of each romance on the faults of his most recent conquest, supposing that the next one will fill the void in his heart; the ambitious man attributes his reverses to a want of power, and blindly pursues the same self-contradictory course. As Rousseau describes him, the bourgeois lacks the single-mindedness of these exemplars of avarice, lust, and ambition. As we have seen, the bourgeois soul is not so much gripped by vice as it is indifferent to virtue: he self-consciously seeks his own welfare, generally avoiding wickedness but only for fear of the consequences of getting caught. But unlike the other figures just considered, the bourgeois does not necessarily have any single, fixed notion of where his welfare lies: Rousseau describes him as "floating" through life, meandering haphazardly from one project to another.[11] In a way, he is less blind than the thoroughly vicious soul since his aimlessness reflects some awareness—perhaps unconscious—that nothing he does satisfies the deepest longings of his heart.

In a few short, cryptic sentences at the beginning of *Emile*, Rousseau explains why those resembling the bourgeois find themselves drifting through life without ever really attaining the happiness naturally longed for:

> [T]he education of society . . . tending to two contrary ends, fails to attain either. It is fit only for making double men, always appearing to relate everything to others and never relating anything except to themselves alone . . .
>
> From these contradictions is born the one we constantly experience within ourselves. Swept along in contrary routes by nature and by men, forced to divide ourselves between these different impulses, we follow a composite impulse which leads us to neither one goal nor the other. Thus in conflict and floating during the whole course of our life, we end it without having been able to put ourselves in harmony with ourselves and without having been good either for ourselves or for others. (E 41)[12]

The feeling of floating arises because we are pulled in contrary directions by two distinct passions (see J 164). If we were moved solely by self-love and reason, we might from time to time find ourselves puzzled about how most efficiently to advance our own well-being, but we should not find ourselves divided, pulled first in one direction then in another. Natural self-love speaks with one voice, telling us to seek our own absolute well-being. But life in society generates a second passion in our souls, distinct from self-love, which deflects us from following the path it indicates.

11. Rousseau was hardly the first to make this observation. Using a virtually identical metaphor, Aristotle notes that good people differ from those who are not good in that "they are in concord with themselves and with each other . . . for their wishes are stable, not flowing back and forth like a tidal strait." *Nicomachean Ethics*, 1167b5–8.

12. Rousseau's account here echoes Aristotle's account of the inner dividedness of vicious people: "they are at odds with themselves, and . . . have an appetite for one thing and a wish for another. . . . Besides, vicious people seek others to pass their days with, and shun themselves. For when they are by themselves they remember many disagreeable actions . . . but they manage to forget these in other people's company. . . . Hence such a person does not share his own enjoyments and distresses. For his soul is in conflict, and because he is vicious one part is distressed at being restrained, and another is pleased [by the intended action]; and so each part pulls in a different direction, as though they were tearing him apart." *Nicomachean Ethics*, 1166b7–22.

That second passion is *amour-propre* inflamed into a concern for how we stack up against others in terms of the goods valued in society. Unfortunately for us, our fellows speak with two voices, professing to value contradictory goods. Our parents, our pastors, and our teachers all tell us to be good for others; they preach the golden rule, admonishing us to tell the truth, obey the law, respect others, and so forth. But we see in the world that people are esteemed and rewarded for their wealth, status, and accomplishments—regardless of how they attained them. As a result, we learn from society that we should seek our own welfare in whatever way we please, so long as we preserve the appearance of justice. From the contradictory education we receive from society, we learn to treat the demands of justice instrumentally: we profess our attachment to justice while making the real principle of our action the pursuit of our own self-interest.

Thus the "different impulses" of nature and men, of self-love and inflamed *amour-propre*, pull us along "contrary routes." Sometimes we genuinely do aspire to be happy and worthy of being so (that is the route marked out by well-ordered nature); at other times, we orient ourselves only by reference to society's values (following the route marked out by opinion). *Amour-propre* is the cause of the moral blindness diagnosed earlier. We who resemble Rousseau's bourgeois soul find it impossible to listen only to the voice of nature because the impressions we receive from society are so vivid and so loudly contradict the advice of the conscience and the heart. But we find no lasting satisfaction in following the guidance of inflamed *amour-propre*. We may for a time find some satisfaction in the money, power, and status we acquire by manipulating others, but those goods do not generate any lasting satisfaction in the heart, and our natural longing for happiness, which can never be eradicated from the soul, makes us feel their inadequacy. We know that we should not cheat on our taxes and our spouses, yet cheating can seem so desirable—and even approved of by the practice of so many famous and esteemed people. Yielding to temptation, we feel guilty; resisting, we feel cowardly and contemptible. Whichever course we follow, the road not taken beckons. Whatever we do, so long as we remain suspended, floating between moralisms we do not believe and an immoralism we cannot relish, we live joylessly, emptily, unhappily. Our longing for happiness occasionally disturbs us as we realize that living as we do, we drift through life without truly *living*—because we no longer know where true happiness can be found.

Rousseau's analysis of *amour-propre* has the further advantage of making it possible to understand why the pursuit of goods such as money and power generally fails to bring happiness and why their pursuit continues nevertheless. Money is a good thing, of course, and Rousseau never denies this: when he reaches adulthood, Emile does not renounce his fortune but only resolves not to become a slave to his money (E 472). It is a good thing, however, only when it is used well—when the motive behind its use springs from a well-ordered development of our natural self-love. Rousseau has a great deal to say about the details of good domestic economy in the letters of *Julie* devoted to Wolmar's management of Clarens, his estate (J 363–386, 492–499). The greedy man, however, takes an entirely different interest in money: he values money not for the sake of the goods it can buy but for the status its possession confers. To long for the esteem of others on account of one's fortune, however, is to set oneself up for perpetual disappointment. The problem is that the comparisons are endless: having kept up with or even surpassed the Jones family next door, one finds that one still has far to go to keep up with the Smith family down the street. However much wealth one possesses, there are always others with more— or others who might come to have more and who must be kept in their (lower) place. *Amour-propre* continually looks upward at those who surpass us because we cannot be satisfied by the esteem of those who are below us. No satisfaction can be had in being richer than someone we deem to be poor: we want someone we acknowledge rich to see how flush we are in turn. Once we have surpassed them, however, we transfer them into the category of the poor whose esteem matters little to us. Our victory proves hollow, and we set out once again to increase our fortune.

Insofar as we view power as a positional good—valuable for the status it confers rather than for the sake of the good one can do with it—the preceding analysis of money applies. We can never have enough of it to secure any lasting satisfaction in its possession. As we observed earlier when considering Rousseau's critique of personal dependence, however, we saw a second difficulty with the pursuit of power: the acquisition of power over others does not enhance one's real ability to do what one desires as much as may be thought. In order to get others to carry out our will, we must attend to what will move others to act: we must present our wishes in a form that appeals to those we hope to persuade, with the consequence that we may find ourselves unable to accomplish precisely what we had desired (E 83–84). Rousseau concludes: "the only one who does his own will is he who, in order to do it, has no need to put another's arms at the end of his own" (E 84).

CONCLUSION: "REASON WITHOUT WISDOM"

Throughout the Clinton presidency, political commentators often voiced surprise that a man of such considerable intelligence should nevertheless have been so morally obtuse. In Rousseau's view, however, nothing could be less surprising than the juxtaposition of great intelligence and bad morals: in his view, "reason without wisdom" is the characteristic condition of that distinctive man of our days, the bourgeois (D2 187). As with Rousseau's society, so also does U.S. society celebrate a certain kind of intelligence and learning. Above all, we value the problem-solving or instrumental rationality that enables its possessor to figure out how to accomplish, at the lowest cost, whatever aim is set before it. Rousseau's account of human nature implies that, beyond a fairly low threshold, the possession of this sort of intelligence has little to do with our capacity to act morally. Morality fundamentally concerns the goodness of the ends we choose to pursue; instrumental reasoning fundamentally concerns identifying the means to our ends. (The efficiency with which we pursue those ends may factor into our moral deliberations, but only secondarily: it is wrong deliberately or recklessly to squander scarce resources). To be moral, we must be able to make the welfare of others our end; to love one's neighbor as oneself, however, is an affair of the heart, not of the head.

Rousseau's model of the soul explains why the cultivation of instrumental reason can so easily prove detrimental to one's capacity to act morally: the problem is that the sense of mastery it generates also flatters our *amour-propre* into a feeling of pride that threatens to undermine our just relationships with others (see E 173–175). The pleasure we feel in exercising power over things and the pride we take in that power can easily translate into the desire to possess power for its own sake, and in this connection, it must not be forgotten that money is also a kind of power. Where the whole educational establishment and the far more influential economic marketplace shower rewards on those who successfully manipulate ideas, things, and even other people ("human resources") in the service of production, that tendency is considerably strengthened. As we have just seen, however, that desire for money or power as an end—which, in the jargon of Rousseau's model of human nature, we can call the passion of inflamed *amour-propre*—is the source of our distinctive propensity to do evil and the reason why we so often lose sight of where true happiness can be found.

We have seen that Rousseau's model of human nature has great explanatory power: it enables us to understand for the first time the true nature of political society and the genuine causes of evil and unhappiness. By demonstrating that inequality and oppression, injustice and unhappiness are not the natural condition of humanity, Rousseau indeed "raises the stakes" for politics. Now that we know that the worst ills are indeed of our own making, the question is: What, if anything, we can do to cure ourselves? That is the topic of the second half of this book.

4 Friendship and Love

ROUSSEAU'S PORTRAITS OF MODERN society and of the bourgeois character make plain the harsh truth that inflamed *amour-propre* tends powerfully to corrode genuinely human relationships. Looking at the polite society of Paris, where the *bels-esprits* competed to see who could shine most brilliantly in the most exclusive salons, Rousseau perceives that among such people there can be no "sincere friendships; no . . . real esteem; no . . . well-founded trust" (D1 8). Although he expresses particular scorn for the vanity of literary men, Rousseau's point is a general one: those who base their self-esteem on their wealth or loftiness of status tend to view others through the distorting lenses of their own disordered *amour-propre*, thus seeing others through the scheme of their own interests and purposes, not as they are.

In contrast to the manipulative relationships he sees as characteristic of the bourgeois and his society, Rousseau envisions two potentially healthful forms of personal relationship—love and friendship, the "two idols of [his] heart" (C 361). To these may be added the relationships among the citizens of a soundly constituted republic, but it is more appropriate to consider Rousseau's conception of citizenship together with his account of civic virtue in chapter 5. Allan Bloom has argued, however, that Rousseau's conception of human nature cannot really account for the possibility of true friendship at all. In his view, Rousseau holds a fundamentally materialistic conception of man and so finds himself forced to treat friendship as nothing more than a "secondary offshoot" of the sexual passion.[1] "One must have a friend to discuss one's mistress"; thus does Bloom disparagingly report the attitude toward friendship he detects in Rousseau's novels.[2] Conceived in this way, friendship is a relationship of little moral significance that cannot be thought to play a substantial part in the life of a serious person. But since he recognizes that better friendships than this do exist and have existed among serious people—Michel Eyquem de

---

1. Allan Bloom, *Love and Friendship* (New York: Simon and Schuster, 1993), 147.
2. It is a paraphrase of E 215, but Bloom applies the remark also to *Julie*, observing that "the rule is strictly followed in the *Nouvelle Héloïse.*" *Love and Friendship*, 147. The next section of this chapter reveals, however, that Bloom has (uncharacteristically) taken this maxim out of context.

Montaigne's essay eloquently testifies to the reality of his friendship with Etienne de la Boétie—Bloom concludes that Rousseau's conception of human nature must be rejected.[3]

Were Bloom's judgment correct that Rousseau's model of the soul cannot account for the observed reality of true friendship, he would be right to insist that we seek a different account of human nature. In fact, however, Rousseau's model of the soul leaves ample room to account for both friendship and romantic love. Although Rousseau's oeuvre contains no single discussion directly comparable to Aristotle's treatise on friendship in books VIII and IX of the *Nicomachean Ethics*, scattered throughout his works are brief remarks about friendship which, when brought together, enable the discernment and articulation of his implicit conception of friendship. That conception bears a surprising resemblance to Aristotle's account, with two noteworthy differences.

First, Rousseau flatly rejects Aristotle's suggestion that "each person would seem to be the understanding part" of the soul (*noûs*), "or that most of all."[4] Although Rousseau recognizes that our intelligence and reason can be a large part of who we are (at least in some people, including himself), he insists that who we are is most profoundly embedded in our character— our tastes, feelings, and dispositions, the parts of ourselves that depend on reason for their development, yet retain a measure of autonomy from the active and conscious faculty of reason that Aristotle identifies as *noûs*. This disagreement about the importance of the calculating part of the soul accounts for many of the specific differences in emphasis between Aristotle's conception of friendship and Rousseau's. The net result of this difference is that Rousseau's account is more "democratic" than Aristotle's. Whereas Aristotle's view culminates in the suggestion that complete friendship arises only in a community of shared knowers (because he supposes the sharing of thoughts to be what brings people most closely together), Rousseau's conception leads to the conclusion that true friendship arises in those able to share their feelings with one another. We must take care not to overstate the difference between Rousseau and Aristotle on this point. Aristotle's account implies that complete friendships include the sharing of affectionate feelings, and Rousseau's account implies that the most complete friendships include reasoned conversations that, at their best, will be genuinely philosophical.

3. Bloom, *Love and Friendship*, 421.
4. Aristotle, *Nicomachean Ethics*, 1166a22–23. Aristotle's own remarks are more modest and hedged with qualification than the conventional reading of his account suggests, and so the difference between Aristotle and Rousseau even on this score may be less than at first appears. Further references to the *Nicomachean Ethics* will appear parenthetically in the text, indicated by the abbreviation NE.

The second noteworthy difference between Rousseau and Aristotle can be traced to the central innovation in Rousseau's account of human nature—the discovery of *amour-propre*. His reflections on the role of *amour-propre* in the soul lead Rousseau to reject Aristotle's categorization of friendships into three species; Rousseau in effect denies that there can be friendships based on either utility or pleasure. Moreover, Rousseau's model of the soul has one clear advantage over Aristotle's: whereas Aristotle treats erotic passion as a kind of friendship formed for the sake of pleasure (NE 1156a32–1156b6), Rousseau rightly sees romantic love as something entirely different from friendship, grounded on different psychological principles and producing different behavioral effects. In his view, friendship stems from the natural expansiveness of our innate self-love whereas romantic love is constituted by the heightened self-consciousness of *amour-propre*. Friends do not feel self-conscious before each other, since each regards the other as almost a part of himself. In contrast, a lover is utterly dependent on the judgment of his beloved: he wants to please her because he wants—he needs—to be preferred by her over all others (E 214). This crucial difference between the psychology of love and that of friendship accounts for the different moral effects of the two passions. It explains why Rousseau presents friendship as the sole relationship within which education to virtue can take place whereas he portrays sexual love—even with a person of excellent character—as a threat to virtue in a way that friendship can never be. It must be emphasized that Rousseau does not assert that all friendships are morally beneficial; he recognizes (and, in his correspondence and autobiographies, frequently laments) that friendships with persons of bad character are often both painful and morally corrupting.

FRIENDSHIP

The idea that Rousseau maintains any coherent conception of friendship may surprise those readers who are familiar only with the *Social Contract* and the *Discourse on Political Economy*. It may be even more shocking to those who are in any way acquainted with his autobiographical writings. Arguably the most famous events of his life are the rupture of his friendship with Denis Diderot and his tumultuous relationship with David Hume, under whose auspices he had received protection in England from persecution on the Continent. It is true that Rousseau was a difficult man to both have and keep as one's friend, even in his early days in Paris, and he became much more difficult later, as the shattering impact of the political persecution he suffered in France and Switzerland after the publication of *Emile* took its toll on his psychological well-being.

Nevertheless, he wrote a surprising amount about friendship, and, as an examination of those writings reveals, friendship occupies an important place within his system of thought. Several discussions of friendship appear in *Emile*, and in that work Rousseau explains most clearly how his understanding of human nature accounts for the reality of friendship. He describes two of the central relationships in that work—that between Jean-Jacques in his role as tutor and his pupil, Emile, and that between the Savoyard Vicar and a younger version of Jean-Jacques, the author—as friendships. In both cases, as the arguments of chapters 6 and 7 demonstrate, the nature of the relationship proves vital to the success of the educational project being undertaken. Friendship also figures as one of the principal themes in his other novel, *Julie*, where the connection between friendship and moral education is again explored.

It has already been noted that Rousseau writes at length about his friendships in his autobiographies, and much can also be learned about Rousseau's own attitude toward friendship by reading his letters. The letters must be used with a degree of caution, however. Just as Rousseau never succeeded in living up to the principles of virtue he preached, so also did Rousseau never live up to his own ideal of friendship. In fact, those failures turn out to be linked: he failed most conspicuously as a friend when and because he most conspicuously failed to live up to the demands of virtue.[5] Because the historical Jean-Jacques Rousseau cannot be regarded as an exemplary friend (despite his protestations to the contrary), references here to his letters and autobiographical writings are made to illustrate the principles developed in his system and to show that he tended to think about his own personal relationships in the terms his intellectual system made available to him.[6]

Aristotle on Friendship: An Introduction

Before we consider what Rousseau has to say about friendship, it will be helpful to begin with a summary of Aristotle's account, which will serve

5. Rousseau's great failure of virtue occurred when he became romantically involved with Sophie d'Houdetot who despite being married to another man was romantically linked with one of Rousseau's friends, Jean-François de Saint-Lambert. Rousseau's disgraceful behavior in this affair (he betrays and lies to his friend, Saint-Lambert; he seems to have hurt the feelings of his friend and patron, Louise-Florence d'Epinay, or at least wounded her vanity, by ignoring her own attentions for him and falling in love instead with her sister-in-law; and his conduct throughout demonstrated a total disregard for Therese) did much to contribute to his break with Mme. d'Epinay, Melchior Grimm, and eventually Diderot and the whole philosophic circle around the Baron d'Holbach. Rousseau would eventually admit that he was less able to subordinate his desires to his duties "than any other man in the world" (RW 77).

6. The most important such letter is the one he wrote to Sophie d'Houdetot on 17 December 1757 (CC 4:592) to justify his ending of his friendship with Mme. d'Epinay and his abrupt departure from the "Hermitage" on her property in which he had been living for about two years.

as a useful point of reference for the analysis to follow.[7] It must be noted at the outset, however, that the Greek word *philía*, translated here as friendship, includes a wider range of human relationships than we would normally refer to in English as friendships. Not only those whom we consider friends in the narrow sense but also our parents, our children, our business associates, our traveling companions, and even our fellow citizens (NE 1159b25–30), and in a way, all human beings (NE 1155a20–22, 1161b7) are our *philoi*. This usage becomes more intelligible when we bear in mind that the noun for "friend," *philos*, is related to the verb "to love," *philein*. Our *philoi* are all those with whom we share or jointly create some form of community, pursuing together a narrower or wider range of goods in common; in short, our *philoi* are those who love what we love.

Aristotle identifies three species of friendship, differentiated according to the three objects that can inspire love, namely: pleasure, utility, and goodness (NE 1155b16–1156b35). To be in a relationship of friendship with another, one must: (1) have goodwill for the other, which is to say that one must wish good things for him, (2) the other must have a like goodwill in return, and (3) each must be aware of the other's goodwill (NE 1155b28–1156a6). Because it requires reciprocity, friendship also demands a measure of equality between the friends.

In every case, the origin of friendship lies in our recognition of something lovable in another. It may be that we take pleasure in each other's company: we delight in each other's wit, enjoy playing sports together, or even admire each other's bodies. Such relationships for the sake of pleasure are the typical friendships of the young, Aristotle observes. But since these relationships are based on feelings, which in young people readily change, they tend not to last (NE 1156a32–b5). Another sort of friendship arises when we find association with another to be advantageous or useful to us. Aristotle seems to include among friendships for the sake of utility virtually every sort of economic relationship—not only relationships between partners in a business enterprise whose mutual confidence is such that they feel no need to put the terms of their partnership into writing, but also the legally enforced contractual relationship between a creditor and a debtor (NE 1162b25–30)—which plainly does not much resemble our ordinary notion of friendship. Friendships for the sake of advantage are less perfect than friendships for the sake of pleasure: in the latter case, the

7. Of a vast literature on Aristotle's conception of friendship, the following three works proved most helpful in preparing the summary account presented here. John M. Cooper, "Aristotle on Friendship," in Amélie Oksenberg Rorty ed., *Essays on Aristotle's Ethics* (Berkeley: University of California Press, 1980); A. W. Price, *Love and Friendship in Plato and Aristotle* (Oxford: Oxford University Press, Clarendon Press, 1989); Bernard Yack, *Problems of a Political Animal: Community, Justice, and Conflict in Aristotelian Political Thought* (Berkeley: University of California Press, 1993).

friends exchange the same thing with each other and desire to spend time with each other (NE 1158a18–23). But friendships for the sake of utility grow out of the exchange of different goods. Moreover, such friends need not even take pleasure in each other's company (NE 1156a27), they typically do not seek to spend time together, and their association with each other lasts only as long as the advantage continues on both sides (NE 1157a14–16).

The best form of friendship—Aristotle calls it complete friendship (*teleía philía*)—is friendship for the sake of another's good character (NE 1156b6–13). It is complete because it includes the advantages of the lesser forms of friendship: such friends are also useful and pleasant to each other. Only those who are friends for the sake of each other's good character truly embody the highest aspiration of friendship: to love each other for their own sakes.[8] This is so because a man's virtues are constitutive of his being in a way that his wealth or handsome appearance is not. These friendships arise out of the goodwill inspired by the perception of the other's good qualities (NE 1167a4–20). Both friends jointly love what is good, in this case the virtues of character and thought that both embody. But that is not to say that they do not love each other for themselves: it is not just that my friend loves the ideal of justice, which I happen to embody (let us suppose); it is that he loves *my being just*—as I love his being just. Since each of us also loves himself, we both share the same loves: I love my friend's virtuous character, as he loves his own character, and he loves my character, as I love my own.

But such friendships are not formed all at once: although the "wish for friendship" may arise quickly, the state of friendship cannot arise "until each appears lovable to the other and gains the other's confidence"—which takes time (NE 1156b26–30). Although any sort of person can form any of the inferior sorts of friendship with any sort of person, only two good people can form the best sort of friendship. A good person would be pained by a bad person's vices and so would not wish to spend time with him, and a bad person would find no enjoyment in his association with the better person unless he derived something he would recognize as advantageous (such as money) from the association (NE 1157a15–20), which he would not do, since good people "neither request nor provide assistance that requires base actions" (NE 1159b5–6). The friendships of those "who are similar in being virtuous" are the most enduring: first, because each loves the other for his character, which is firm and slow to change (NE 1159b4–5), and second, because of their well-founded trust for each other,

---

8. Price, *Love and Friendship in Plato and Aristotle*, 101–110. For a contrasting view, see Cooper, "Aristotle on Friendship."

their relationship is "immune to slander" (NE 1157a20). There is another reason: good people help one another to avoid error and to improve their character (NE 1159b6–8, 1170a10, 1172a10–15). They want to aid one another in this way because they delight in what is good and wish only what is good for their friends.

We must not be misled by the dry tone of Aristotle's treatise into thinking that his idea of a complete friendship is an edifying but joyless association between a pair of priggish and stuffy old pedants. In fact, Aristotle observes on more than one occasion that both old and "sour" people have difficulty making friends because their company is harder to enjoy (NE 1157b15, 1158a1–11). Aristotle's notion of friendship requires that the friends delight in each other's presence and indeed love each other: "loving is the virtue of friends" (NE 1159a35). Friendship, after all, is a relationship sustained by no bond other than the free choices of the friends to remain together.[9] One clear sign of such a friendship is the wish to spend time together: "what friends find most choiceworthy is living together" (NE 1171b32–34). No one wishes to spend time with someone who is not in some way pleasant to be with. What friends do together depends on what activities they most enjoy doing—what they judge, all things considered, to be the most truly worthwhile and genuinely satisfying: "whatever someone [regards as] his being, or the end for which he chooses to be alive, that is the activity he wishes to pursue in his friend's company" (NE 1172a1–5). Having friends is part of what makes life worth living, especially for those of excellent character. In such people, self-love is part of what motivates their devotion to their friends. Happiness "is found in living and being active" (NE 1169b30) but it is hard to be active all the time when one is alone (NE 1170a5–7). In the company of others it is easier, and besides, the good person delights in his friend's good actions both because they are good and because they are, in a way, his own (NE 1170a1–2). For, as Aristotle has famously observed, "a friend is another himself" (NE 1166a30, 1170b7).

Rousseau on Friendship: An Introduction

Rousseau's account of the friendships of "decent people" (*honnêtes gens*) evidently resembles Aristotle's conception of complete friendship: in his view, friendship is the reciprocal attachment of two individuals each of whom feels a sense of emotional identification with the other and knows that the other feels the same way for him. In *Emile*, Rousseau elucidates the nature of friendship as follows:

9. At least this is true of the best sort of friendship, which Aristotle treats as the paradigmatic case.

> Attachment can exist without being returned, but friendship never can. It is an exchange, a contract like others, but it is the most sacred of all. The word *friend* has no correlative other than itself. Any man who is not his friend's friend is most assuredly a cheat, for it is only in returning or feigning to return friendship that one can obtain it. (E 233n)

Although Rousseau likens friendship to a contract, Rousseau's conception of friendship as a "most sacred" contract *excludes* relationships entered into for the sake of gain or advantage. One of Rousseau's firmest convictions is that "neither a friend nor a mistress can be bought" (E 348). The only contract friendship resembles is the genuine social contract.[10] The two contracts are alike in that both create communities ("moral persons") by altering the identities of the contracting parties: the ideal friend, like the ideal citizen, thinks about himself not as an isolated *I* but as part of a collective *we*. As with the social contract, the "most sacred" contract of friendship demands perfect reciprocity between the partners as free and equal members of a fully voluntary association. Friendship, like the social contract, may be thought to create a measure of equality between the friends, with one important difference: once the social contract brings a new political order into existence, the laws may dictate the legal equalization of property (as where the laws of Lycurgus established equality in Sparta, which had previously known great inequality of fortune). Friendship may enable two friends of unequal fortune to *feel* that their properties jointly belong to them both, but as long as one retains title to his estate while the other remains poor, the inequality of their fortunes will always be a potential sore point in the relationship. It is hard for the poor friend not to feel envy and hard for the rich not to feel that the goods he is sharing with his friend authorizes him to expect a certain recompense for his generosity.[11]

Friendship and the Soul

Rousseau offers two distinct accounts in *Emile* of the genesis of friendship. In the first, he explains how the false friendships characteristic of high society arise; in the second, he explains how the interaction among our natural self-love, our moral sensitivity, and our imagination makes possible the formation of true friendships. Bloom reaches an excessively pessimistic conclusion about the capacity of Rousseau's model of human nature to account for the phenomenon of friendship because he fails adequately to dis-

---

10. See William Acher, *Jean-Jacques Rousseau: Ecrivain de l'Amitié* (Paris: Editions A.-G. Nizet, 1971), chapter 6.

11. One of the things Rousseau most prized about M. le Maréchal-duc de Luxembourg was the facility and sincerity with which the duke put himself on a "footing of equality" with him and "took [him] at [his] word about the absolute independence in which [he] wanted to live" (C 435, 437, 447).

tinguish these two accounts. In the first, Rousseau writes that "from the need of a mistress is soon born the need for a friend," depicting friendship as a "secondary offshoot" of the sexual passion, just as Bloom maintains (E 215). But an examination of the context of that remark makes clear that Rousseau is describing the passions that move the hearts of fashionable young men in society, not those that arise in the heart of "a carefully raised young man" (E 220). Here is the text of the relevant passage from the first account:

> As soon as man has need of a companion, he is no longer an isolated being. His heart is no longer alone. All his relations with his species, all the affections of his soul are born with this one. His first passion soon makes the others ferment . . . .
>
> To be loved, one has to make oneself lovable. To be preferred, one has to make oneself more lovable than another, more lovable than every other, at least in the eyes of the beloved object. This is the source of the first glances at one's fellows; this is the source of emulation, rivalries, and jealousy. A heart full of an overflowing sentiment likes to open itself. From the need for a mistress is soon born the need for a friend. He who senses how sweet it is to be loved would want to be loved by everyone; and all could not want preference without there being many malcontents. With love and friendship are born dissentions, enmity, and hate. From the bosom of so many diverse passions I see opinion raising an unshakable throne, and stupid mortals, subjected to its empire, basing their existence on the judgments of others.
>
> Extend these ideas, and you will see where our *amour-propre* gets the form we believe natural to it, and how self-love, ceasing to be an absolute sentiment, becomes pride in great souls, vanity in small ones, and feeds itself constantly in all at the expense of their neighbors. (E 214–215)

In society as it is currently constituted, we learn to compare ourselves to others before we acquire the wisdom to distinguish those things that are truly good from those that merely appear to be so. Thus we ask ourselves how we measure up against others in terms of wealth or influence, rather than focusing on such unconditional goods as happiness and virtue. Thanks to our premature introduction to sexuality, we no sooner feel the first stirrings of sensitivity to others of our kind than we conclude that what we are feeling is the desire for sexual intercourse (E 214–220). Viewing ourselves as we think others of the opposite sex must see us, we do what we can to make ourselves appealing to those whose hearts we hope to win. Competing with our fellows to win the affection of the most desirable woman, we seek to distinguish ourselves by our wealth, attire, wit, or in some other way, and so we put ourselves at odds with them, creating a fertile ground for "dissentions, enmity, and hate" to arise. Once we have begun to view our fellows as rivals and competitors, we naturally (pre-dictably) wish to have friends and allies—as many as possible—because they can provide useful services and because having a great many who call themselves our friends is a way of showing our social prowess, and, as Rousseau indicates, so that we will have an audience before whom to vaunt our sexual conquests. Such may be the friendships of society, but those crass relationships in no way correspond to Rousseau's exalted conception of true friendship.

He subsequently explains that "the first sentiment of which a carefully raised young man is capable is not love; it is friendship" (E 220). It is true that Rousseau sees the biological changes that take place during puberty as the physical basis for the emergence of our active and moral sensitivity, which makes it possible for us to love other persons. But it is not correct to conclude from this observation, as Bloom does, that Rousseau supposes that the task of education is to redirect or, as he more polemically suggests, to *misdirect* sexual desire into the sentiment of commiseration and the ca-pacity for friendship.[12]

In mentally developed human beings, *all* of the complex passions we ex-perience are constituted by the interaction between the biological impulses we receive from our bodies and the ideas we have in our imagination. Self-love, which is the most basic principle in the soul of any animate creature, is itself manifested in increasingly more sophisticated forms as the mind develops: first, we seek our welfare only in what is pleasant; later, we pur-sue also what is useful; finally, we seek also what reason tells us is right and good (E 39). The interaction between reason and sensitivity enables us to formulate gradually more expansive conceptions of our self. First we discover that we can attach ourselves to things, as Emile does when he be-gins to cultivate his garden (E 98). Later, as we will soon see, Emile learns to attach himself to other people so that he feels that what is good for them in some way contributes to his own well-being.

It is a mistake, therefore, to suppose that Rousseau regards sexual de-sire *as we experience it* to be somehow more natural or more real than the desire for friendship. Neither is absolutely natural to human beings, as a glance back to the primitive humans of the earliest state of nature confirms, but both can be natural for human beings under certain conditions. Emile's education aims less at misdirecting the boy's nascent sexuality than it does at preventing society from stunting the development of his nascent sensi-tivity by reducing it to nothing other than the desire for sexual intercourse. His education aims to follow the "true course of nature, [which] is more gradual and slower" than the education of society. In the natural course of

12. See Bloom, *Love and Friendship*, 91, 93.

events, unhastened by the "premature instructions" of others: "the blood ferments and is agitated; a superabundance of life seeks to extend itself outward. The eye becomes animated and looks over other beings. One begins to take an interest in those surrounding us; one begins to feel that one is not made to live alone. It is thus that the heart is opened and becomes capable of attachment" (E 220).

If young people become sexually experienced too early, Rousseau fears, "their imaginations" will be "filled by [this] single object" and will "reject . . . all the rest" (E 220). Notice that Rousseau focuses on the danger premature sexuality poses to the *imagination*. All human relationships are mediated by the imagination, which by "transport[ing] [us] out of [ourselves]" enables us to feel what another is feeling and thus is essential to the transformation of our innate, passive sensitivity to the active and moral sensitivity which all normal adults in society possess (E 223). As with the longing for friendship and sensitivity to the sufferings of others, the feeling of sexual *desire* exists substantially in the imagination. Unlike the experience of friendship and pity, however, sexual *satisfaction* is powerfully physical. The premature experience of sex is corrupting because it teaches us to regard the bodily satisfaction of sex as the measure of all human relationships—a lesson that makes it far more difficult for us to sense in our hearts the more refined pleasures of commiseration and friendship.

Because friendship requires us to identify in our feelings with our friend, Rousseau regards the cultivation of pity as one step on the road to becoming capable of friendship (see E 220–233). This is why he rightly refers to pity in the *Discourse on Inequality* as the foundation of friendship (D2 153). Commiseration and friendship are alike in that both rest on the apprehension of similarities among men, and both are sentiments that draw us out of ourselves. Emile's tutor does not shield him from the sufferings of others, but rather brings him to witness them—all the while making Emile realize that he is not exempt from the suffering that he witnesses and that the poor, whose sufferings are so readily visible, are no less pained by the "rigor of their lot" than he would be if he were in their place (E 223–226). Rousseau presents the development of Emile's sensitivity as a natural development of his innate capacities:

> To excite and nourish this nascent sensitivity, to guide it or follow it in its natural inclination, what is there to do other than to offer the young man objects on which the expansive force of his heart can act—objects which swell the heart, which extend it to other beings, which make it find itself everywhere outside of itself—and carefully to keep away those which contract and concentrate the heart and tighten the spring of the human *I*? (E 223)

Knowing the principles of the passions, Jean-Jacques governs his pupil so that he experiences no passions that would put him in contradiction with himself by opposing his natural inclination for happiness or by putting his interests in opposition to those of others. Instead, Emile is encouraged to feel only those passions that incline him to act in ways that enhance his genuine well-being and dispose him to find his own happiness in working to increase the happiness of others.

Allan Bloom has rightly insisted that Rousseau hard-headedly teaches the limits to our capacity for sympathy with others and that part of what makes the feeling of pity so sweet is that the perception of another's weakness is typically accompanied by a feeling of our own strength (E 221).[13] But he wrongly judges that Rousseau thereby commits himself to the judgment that "nobody can share the happiness of even his best friend without envy." Bloom continues: "Aristotle would say that the true friend, although rare, is possible, that he could rejoice in his friend's good luck, whereas Rousseau insists that this is simply impossible."[14] Rousseau certainly does see that the sight of a happy man "inspires in others less love than envy" and in the process wounds *amour-propre* because it makes "us feel that this man has no need of us" (E 221). But that observation does not foreclose the possibility of genuine friendship because Rousseau's account of the soul implies that no human being can enjoy a perfect and self-sufficient happiness (E 221).[15] What "truly belongs to man" is *suffering*: all of us feel the pains of injury and illness, all of us experience misfortune and injustice, and all of us eventually die (E 222; see also E 80–82). Part of what it takes to be a friend is the ability to see past the appearance of happiness that the possession of external goods confers in order to read the heart of another.

So long as "the rich or noble man" continues to prosper, "he has as a true friend only that man who is not the dupe of appearances, and who pities him more than he envies him, in spite of his prosperity" (E 223). We share our sympathies with our friends when they are suffering, and when they enjoy good fortune, we "appropriate a part of [their] well-being," enjoying it with them; and they do the same in relation to us (E 223). What particularly troubles Rousseau in the passage Bloom finds so objectionable is the case of a friendship between two people of very unequal status. In such a relationship there can be no reciprocity in the exchange of anything but

13. Ibid., 68–69.
14. Ibid., 68.
15. He does claim in the *Reveries* to have himself discovered the secret of a self-sufficient happiness, but those claims consistently prove hollow. See Joseph R. Reisert, "Justice and Authenticity in Taylor and Rousseau," *Polity* 33 (Winter 2001): 305–330.

thoughts and feelings, and the inequality of status that divides them must constantly threaten the relationship.[16] That is why Rousseau insists that such a friendship can exist only as long as the force of commiseration tends to unite the friends.[17] In any case, the contrast Bloom seeks to draw between Aristotle and Rousseau is overdrawn, since Aristotle is well aware of the difficulty of maintaining friendships between unequals,[18] and just as hard-headedly as Rousseau, he too acknowledges that a core of selfishness exists in the human heart that complicates but does not altogether preclude the foundation of true friendship.[19]

The Genesis of Attachment

Rousseau sees that friends are attracted to one another not primarily by the similarity of their ideas but rather are drawn to one another by a more comprehensive attraction. Friendship is not primarily a relationship between minds, in his view, but between whole *persons*. He writes that friendship arises when two people find a certain "agreement of tastes" or when "suitableness of characters" draws them together; above all, it is agreement in "moral taste" that unites friends (E 339, 348, 413). Taste is the faculty of judging what is pleasing so that one takes pleasure in the appropriate objects of perception (E 67). Reason is involved in the judgment of what pleases, but a person of taste literally takes pleasure in the perception of something delightful—without having to deliberate consciously about the object of his delight. One does not think about and then consciously decide that the appropriate response to a Mozart sonata would be to enjoy it: one just listens and enjoys. In like fashion, a person of sound moral taste simply delights in the perception of what is morally good. A man such as Emile, for example, suffers when he witnesses the unjust suffering of others.[20] Thus he is moved to tears when he hears of the devotion Sophie's father exhibited toward his wife in adversity because he immediately recognizes it to be a sign of the man's excellent character (E 414). As one would expect, reason plays a decisive part in determining these emotional re-

16. For evidence of Rousseau's fears that the great difference in status between them would fatally undermine his friendship with the Maréchal and Maréchale de Luxembourg, see the letter he wrote to the Maréchale on 13 August 1759 (CC 6:849), quoted in C 446–447.

17. The same point figures prominently in Rousseau's letter to Sophie d'Houdetot (CC 4:592), referenced in this chapter, n. 7.

18. Aristotle, *Nicomachean Ethics*, 1158b32–1159a3: "if friends come to be separated by some wide gap in virtue, vice, wealth, or something else; for then they are friends no more and do not expect to be."

19. Aristotle, *Nicomachean Ethics*, 1159a10–13 (emphasis added): "Hence it is to his friend as a human being that a friend will wish the greatest goods—*though presumably not all of them, since each person wishes goods most to himself.*"

20. This is not the case when he witnesses the suffering occasioned by the just punishment of a duly convicted criminal. See E 253.

sponses, as Rousseau notes explicitly (E 341); it operates unconsciously, however.

Those who have the same tastes in literature, in music, and in other recreational activities are those who delight in the same activities, and such people find many occasions for enjoying each other's company. Those who have the same *moral* tastes find themselves in an even more comprehensive harmony with each other. Since nearly every human activity has a moral dimension, those who have sharply different moral tastes find it much harder to take pleasure in the same things.

Rousseau consistently identifies the similarity of moral tastes and temperaments as crucial to the genesis of the friendships he describes. He observes that Emile becomes friends with those "whom he observes to have ways of thinking and feeling clearly in common with him" (E 233). In the *Confessions*, he describes the genesis of his own friendships in the same terms; thus, for example, he attributes the rapidity with which he and George Keith became fast friends to their "great similarity of character" (C 499). Likewise, he tells us in the *Nouvelle Héloïse* that Claire and Julie became fast friends because they share "the same blood, the same age, and a perfect conformity of tastes and humors."[21] Rousseau describes the beginnings of the friendship between Lord Edward and Saint-Preux in similar terms. The two men met by chance at an inn and struck up a conversation. After hearing Bomston speak about the men and morals in the countries he had visited, Saint-Preux was impressed; when he heard him talk about art and music, he knew Lord Edward to have a "sensitive soul" like his own (J 103).

It is not only similarity of character that draws people into the best sort of friendships, according to Rousseau, but similarity of *good* character. On this point, Rousseau and Aristotle agree, but this principle is what leads Rousseau ultimately to deny the existence of friendships for the sake of utility or for the sake of pleasure. Part of the problem, as Rousseau sees it, is that people whose moral tastes have been corrupted by inflamed *amour-propre* are not sufficiently sensitive to the signs and pleasures of friendship. Those obsessed with social or professional status see others through the distorting lens of their own narrow interests: the other will be a competitor, perhaps, or a useful ally—but hardly a friend (see D 157). Such men cannot form genuine communities with others because they cannot wholeheartedly devote themselves to any truly common good.

21. He notes, however, that the young women also have "contrary temperaments." Julie is more serious and "romantic," whereas Claire is more lighthearted and easygoing. He suggests that this complementarity of differences within a fundamental similarity of moral character strengthens their friendship, but since he does not particularly stress the complementarity of other pairs of friends he discusses I do not take it to be crucial to his understanding of friendship.

When two men, each of whom bases his self-esteem on the amount of his wealth, form some sort of economic relationship (contractual or otherwise), they bring to the table necessarily conflicting goals: each wishes to get the better of the other. To be sure, their interests must agree on some particular point—for example, the one must want the money to be gained by selling a car, and the other must need the car more than the cash he will use to buy it—but their underlying aims set them necessarily at odds. The seller, wanting to maximize his profit, has every motive to hide the true condition of the car; the buyer, in contrast, wanting to minimize his expense, has every motive to deceive the seller into thinking the car is worth less than its true value. Rousseau denies that any such relationship can be a friendship because there is no genuine community in it: the goods that both parties most of all hope to gain (the life-projects they hope to advance by means of the economic relationship) are not common but mutually exclusive. Even an economic exchange from which both parties walk away satisfied cannot be described as having brought into being any community: rather, each of the two happy contractors is satisfied that he has been used in proportion to the benefit he has gained by using the other.

The economic relationships of good people (those who are not gripped by avarice or ambition) need not be conflicted in this way, but Rousseau nevertheless declines to speak of them as friendships. There is no reason to suppose that Emile's working for a master carpenter is in any way morally corrupting, but he is nevertheless not really his employer's friend. Their relationship is not like the economic relationships of greedy people: unlike the avaricious, who aim at taking advantage of one another and so aim at necessarily conflicting ends, Emile and his employer share a genuinely common interest in that both aim to produce good work. Nevertheless, they have in common only one small part of themselves: to be friends, they would have to be drawn to each other in virtue of their overall characters. But in light of Emile's superior taste, unusual habits of thought, and wider range of interests, it is not likely that he would find a soulmate in an employer or one of his peasant neighbors. If Aristotle's account of friendship is to be faulted for insufficiently distinguishing between a genuine community of interests and relationships in which each party uses the other, Rousseau's may equally be faulted for failing to stress the similarity of friendship to other relationships based on the shared pursuit of common goods.

As we have seen, Rousseau maintains that true friendships are based on an attraction to another person's whole character and being. To take lasting pleasure in another person's character, however, one must find that character worthy of esteem (D 196, 225, 244). Thus Rousseau writes of Emile:

He loves men because they are his fellows, but he will especially love those who resemble him most because he will feel that he is good; and since he judges this resemblance by agreement in moral taste, he will be quite gratified to be approved in everything connected with good character. He will not precisely say to himself, "I rejoice because they approve of me," but rather, "I rejoice because they approve of what I have done that is good. I rejoice that the people who honor me do themselves honor. So long as they judge so soundly, it will be a fine thing to merit their esteem." (E 339)[22]

Rousseau does not deny the obvious fact that people can be attracted to others for reasons having nothing to do with good character. He tells us in the *Confessions*, for example, that he had as a youth found himself inexplicably drawn into friendship with the "charming rake," Venture de Villeneuve, and other similarly shady characters (C 83–86, 104–105). When we find ourselves drawn to such people, it is because we find something about them delightful; even if we recognize, when we stand back and think about it, that they are probably not going to be a good influence on us, we still feel some attraction to them. These friendships of Rousseau's youth resemble the friendships Aristotle describes as friendships formed for the sake of pleasure. Such friendships do not endure unless the friends mature so that they come to feel fondness for one another because of their mutual esteem. Typically, however, they do not last. When, later in his life, Rousseau encountered Venture again, he found nothing to admire in his old acquaintance, "and [they] parted rather coldly" (C 334).

In contrast with Aristotle, who insists that friendships form only slowly, Rousseau often stresses the rapidity with which kindred souls recognize one another and become friends. Aristotle explains that the best friendships form slowly because it takes time for people to know each other's character well enough to judge it accurately; only after a long acquaintance can one confidently conclude that one's friend in fact possesses the good character his observed behavior promises. "Those who are quick to treat each other in friendly ways wish to be friends, but are not friends," Aristotle writes, "unless they are also lovable and know this; for though the wish for friendship comes quickly, friendship does not" (NE 1156b30–35). Rousseau's distance from Aristotle on this point is more apparent than real, however. He does insist on the rapidity with which friendships arise (C 11–13, 83, 104–105, 244, 498–500), but he also acknowledges the difficulty of coming to know someone well.[23] Although he suggests in the *Dialogues*

---

22. Compare Aristotle, *Nicomachean Ethics*, 1159a20–25.

23. This is, in effect, the problem that the whole of the *Dialogues* may be said to confront. See esp. D 95–96. Throughout his letters and his autobiographical writings Rousseau continually laments, after the failure of his friendships, how mistaken he had been in his judgments regarding the character of the people he had befriended.

that those sensitive souls who—like himself[24]—are naturally most disposed to be friends can infallibly recognize one another by the presence of a "characteristic sign" that "cannot be counterfeit," there is good reason to suppose that this profession of belief in the existence of 'the sign' should not be taken literally but rather seen as a testament to the depth of his longing for the kind of perfectly transparent and harmonious relationships its existence seems to promise.[25]

Rousseau insists on the rapidity with which friendship is established in order to emphasize the powerful role the feeling of attraction to another person plays in the origins of friendship. He simply does not distinguish between the wish for friendship and the actuality of friendship, as Aristotle does. He does not do so, because he maintains that we should treat those whom we wish to be our friends as if they already were our friends. He holds that friendship can only grow if the two would-be friends accept the emotional risk involved in treating each other with sincerity and openness. Nor does Rousseau seek to differentiate species of friendship, as Aristotle does, based on what we find lovable in the other. He maintains that all real friendships begin out of a pleasure we take in the other's whole person. The tragedy of friendship is that we can never know at the beginning of any association who will turn out to be a true and lasting friend. Only in hindsight can we truly know whether a friendship was based on a genuine esteem for good character or whether it was only a transient enthusiasm.

The Activity of Friendship

Perhaps nowhere is the idiosyncrasy of Rousseau's conception of friendship more evident than in his account of what friends do together. Whereas traditional accounts of friendship emphasize the shared conversation and activity of friends, Rousseau speaks much more about the passive, emotionally intense, and intimate moments only friends can share. His description in *Julie* of the "breakfast in the English manner" at Clarens paints a portrait of friendship that seems remote from anything in Aristotle. We must be careful, however, lest attention to what is distinctive in Rousseau's account of friendship obscure the other, strongly traditional elements in his understanding of the proper activity of friendship. Even in his most rapturous celebration of the silent exchange of sentiments, Rousseau does not suggest that shared conversation is irrelevant to friendship, as Bloom suggests; rather, Rousseau seeks to enhance and deepen the tra-

24. In the fragmentary autobiographical essay, "Mon portrait," Rousseau laments that he "was made to be the best friend that ever was, but the one who should have responded to [him] was still to come" (MP 1124; see also RW 1; C 88).

25. See Jean Starobinski, *Jean-Jacques Rousseau: Transparency and Obstruction*, translated by Arthur Goldhammer (Chicago: University of Chicago Press, 1988).

ditional conception of friendship by emphasizing its previously neglected emotional aspect.

Friends, who are reciprocally attached to each other and who share similar characters and moral tastes naturally wish to spend their whole lives together. He describes the friends Julie and Claire as the Inseparables; at Clarens, Julie creates an estate where all her friends can live together. When, in *Emile*, Rousseau imagines what he would do if he could live as he pleased, he imagines himself living in the country surrounded by friends. He would lead an active life, filled with an assortment of rustic games and activities, with the aim of living as delightfully as possible (E 351–353). Although he occasionally seems to reject it, Rousseau in fact agrees with the traditional maxim that friends should share their goods.[26] He adds to the traditional sentiment, however, the idea that good people— those who are capable of real friendship—should not value property and material things very much. In *Julie*, for example, the community of friends living together scarcely ever discuss their finances, and there is no hint of any suggestion that Wolmar's position as head of the household at Clarens[27] should confer any particular authority on him to direct the lives of his friends who live with him.

Rousseau insists in his letters and autobiographical writings that he does not want money and services from his friends; he wants only "a sweet sentiment, a tender outpouring [of affection]" (MP 1126). Rousseau frequently expresses his suspicion of and resentment at those who, offering him money and other goods, claimed his friendship in order to gain a right to his gratitude. But he writes that "as for true friendship, it is another thing entirely. What does it matter that one of two friends should give or receive, and that common goods pass from one hand to the other; one remembers that one is loved and all is said, one can forget all the rest" (MP 1127). After all, Rousseau points out, one owes assistance to the needy as a matter of moral duty; to give goods to friends or to do favors for them is not remarkable. Love is what friends, as friends, owe to each other, and he insists that friends should demonstrate their affection for their friends rather than concern themselves with what they are owed in return (CC 4:592).

For good people to live their lives in common is to strive together to live well. Friendship is a "sacred trust"—all too often violated, in Rousseau's own experience (D 189). By becoming someone's close friend, by taking

26. In the first part of the novel, when Saint-Preux is still Julie's lover, he refuses to take a small gift of money from her; she insists that he take the gift, however, writing (and clearly expressing Rousseau's own sentiment): "between two united hearts, community of property is justice and duty" (J 55).

27. Insofar as he exercises authority over them, he does so in virtue of his wisdom, which is universally recognized by the others in the novel.

that friend into our confidence, by making our own happiness dependent on our friend's, we give our friend a degree of responsibility for our welfare. We can think of a close friend as a trustee of our happiness and well-being, with a responsibility to look out for our welfare, just as we have a responsibility to look out for the welfare of our friend. Rousseau insists particularly that friends, as trustees of our welfare, must keep the confidences with which we have entrusted them.[28] At times of particular difficulty, a friend might even make the idea of the trust explicit and insist that the friend act directly on his behalf. Knowing that Saint-Preux must be sent away to avoid a scandal, but unable to act herself, Julie implores her friend Claire to act for her: "Be so good as to think, speak, act for me; I place my fate in your hands; whatever choice you make, I endorse in advance everything you will do" (J 145).

Rousseau insists, however, on the limits to the authority we can delegate even to our friends. We cannot enslave ourselves even to a friend. If we ask our friend to act for us, he must still remember that he is our trustee, and he owes us an account of his actions. Exemplary friend that she is, Claire renders a full accounting to Julie of her efforts to dismiss Saint-Preux (J 147). Similarly, when Jean-Jacques agrees to take responsibility for the completion of Emile's education he gives an accounting of what he has already done on Emile's behalf, and he promises to explain any commands he will issue (E 318, 326). There are also times when our friends recognize that they can only help us by forcing us to make the difficult choice we seek to avoid.[29] Any effort to influence a friend's decision making can be dangerous to the friendship because it may reveal differences between the friends that had gone unnoticed until then. Being perfect friends (according to Rousseau's design), Julie and Claire do not come into any conflict; even when Claire refuses Julie's advice to marry Saint-Preux herself, she recognizes the good intentions that motivated her friend's suggestion.

Throughout his autobiographical writings, Rousseau complains that his friends were constantly trying to get him to do things he did not want to do.[30] He particularly resents their interference, not because he thinks friends should be indifferent to one another's moral and physical well-being, but because the particular measures his friends would propose often

28. As a consequence, he complains bitterly throughout his autobiographical works about the confidences of his that his former friends had betrayed.

29. Uncertain whether to go to Yorkshire to marry Saint-Preux and live on Bomston's estate or to remain with her parents, Julie once again asks Claire to decide: "Tell me therefore what I will, and choose for me, when I no longer have strength to will, nor reason with which to choose" (J 201). Claire refuses, and explains that she could not do this for her friend although she had never before refused any of Julie's requests. She does seek to influence Julie's decision, however.

30. See, for example, C 320, 333, 357, 382, 400, 421, 435–436.

did not accord with his own judgment of what would be best for himself.[31] To take the most famous such quarrel, let us consider Rousseau's refusal to accept a pension from King Louis xv (C 318–320). Diderot strongly urged Rousseau to accept, and if necessary, to solicit the pension—on the grounds that Rousseau had an obligation to provide for the financial support of his longtime companion, Therese, and her mother. Rousseau refused, fearing that accepting royal support would entail a loss of the independence necessary for him to speak and write in accordance with his own principles. Rousseau accurately recognized in Diderot's efforts a fundamental disagreement about how best to live—Diderot being far more "bourgeois" than his Genevan friend—but it is not at all clear that Rousseau was altogether right to disregard Diderot's advice. By inducing Therese to become dependent on him, Rousseau had already compromised the independence he sought to preserve, and in this episode, as he would so often, he simply subordinated her own interests to his own. It is true that Rousseau rightly found much to dislike in Diderot's worldliness, but it must have been impossibly exasperating for Diderot to put up with Rousseau's criticisms while at the same time observing how inconsistently the Citizen of Geneva lived out the lofty virtue he so loudly professed.

Rousseau's view of friendship as a relationship based on the shared affections of two people of similarly good moral character leads him also to conclude that the sharing of intimate feelings and tender moments must be central to the practice of friendship. Rousseau agrees with the traditional idea that friends should spend their leisure together in pleasant communication with each other. Rousseau's idea of communication, however, includes more than conversation and letter writing—forms of communication that necessarily involve the mediation of language. Friends share their feelings with each other in addition to their ideas; in so doing, they open their whole beings to each other. This sharing of emotions can involve speech, but it can also be entirely nonverbal. In a time of sorrow (perhaps after the death of a child), a friend's embrace and even a friend's presence can be more comforting than any words might be.

Perhaps the most famous depiction of friendship in all of Rousseau's works is his depiction of a breakfast taken "in the English manner" at

---

31. Not only did Rousseau depict his exemplary friends in *Julie* as interfering materially in the conduct of one another's lives (to the incidents already mentioned could be added Lord Edward's efforts to dissuade Saint-Preux from suicide and Saint-Preux's efforts to prevent Lord Edward from marrying the reformed prostitute, Laura), he personally interfered most heavy handedly in the life of young Alexandre Deleyre, seeking (unsuccessfully) to dissuade the younger man from marrying a woman of whom he disapproved. See Maurice Cranston, *The Noble Savage: Jean-Jacques Rousseau, 1754–1762* (Chicago: University of Chicago Press, 1982), 170–171.

Clarens. Saint-Preux writes his absent friend, Bomston, to describe his time alone with Julie and Wolmar:

> After six days wasted in frivolous discussions with indifferent people, we have today spent a morning in the English manner, gathered in silence, enjoying at once the pleasure of being together and the bliss of contemplation. How few people know the delights of that state! I saw no one in France who had the slightest notion of it. Conversation among friends never runs dry, they say. It is true, the tongue furnishes mediocre attachments with a facile babble. But friendship, Milord, friendship! Powerful and heavenly sentiment, what words are worthy of thee? What tongue dares be thine interpreter? Can what one says to one's friend ever equal what one feels by his side? Oh God! How many things a clasped hand, a spirited look, a tight hug, the sigh that follows it say, and how cold after that is the first word that is uttered! . . .
>
> It is certain that this state of contemplation constitutes one of the great charms of sensitive men. But I have always found that outsiders keep one from enjoying it, and that friends need to be without witnesses if they are to be free to say nothing to each other, as they wish. They need to be collected, so to speak, within each other: the slightest distractions are dismaying, the slightest constraint is unbearable. If the heart sometimes brings a word to the lips, how sweet to be able to utter it without second thoughts. It seems that one dares think freely only when one can similarly speak: it seems that the presence of a single stranger holds back sentiment, and oppresses souls that would consort so well without him. (J 456)

The perfection of friendship is found not in philosophical or any other sort of conversation, he maintains, but in moments of shared silence in which the friends briefly become one by mutely communicating their feelings. Words alone cannot suitably express the depth of emotion true friends feel for each other nor adequately express the various forms of love that they share. Indeed, to say what should be left understood or expressed in a loving glance would be to debase the sentiment and to cast doubt on the sincerity of the feeling expressed (J 456; C 294). In part, Rousseau scorns the mediation of words because he finds them more easily falsified than the expressive language of the body, but, more fundamentally, because our conscious rationality is only one, small part of who we really are.

This passage points to the central role of the imagination in friendship. In his letter to Lord Edward, Saint-Preux mingles his appreciation for the company of Julie and Wolmar with his fond memories of Bomston's friendship for him. Because friendship is based on a kind of identification that proceeds through the imagination, Saint-Preux can take some pleasure in thinking about Bomston's friendship for him, even in his friend's absence. He recalls and contemplates the past affections his friend has shown for him. Once again, too, we see that the intimacy of friendship is opposed to the self consciousness of *amour-propre*. In most circumstances of everyday life, long moments of silence in a social encounter are uncomfortable: we spend the time wondering why the other will not speak, fearing that we look or sound foolish, and generally wondering how we appear in the eyes of the other. In contrast, we remain comfortable even during long moments of silence with our friends because we need not worry about how we appear in our friend's eyes. My friend knows me so well that I have nothing to hide from him, as I might from others. That is why friends can most fully enjoy each other's company only when no one else is present (J 456, 354).

Certainly thought and conversation do matter a great deal to Rousseau. The previous celebration of silence occurs in a letter written to a friend, and despite Saint-Preux's reference to two hours spent in "ecstatic immobility," the truth (as the balance of the letter makes clear) is that the two-hour breakfast was spent neither in perfect silence nor in inactivity. Saint-Preux's letter is certainly written in a style and with an enthusiasm that has little in common with contemporary sensibilities. But the experience he describes is hardly as exotic as the language he uses to describe it. For much of the time, the men were reading the newspapers and Julie was working on a piece of embroidery and looking after the children, who were busy playing. From time to time, they would have a few words to say to one another. Reading a portion of the paper aloud, Wolmar caught the attention of his wife and took the occasion to express his love for her. In reply, she put down her work and "cast on her husband such a touching look, so tender, that I myself [writes Saint-Preux] thrilled at it. She said nothing: what could she have said equal to that look? Our eyes also met. I could tell from the way her husband clasped my hand that we were all three caught up in the same emotion . . ." (J 457). Having fallen silent, the adults remained so, watching the children play for what could have been no more than a couple of minutes, until their silence was interrupted by the children's boisterous play.

The intimate moments passed in silence may be the ones remembered most affectionately, but Rousseau makes clear that they constitute only a small part of the activity of friends. After the moment of silence was interrupted by the children, Saint-Preux commented on the ease with which Julie disciplined the children and thought to ask her about child rearing, whereupon a discussion ensued in which Wolmar and Julie spoke with him at length, and in great philosophical depth, about the principles of education. Rousseau recognizes plainly enough that thinking matters a great deal in human life and thus in our relationships: he insists only that it is not everything and devotes all his considerable literary talent to celebrating the emotional aspects of friendship that he felt were insufficiently prized. He goes so far as to say in *Emile* that there is only one important natural distinction among people: some people think, and others do not.[32] A man who thinks ought not to marry a woman who does not: "for the greatest charm of society is lacking to him when, despite having a wife, he is reduced to thinking alone" (E 408). Rousseau knew what he was talking about, for his Therese could not follow his ideas (C 354).

Rousseau insists on the element of intimacy in friendship because the place of conversation and activity were so misunderstood. He was quite sure that the polite conversations in the salons had nothing to do with any real friendship, and he thought that the bustling activity of men of affairs likewise did more to destroy than to cement real friendships. Because these practices were so corrupted by *amour-propre*, he denounced them for their incompatibility with friendship. He was quite right to do so. We must not, however, forget that his notion of friendship—the reciprocal attachment of two people each of whom loves the other for his whole character—does not exclude, but rather requires that intellectual connection be a part of friendship.

Rousseau, Montaigne, and the Nature of Complete Friendship

Because Rousseau supposes that our sense of ourselves is naturally expansive, his understanding of human nature leaves open the possibility that we can perceive another person almost as a part of our selves, so that our natural self-love manifests itself as affection for our friend. Nothing in Rousseau's account of friendship or of human nature excludes the possibility of philosophic friendship—the friendship of two individuals who seek wisdom together. From what Rousseau says about the *philosophes*, it is clear that he thought that career-minded, philosophical professionals could not be true friends any more than other competitors can. But this judgment, as with all his attacks on the *philosophes*, is based on his perception that they were not true lovers of truth or wisdom.

It has been noted that Rousseau denies that true friendship can be based on intellect alone: friends must love one another's whole selves; although the conscious understanding is an important part, and perhaps the most important part of who we are, it is not the whole. Our tastes, virtues and vices, and capacities are just as much a part of who we are. But this conception does not prevent Rousseau from understanding a great friendship such as the one between Montaigne and Boétie. On the contrary, although Bloom makes an impressive effort to unearth the intellectual roots of their friendship, he fails to show that their friendship was exclusively or even primarily intellectual. I would not deny that the overwhelming attraction Montaigne describes for Boétie could be based on his appreciation of the

32. Bloom, *Love and Friendship*, 123.

older man's mind, as Bloom suggests. But Montaigne writes primarily about the effect of his friendship on his will: "It is I know not what quintessence of all this mixture, which, having seized my whole will, led it to plunge and lose itself in his; which, having seized his whole will, led it to plunge and lose itself in mine, with equal hunger, equal rivalry. I say lose, in truth, for neither of us reserved anything for himself, nor was anything either his or mine."[33] Their wills became one because their very *selves* became one; not only their thoughts and judgments were in common, but their whole moral beings as well were united. "Our souls pulled together in such unison, they regarded each other with such ardent affection, and with a like affection revealed themselves to each other to the very depths of our hearts, that not only did I know his soul as well as mine, but I should certainly have trusted myself to him more readily than to myself."[34] Despite Bloom's arguments to the contrary, Montaigne's account of his friendship with Boétie so accords with Rousseau's teaching that the passages just quoted could just as easily have been taken from one of the letters in *Julie*.

LOVE, FRIENDSHIP, AND THE FAMILY

If the characteristic manifestation of friendship is emotional intimacy, one may well wonder whether Rousseau can distinguish friendship from romantic love. Some readers have concluded that Rousseau does not consistently distinguish these relationships.[35] Not only do the characters in Rousseau's fiction frequently use the language of friendship to advance their romantic and erotic projects, so too does Rousseau himself frequently mingle the language of friendship, family, and romantic love when he describes women he loves. It is fair to say that Rousseau deliberately sought, under the guise of being no more than her friend, to make Sophie d'Houdetot his lover. Nevertheless, an examination of the works comprising Rousseau's system of thought reveals that he adheres with reasonable consistency to a distinction between them: erotic, romantic love is based on *amour-propre*, and friendship grows from natural self-love. There is no reason to expect this to be a sharp, exhaustive distinction: we can feel both passions at the same time to different degrees, and we are not always even the best judges of our own feelings. The love of parents and children is, in this scheme, a kind of friendship; the relation of spouses begins in romantic love but ends, as passion cools, in friendship (E 479).[36]

33. Michel de Montaigne, "On Friendship," in *Complete Essays of Montaigne*, translated by Donald M. Frame (Stanford: Stanford University Press, 1943), 139.

34. Montaigne, *Essays*, 140.

35. See, for example, Acher, *Jean-Jacques Rousseau: Ecrivain de l'Amitié*, 38.

36. In *Julie*, Claire and M. d'Orbe are never more than friends: she feels no passion for him, though she esteems him and enjoys his company.

We can see the tendency to mingle the language of friendship with that of love in Saint-Preux's early relationship with Julie. Even after they have become lovers, they address each other as friends.[37] After consummating his love for Julie, Saint-Preux mingles the languages of love, friendship, marriage, and family in his expressions of affection for her (J 120–22). Of course, Rousseau is himself notorious for having consistently referred to his first lover, Mme de Warens, as *Maman*—that is, as "mom." Rousseau thought his relationship with Mme de Warens was unique and entirely unprecedented, and based on what he writes in the *Confessions*, it is hard to disagree with that assessment. It was a love affair in the physical sense, but Rousseau insists that he never felt for Mme de Warens the violent passions he associates with romantic love. It was a kind of friendship sweetened by sexual attraction and intimacy, and he declares that this feeling of tender friendship for someone to whom one is sexually attracted is the most delightful of all human relationships. He writes:

> I will dare to say it; whoever feels only love does not feel what is sweetest in life. I am acquainted with another feeling, less impetuous perhaps, but a thousand times more delightful, which is sometimes joined to love and which is often separate from it. This feeling is not friendship alone either; it is more voluptuous, more tender; I do not imagine that it can take effect for someone of the same sex; at least I have been a friend, if ever a man has been, and I have never experienced it with any of my male friends. (C 87–88)

Rousseau's relationship with Mme de Warens was more perfect, more complete, than either his relationship with Therese or his affair with Sophie. Like Therese, his *Maman* did not make him feel self-conscious: they could simply be themselves without regard for appearances. But like Sophie and unlike Therese, his *Maman* was sufficiently intelligent and well educated as to make genuine conversation possible.

Later in the *Confessions* Rousseau writes Sophie d'Houdetot was "the first and only [love] in [his] whole life" (C 369). His reason for this judgment is that he was seized by such a passion for her that he was constantly agitated and dreamed always about her. He adds that thoughts of her "set [his] blood on fire to such a point that [his] head became cloudy, a dizziness blinded [him], [his] trembling knees could not hold [him] up" (C 374). Inspired by what he felt while he was writing *Julie*, Rousseau's passion for Sophie d'Houdetot obviously has much more in common with Saint-Preux's amorous passion for Julie than the calm friendship of Claire and her husband, M. d'Orbe. Both lovers are constantly concerned about what their beloveds think of them, and they seek in whatever way possible to

37. See, for example, *Julie*, 118–119, 120–122, 124–131. Julie more consistently addresses Saint-Preux as "ami" (friend); Saint-Preux more typically refers to her as "ange" (angel).

win their affections. When the women resist the men's advances, as Sophie does successfully and Julie unsuccessfully, the men's *amour-propre* becomes all the more engaged: it becomes a point of pride with them to succeed (E 433, 358).[38] Spouses who have been married a long time can become friends whose relationship somewhat resembles Rousseau's relationship with Mme de Warens (at least if we can imagine that relationship shorn of its disturbingly Oedipal aspect). When the sexual passion no longer makes itself felt in all its potentially tyrannical fury, the love of husband and wife can mature into a "tender friendship." Jean-Jacques tells Sophie: "When you stop being Emile's beloved, you will be his wife and his friend. Then, in place of your former reserve, establish between yourselves the greatest intimacy" (E 479).

Just as the relationship between spouses ultimately should mature into friendship, so too should the relationship of parents and children. Once children become adults, they owe their parents love and respect, but not obedience. He explains that a father should rear his own son so that he can shape him into a man fit to be a friend (E 50). On this point, Rousseau follows the teaching of his great predecessor, Locke, who writes that "everyone will judge it reasonable, that their children . . . , when they come to riper years, . . . should look on them as their best, as their only sure Friends."[39] In contrast, Montaigne holds that the inequality between parents and children must forever prevent the complete intimacy that friendship presupposes.[40] Perhaps the greatest obstacle to friendship with one's father is the matter of the family property; Montaigne observes that, "by nature the one depends on the destruction of the other."[41] To this Rousseau replies that fathers' and sons' interests are opposed only in society; he insists that men are capable of real friendship at all only to the extent that they are indifferent to the wealth and social prerogatives that could divide them.[42] Rousseau presents Sophie and Emile, after they are married, as living in friendship with Sophie's parents; the Baron d'Etange lives in friendship at Clarens with his daughter and even with her former lover, Saint-Preux. In addition, Emile and Jean-Jacques—who at times call each other father and son—are also depicted as friends.

38. For a more detailed account of the Rousseauian psychology of love, see Joel Schwartz, *The Sexual Politics of Jean-Jacques Rousseau* (Chicago: University of Chicago Press, 1984).

39. John Locke, *Some Thoughts Concerning Education*, edited by John W. Yolton and Jean S. Yolton (Oxford: Oxford University Press, Clarendon Press, 1989), 109.

40. Montaigne, *Essays*, 136.

41. Ibid., 136.

42. Locke, too, supposes that the opposed economic interests of fathers and sons does pose a danger to their relationship but observes that it need not preclude the possibility of friendship between them. Locke, *Some Thoughts*, 109–110.

THE FRIENDSHIP OF EMILE AND JEAN-JACQUES

In light of the great inequalities that divide them, one may well wonder whether the relationship between Emile and Jean-Jacques is a friendship at all. Jean-Jacques is much older than his charge: he is a young man—probably in his twenties—at Emile's birth.[43] Jean-Jacques also possess a measure of intelligence and of virtue that Emile, with his "common mind," will never equal (E 52). If these natural differences were not sufficient to cast doubt on the suggestion of friendship, further problems require consideration. The early education of Emile requires that Jean-Jacques manipulate the child's desires by controlling his environment and teach him hard lessons by allowing the lad to suffer the painful consequences of misfortunes the tutor could have prevented. Even after Emile has become an adult, Jean-Jacques seems at times to toy with his friend's feelings in ways that do not seem to us directly related to the cause of his education.

Despite these difficulties, one compelling reason to regard the relationship between Emile and Jean-Jacques as one of friendship is that Rousseau consistently characterizes the relationship as a friendship. Indeed, Rousseau specifically indicates the moment, late in Emile's adolescence, at which their relationship matures from one of potential friendship to a genuine relationship based on an approximate measure of equality (E 323). Before this moment, and even during Emile's earliest childhood, Jean-Jacques is to prepare the groundwork for this friendship by becoming "his pupil's companion and attract[ing] his confidence by sharing his enjoyments" (E 51). Rousseau adds:

> I would even want the pupil and the governor to regard themselves as so inseparable that the lot of each in life is always a common object for them. . . . When they regard themselves as people who are going to spend their lives together, it is important for each to make himself loved by the other; and by that very fact they become dear to each other. The pupil does not blush at following in childhood the friend he is going to have when he is grown. (E 53)

It is easy to see how this age difference would gradually become less important as Emile advanced into his late teens and young adulthood, when the crucial part of his education takes place. Although Jean-Jacques surely manipulates his young charge (in ways that differ greatly in degree, if not necessarily in kind, from what modern parents ordinarily do), it is clear that he does so only for Emile's benefit. Whether or not any such education could succeed as fully as Rousseau imagines, the condition Rousseau introduces to judge the legitimacy of that manipulative, early education is

43. This is the age differential between Saint-Preux and the *enfants* Wolmar, who are to become his pupils.

sound. When Emile is old enough to understand, Jean-Jacques explains what he has done for the boy and why, leaving Emile to judge for himself whether he is glad to have received his unique education.

Just as their inequality in age becomes less manifest, however, Emile becomes able to perceive the other, more significant inequality that divides him from his tutor: Jean-Jacques is wise, whereas Emile will be "led to wisdom in spite of himself" (E 431). After his education is complete, Emile continues to recognize his tutor's superior wisdom and begs for his continued assistance: "Remain the master of the young masters . . . As long as I live, I shall need you . . . Guide me so that I can imitate you" (E 480). It is also hard to see any intimacy in their friendship, and whether their friendship can ever be fully reciprocal. These problems arise in virtue of the inequalities of age and wisdom that separate them. Nevertheless, Rousseau shows that Emile and Jean-Jacques do manage to achieve a degree of both intimacy and reciprocity. They do not luxuriate in the deeply emotional intimacy that Saint-Preux indulges with Bomston, Claire, and even with Julie after his cure by Wolmar. Nevertheless, we see hints in *Emile* that they do experience something like it. As they depart from Paris, Emile complains that his tutor is unmoved by the suffering his unsatisfied longing for Sophie causes him. Jean-Jacques does not reproach him for this, but asks whether he really believes in the truth of this accusation. Emile says nothing, but answers only by embracing his tutor and hugging him in his arms (E 410). Here too, the strongest feelings are communicated not by words, but by more natural signs.

Although it is easy to see how Emile could delight in his older companion's company, it is less clear that the tutor can really find happiness as the adopted father of a much younger man. We must assume that Jean-Jacques has other adult friends whose existence is irrelevant to the narrative of Emile and so are not shown—just as Saint-Preux continues to be friends with Wolmar, Lord Edward, and Clare when he becomes the tutor to the *enfants* de Wolmar. Rousseau insists his quasi-paternal role is deeply satisfying, and his assertions are mostly credible (E 159, 323, 407, 421, 423–426, 480). Jean-Jacques delights in watching the development of Emile's potential, and he takes pleasure in Emile's happiness, which he knows he is responsible for having preserved. He insists also, however, that he delights in serving as Emile's go-between in his relationship with Sophie. Given that the real Jean-Jacques Rousseau fell passionately in love with Sophie d'Houdetot as he listened to her declarations of love for his friend Saint-Lambert (C 370), the psychological plausibility of these particular assertions is doubtful. The difference between the real Jean-Jacques and Emile's tutor, of course, is that Rousseau endowed his fictional alter ego with all the virtues—and indeed with the singular attribute of virtue—that he himself so conspicuously lacked.

5 Justice, Happiness, and Virtue

ROUSSEAU'S PORTRAIT OF THE bourgeois presents the terrible and paradoxical image of a man unable to find happiness even though he is willing to do anything, whether it be just or unjust, to attain it. The bourgeois is not ignorant of what morality demands, but he does not love justice for its own sake, which is why he is willing to sacrifice it for the sake of whatever he thinks will bring him happiness. He has been taught always to act justly, but those instructions do not move him as do the lessons derived from studying the actions of men in society. Wherever he looks, he sees few who happily fulfill the hard duties they so easily preach, observing instead that wealth, power, and fame are everywhere admired, regardless of how they were won. Seduced by this spectacle, he fancies that these goods are the real keys to happiness, and he makes these goods the object of all his striving and the basis of his self-esteem. Desiring money, power, and celebrity above all else, he feels the demands of law and justice as an alien yoke, at odds with his longing to be happy. In his eagerness to succeed, the bourgeois does have an instrumental motive to act justly and to obey the laws—it is hard to enjoy wealth or power from the confines of a jail cell—but he does what justice requires only as a concession to necessity, and in his secret heart he looks for ways to get away with as much as he can. Lacking the willingness to do what is right because it is right, the bourgeois is truly said to lack virtue and to possess instead the vice of injustice.

Rousseau's account of human nature enables him to demonstrate that the unfortunate condition of the bourgeois is not paradoxical at all: he is not unhappy despite the injustice in his heart; he is unhappy because he will stop at no unjust deed in order to satisfy his desires. Actually, it would be more correct to say that *the same cause* accounts for both his unhappiness and his injustice; that cause is his disordered *amour-propre*. The soul of the bourgeois is dominated by *amour-propre* inflamed into the desire for money, power, and celebrity; he makes these goods the foundation of his own sense of who he is and the basis of his self-esteem. Consumed by this inflamed *amour-propre*, the bourgeois maintains an instrumental attitude toward morality: he perceives that it can be advantageous to him to be seen to do what justice requires, but he also feels that greater advantages are gained by evading the demands of law and justice, when he can do so secretly and with impunity. But the goods he desires—money, power, celebrity—receive all their value from human opinion; they flatter his *amour-propre*, but they do not really satisfy the most fundamental longing of his heart, his desire for well-being. The bourgeois fails to find happiness or to love justice because his incoherent desires leave him in contradiction with himself: attracted by the goods of opinion, but naturally drawn toward more truly satisfying goods whose worth he no longer appreciates, he finds himself pulled first in one direction, then in another. He "floats" and "drifts" between the opposed imperatives of self-love and disordered *amour-propre*. Not "in harmony with [himself]," he lives and dies "without having been good either for [himself] or for others" (E 41).

Repelled by the unattractiveness of the bourgeois way of life, Rousseau asks: What, if anything, can be done to cure the disorder that disturbs the soul of the bourgeois or to prevent this disorder from arising in those who, although living in the civil order, nevertheless substantially retain their natural goodness? Rousseau's ultimate answer to both parts of this question is the same: one must cultivate the state of soul he calls virtue. In the *First Discourse* and the *Discourse on Political Economy*, however, it appears that virtue can exist only within a republican political order such as those that once existed in Sparta and Rome, where it was fostered and sustained by a rigorous, institutional process of civic education (see PE 20–22). Moreover, neither of those early works offers much reason to expect that this civic virtue can exist in any substantial number of people outside of republican regimes, nor does either work lend much support to the hope that those who have already been corrupted by vice may be cured and brought to virtue. In *Emile*, Rousseau offers more reason for hope. That work depicts the domestic education of an ordinary young man who is brought to know and to love virtue through the efforts of an exemplary tutor. Although the domestic education it depicts is in practice unrealizable, *Emile* nevertheless also holds out the promise that those of us who are "sick with evils that can be cured" may learn to take advantage of the help "nature herself" offers us "if we wish to be improved" (E 31 and n. 2).

"Explaining this much profaned word": Rousseauian Virtue Defined

Despite the obvious differences between them, the civic virtue of the selfless Roman and Emile's human virtue are nevertheless closely related, sharing the same basic nature and structure. In both cases, the essence of virtue is a kind of strength of will or character—the ability to make oneself do what one knows to be one's duty (E 444–445; D1 7). Strength of will, however, is only truly a virtue when it is put in the service of good ends: Catiline, the Roman politician and conspirator, and Oliver Cromwell may have had strong wills, but neither man can be said to have possessed virtue.[1] Thus the first component of Rousseauian virtue is a certain kind of knowledge or belief: the man of virtue must know and understand what it is that his duty requires of him in more or less specific contexts, and he must also recognize more generally that the claims of duty are uncondi-tional. To know what he must do in specific contexts requires that he pos-sess substantially good habits and desires—i.e., that he possess a number of particular virtues (such as courage, justice, moderation, and so forth). He whose moral judgment is generally sound can also be said to have a well-formed conscience. In addition, the man of virtue must know and be-lieve (and so feel in his heart) that he ought to choose to do what is right *because it is right*, not because it would be advantageous to be seen doing what is right. In other words, he must not think and feel that the demands of justice are limitations on his ability to find his own happiness; he must feel that being just is a constitutive aspect of what it means to live fully and well. Civic virtue and human virtue differ, however, with respect to the content of the duty on which they are based. The citizen's duty is emphat-ically parochial: it is to respect the laws of his city and to promote his city's welfare, without any particular regard for noncitizens; civic virtue is the "conformity of the particular will to the general will" (PE 13). Human virtue is universalistic: its content is defined, not by the laws of any par-ticular community, but by the moral law or the law of reason.

Some contemporary interpreters have found Rousseau's enthusiasm for the ancient republics of Rome and Sparta to be wholly incompatible with his professed belief in universal principles of justice,[2] but, in fact, the two are easily reconciled. To be sure, neither the Spartan citizen nor the Roman citizen adhered perfectly to the universalistic morality Rousseau deemed to be required by reason and by the Christian faith: to "do unto others as we would have them do unto us" and "to love one's neighbor as oneself" (D2 154; E 251–252).[3] Indeed, many of the ancient citizens' actions are down-

---

1. In DV 309, Rousseau calls these men "scoundrels" and criminals, though he concedes that they were courageous. Although Rousseau argues in the *Discourse on the Virtue Most Nec-essary for a Hero* that these courageous men nevertheless did not possess the strength of will that is essential for virtue, that effort does not wholly succeed. It would be more accurate (and more consistent with what Rousseau says later in the *Discourse*) to say that Catiline and Cromwell did possess strength of will or force of character but that, since their strength was directed toward bad ends, they did not possess true virtue. Rousseau suggests something sim-ilar later in that discourse, when he observes that bravery "is a virtue in a virtuous soul and a vice in a wicked one" (DV 312).

2. Carol Blum, for example, sees him as glorifying in the "virile militarism" of antiquity. *Republic of Virtue*, 40. Arthur Melzer suggests that Rousseau's refusal to condemn the real in-justices committed by the Spartans and the Romans amounts to a decisive refutation of "those who would see in Rousseau a Kantian moralist." *Natural Goodness*, 62–63.

3. See also E 235n: "Love of men derived from love of self is the principle of human jus-tice. *The summation of all morality is given by the Gospel in its summation of the law*" (emphasis added).

right shocking: Sparta brutally enslaved the Helots, and Rome forcibly sub-jugated all of the political communities within her reach. Rousseau plainly delights in horrifying his readers by presenting the fierce men who did such terrible things as moral exemplars, but he does so in order to make an important point about moral character. Yes, he tells us, the Spartans and Romans did act unjustly toward foreigners, but, he claims, they were nev-ertheless better men than we are in one decisive respect. The ancient citi-zens were truly just to those whom they recognized as their fellow citizens, whereas we who profess the lofty principles of Gospel morality, or its con-temporary secular equivalents, love no one as we love ourselves. If we do less harm to others than did the ancient citizens (itself a big "if" in Rous-seau's view—see D2 197–204), our forbearance does not redound to our credit because we are restrained by our selfishness and cowardice, rather than by any real concern for the well-being of others. In *Emile*, Rousseau makes this point explicitly. He does not deny the injustice of the Spartan or Roman to foreigners, but he does *excuse* it: "Every patriot is harsh to for-eigners," he writes, adding: "*This is a drawback, inevitable but not compelling. The essential thing is to be good to the people with whom one lives. Abroad, the Spartan was ambitious, avaricious, iniquitous. But disinter-estedness, equity, and concord reigned within his walls*" (E 39, emphasis added).

The second component of Rousseauian virtue is a matter of motivation or disposition. The virtuous man's first-order desires must be such that they generally conform to the requirements of his duty and he must, in ad-dition, possess the second-order desire to possess and to act on only those first-order desires that correspond to the demands of duty (whether that duty is defined by the laws of his city or by the moral law). This second-order desire is a certain refinement of *amour-propre* that generates in the heart of the virtuous man the strength of character and will to make him-self do what is right because it is right, even in defiance of any temptation to do otherwise. *Amour-propre* is a reflexive and partially malleable passion, the desire to be esteemed by others for whatever it is about ourselves that we most prize. As the desire to be admired for one's money or power, it be-comes the vices of greed and ambition that underpin both the bourgeois soul's instrumental regard for the rights of others and his contradictory de-sire to disregard those rights in pursuit of his own advantage. In contrast, as the desire to excel in devotion to the common good of one's polity it be-comes patriotism (PE 15–16); and as the desire to excel in devotion to the sublime principles of reasoned justice, *amour-propre* becomes what Rous-seau calls the "passion for virtue" (E 445; J 405). Rousseau supposes that either of these latter passions may support a genuine regard for the rights and welfare of others because neither of them sets us at odds with our fellows, nor does either put us in contradiction with ourselves (as long as they arise in the heart of one whose conscience is well-formed).[4]

Rousseauian virtue bears a certain resemblance to the Aristotelian virtue of *phronesis* (practical wisdom), but in other respects resembles the state Aristotle calls continence (*enkrateia*). Like *phronesis*, Rousseauian virtue is a second-order virtue the possession of which is equivalent to possessing a comprehensively good moral character. Unlike the Aristotelian *phronimos*, however, the Rousseauian man of virtue must sometimes compel himself to do what he knows he ought, but does not want, to do. In other words, the Rousseauian man of virtue is sometimes tempted to do wrong or to pursue illusory goods in a way that the Aristotelian *phronimos* is not. Rousseau does not orient his practical teachings around the idea of full practical wisdom because he fears that it is too difficult for most of us to attain: "no one has ever made a people of wise men" (PE 16). If we cannot hope to become so wise as to be immunized against temptation, we can aspire to a second-best ideal: we can learn to know what our duties are and become sufficiently devoted to them that we are enabled to do what is right, even when we feel tempted to do otherwise. Although Rousseau calls this state of self-commanded attachment to duty *virtue*, it is precisely what Aristotle calls continence.[5]

Rousseau teaches that the education of ordinary souls must aim at cultivating this self-commanding virtue because he maintains that attaining their natural ends without it is impossible. He holds that no civilized person can live happily who does not possess a well-formed conscience and the strength of will to cleave steadily to what his conscience tells him is right (see, e.g., E 446; PE 15–16; DV 306; LO 264–265).[6] Although he sometimes suggests that the possession of virtue is a sufficient condition of happiness, Rousseau's model of the human soul in fact supports only the more modest conclusion that virtue is necessary for happiness. Why this should be so is not immediately apparent. Our natural end is specified by the most basic principle in our souls, natural self-love, and this principle directs us to seek our own welfare. By nature, we long for happiness with every fiber of our being, and this longing can never be eradicated from the human soul

---

4. Compare Aristotle, *Nicomachean Ethics*, 1168b24–28: "If someone is always eager to excel everyone in doing just or temperate actions or any others expressing the virtues, and in general always gains for himself what is fine, no one will call him a self-lover or blame him for it."

5. See e.g., Aristotle, *Nicomachean Ethics*, 1151b35–1152a5: "the continent person has base appetites" but is not "led by them."

6. Rousseau aspires to find a way to live happily without virtue (and without practical wisdom or *phronesis*) in the *Reveries of the Solitary Walker*, but although that work testifies to the ardor of Rousseau's desire to realize this aspiration, it also illustrates Rousseau's failure to realize this aim. Reisert, "Justice and Authenticity."

(E 442). But if we long only for "our well-being and our self-preservation" (D2 127), it would seem that we should have no need of virtue as either Aristotle or Rousseau understands it. Even according to the Aristotelian account, according to which the good man need never deny himself anything he desires (since he will only desire what is good), the virtuous man must prefer suffering injustice to doing it—a preference that may, in particularly unfortunate circumstances, require of him even the sacrifice of his own life.[7] Rousseau's praise of men like Cato and Socrates, who chose death rather than violate their principles, demonstrates that he too, accepts this hard conclusion. How can a virtue that may require of us the sacrifice of our own life nevertheless be necessary for happiness? Rousseau's self-commanding virtue is more demanding than the Aristotelian state of full virtue because it not only requires that one prefer suffering wrong to doing wrong, but it also calls for one to make more frequent sacrifices. The man of Rousseauian virtue is often tempted to pursue goods he desires but that his conscience and reason forbid; in these cases, his virtue compels him to forfeit many possible pleasures. Once again, the question arises: How can the sacrifice of pleasures be necessary for the achievement of happiness?

Before attempting to make sense of Rousseau's ultimate answer to these troubling questions, it will be helpful to approach the problem in a preliminary way by examining what he says about them in his early works.

"THE GREATEST MARVELS OF VIRTUE"

In his earlier political works, Rousseau primarily conceives virtue as civic virtue, and although he does not provide much detail, he offers some instructive glimpses into the soul of the citizen. It has rightly been said that the ancient citizen, as Rousseau depicts him in the *First Discourse* and elsewhere, is almost a mirror image of Rousseau's unflattering image of his contemporaries, the bourgeois.[8] As with his portrait of the bourgeois and as with his depiction of the savage, Rousseau's image of the citizen is an idealization, illuminating certain features of our moral psychology and thereby serving a didactic purpose. As Judith Shklar has shown, the citizen and the savage (and, it may be added, the bourgeois) are models against which we are to compare ourselves in order to discover our own shortcomings, rather than exemplary figures whom we are invited to emulate.[9] Completely devoted to the welfare of his own city, the ancient citizen is Rousseau's first image of the virtuous soul; devoted to his own

7. Aristotle, *Nicomachean Ethics*, 1138a28–b5.
8. Shklar, *Men and Citizens*, 13.
9. Ibid., 13–14.

independence and absolute well-being, the savage is Rousseau's image of the naturally good soul; devoted to his own standing within society, the bourgeois is Rousseau's image of the morally corrupt or vicious soul.

These three figures are not arbitrarily drawn; in fact, they represent the fundamental human possibilities as Rousseau conceives them in his early works. (Rousseau only draws a clear distinction between human virtue and civic virtue in *Emile*.) In the savage soul, *amour-propre* is as yet minimally developed; the savage "lives within himself" (D2 187). In the soul of the citizen and the bourgeois, however, *amour-propre* has come to predominate. In these two figures, however, it takes fundamentally opposed directions and has very different consequences. The bourgeois cares fundamentally about himself, basing his self-esteem on the amount of money or power he possesses. The citizen cares fundamentally about others, basing his own self-esteem on the extent of his devotion to his fellow-citizens, their city, and its well-being. There is no solid middle ground between these alternatives. Insofar as we are able to choose between them, only two options exist: either the selflessness of virtue or the selfishness of vice; either the commands of duty are unconditionally binding or they are not. The terrain that appears to lie between these two options disappears when we try to stand on it. Short of devoting oneself wholeheartedly to virtue and doing what is right because it is right, lie only different degrees of vice. Once willing to sacrifice our duty for the sake of some advantage (or, what amounts to the same thing, to avoid some disadvantage), the only question is, How much it will take to get us to prostitute our virtue? If it is true that the bourgeois is wicked and miserable because of his selfishness and if the only alternative to that condition is the state of virtue exemplified by the ancient citizen (leaving aside as impossible any return to the savage state), then indeed Rousseau has gone some way toward establishing the proposition that virtue is a necessary condition of happiness for human beings in the civil order.

Although he insists that a civilized man cannot be happy without virtue, Rousseau's account of citizenship implies that there is a certain austerity to the genuinely civic life. He describes the virtuous citizen as "denatured": rather than devote himself to his own well-being, the citizen's sense of himself is so transformed by his education that he "love[s] the country *exclusive of himself*" (E 40, emphasis added). Rousseau offers a series of examples to illustrate what this extraordinary measure of devotion to the community requires: Regulus counsels the Roman Senate to reject a Carthaginian peace offer that would have spared his own life; Cato kills himself rather than outlast the Roman republic; the Spartan Pedaretus greets the news that he has not won election to the Council of Three Hundred by rejoicing "that there were three hundred men worthier than he in Sparta"; and the

Spartan matron "gives thanks to the gods" on hearing news of a Spartan victory that had cost the lives of her five sons (E 40). In each example, the citizen cares exclusively about the welfare of his community, which he regards as the sole basis of his own well-being; he does not conceive the possibility that he might find any happiness independently of the flourishing of his community. Unlike his ideal savage, Rousseau's virtuous citizen cannot freely luxuriate in "the sweetest sentiments known to man, conjugal love and paternal love" (D2 164). As with the great Roman consul L. Junius Brutus or the unnamed Spartan matron just described, citizens may at any moment find that duty demands them to sacrifice even the lives of their children to the common good of the republic of which they are a part (LR 78–79). How, then, can they be accounted happy?

As Rousseau depicts him, the virtuous citizen does not savor all of the happiness he supposes the savage to enjoy, but he is nevertheless a happier man than the bourgeois. In fact, Rousseau agues, the virtuous citizen's way of life is absolutely better than that of the bourgeois although it does not prove to be in every way superior to that of the savage. The citizen is, Rousseau insists, more truly just than the bourgeois because he loves at least some others—his fellow citizens—as he loves himself, and his existence is not characterized by the aimlessness and futility that prevent the bourgeois from ever truly knowing happiness. In contrast, the citizen feels at one with his fellow citizens and takes a certain pride, if not quite pleasure, in the freedom and strength of his community; as long as his community endures, the citizen knows who he is and why he acts as he does. Because the city will live on after he has died, he can face the prospect of his own death with a degree of equanimity unknown to the bourgeois. (As Rousseau envisions him, the savage thinks little about the future and therefore does not surround the idea of death with all the imaginary terrors the bourgeois associates with it.) There is no doubt in the citizen's heart, and he is troubled by no aching sense that he has wasted his life. He "can say with Cato: 'I do not regret having lived, inasmuch as I have lived in a way that allows me to think that I was not born in vain'" (LV 236). The citizen is fully satisfied with his lot, and to that extent, he can be called happy, even though he never tastes the genuine felicity known to the savage.

"THE ADVANTAGES OF THE NATURAL STATE . . . UNITED WITH THOSE OF THE CIVIL STATE"

If it were true that virtue could exist only in a sound republic, then Rousseau's practical teaching would be as completely pessimistic as Shklar supposes. From the *Discourse on Inequality*, we learn that in society we are less happy than we would have been had we remained savages but discover, in addition, that we cannot return to the savage state. From the *First Discourse*, we learn that we are morally inferior to the selfless heroes of antiquity—who, to our shame, were also less wretched than we. In *Emile*, however, Rousseau suggests a more benign possibility than any he had contemplated in his earlier works: there may be a state that combines the positive felicity of the savage with the moral nobility of the citizen. He envisions this state as a kind of "republic" in which "*all the advantages of the natural state would be united with those of the civil state*, and freedom which keeps man exempt from vices would be joined to morality which raises him to virtue" (E 85, emphasis added). In this fortunate state, no need arises for the "denaturation" required to make a man into a citizen: virtue would not simply demand self–denial; it would, rather, be produced by cultivating and bringing to their full development one's own natural dispositions.

Very early in *Emile*, Rousseau articulates the question he hopes to answer in the course of the volume: "What will a man raised uniquely for himself become for others?" adding that, "if perchance the double object we set for ourselves could be joined in a single one by removing the contradictions of man, a great obstacle to his happiness would be removed" (E 41). The "double object" to which he refers is the aspiration to educate a man to be both "good for himself" (i.e., happy) and "good for others" (i.e., just) (E 40–41). In contemporary society, these two objects generally appear to us to be opposed to each other; this is the most fundamental of the "contradictions" in the human soul Rousseau hopes to overcome. In *Emile*, he depicts a course of education designed to harmonize with the natural sequence of our biological and intellectual development; by following the course of nature, this ideal education aims to enable the pupil to feel the demands of justice as a constitutive element of his own well-being.

Happiness Defined

We begin by returning to the question, first raised in chapter 3, of what Rousseau takes happiness or fullness of life to be. His most precise theoretical definition of happiness appears early in book II of *Emile*; he writes: "To live is not to breathe; it is *to make use of* our organs, our senses, our faculties, of all the parts of ourselves which give us the sentiment of our existence [*qui nous donne le sentiment de nôtre existence*]. The man who has lived the most is not he who has counted the most years, but he who has most felt life [*qui a le plus senti la vie*]" (E 42, emphasis added; OC 4:253). This account of happiness is evidently formal, rather than substantive. It does not prescribe any particular activities as necessary for happiness; it says only that richness of life—happiness—is experienced (sensed, felt: *senti*) in *activity*, in the putting into motion to the fullest extent possible one's whole being. We are happiest, therefore, when our faculties and desires are in proportion, so that our whole being is put in motion and no desire is left unsatisfied: "a being endowed with senses [*un être sensible*] whose faculties equaled his desires would be an absolutely happy being" (E 80).

It follows that "human wisdom or the road of true happiness" requires that we preserve a just proportion between our desires and our powers (E 80). If our desires are too few, we fail to exercise all the parts of ourselves in which we sense our own being; too many, and we expose ourselves to the torment of unsatisfied desire. The great source of human misery, therefore, is the imagination, which tempts us to desire what we can never attain by inviting us to forget the limits of the human condition (E 81, 445–446). The imagination portrays to the inner eye the delights one supposes that more money or power or fame might bring; the imagination deceives us into thinking that the goods of opinion have a real solidity that they lack in fact; the imagination, in sum, seduces us into mistaking apparent goods for real ones. In light of Rousseau's formal definition of happiness, it is easy to see why he presents savages and children at play as his representative images of happiness. Both the savage and the child freely engage in a variety of activities, as it pleases them, and so exercise the whole range of their developed capacities; moreover, neither has the active capacity of imagination to envision new satisfactions he lacks the strength to attain.

Rousseau's formal conception of happiness has two important consequences. First, although it does not specify what one needs to do in order to be happy, it says that, whatever one chooses to do, it must be done with one's whole body, heart, mind, and soul. That is what it means to say that he is happiest who feels most alive, who most completely exercises all of the parts of himself in which he feels his life, his being. Let us call this the *requirement of comprehensiveness*. Rousseau does not maintain that to be happy one must be constantly active in all the parts of one's being all the time: that condition could not possibly be met by any creature, except perhaps by the most primitive micro-organism. He suggests, however, that we can only achieve a lasting happiness by adopting a *manner of living* that provides sufficient opportunities for the exercise of the whole variety of our powers and capacities, without requiring that we make war on our natures by suppressing, silencing, or seeking to eradicate any "part of ourselves which gives us the sentiment of our own existence." It must be added that this activity of soul need not always take outward form: one can put one's heart and mind and soul into motion by daydreaming or simply by luxuriating in the simple but profound pleasure of being alive—the sentiment of existence (RW 69). But Rousseau's theoretical conception of happiness also implies that no reveries, however delightful, can suffice to produce a lasting state of well-being; they can contribute to such a state only if they are a part of a whole way of life that includes other forms of physical and mental activity such that one's entire being is put into activity. When Rousseau claims that the happiest time of his life was spent on Saint Peter's Island in the middle of the Lake Bienne (RW 62), we find that this condition is substantially satisfied: though he describes himself as having been "devoted to idleness," his reveries were indeed only one part of a manner of living that included a great deal of activity.[10] He delighted in conversing with the island's governor and his family, making music with them, undertaking a variety of physical activities, and engaging in the modest but real intellectual activities of botanizing and daydreaming—all in addition to his losing himself from time to time in the total absorption of perfect reverie (RW 62–71).

The second consequence of Rousseau's formal conception implies that *freedom* is a necessary condition of happiness: to be constantly happy, one must be at liberty to satisfy one's desires when and how one pleases. That is to say that one must not be prevented or constrained by some external force from satisfying one's desires. Freedom thus conceived (i.e., as the absence of impediments to motion) is "the first of all goods" because it is a necessary condition of happiness (E 84). For one who has enough strength to satisfy all his desires, freedom is also a sufficient condition of happiness: "whoever does what he wants is happy if he is self-sufficient; this is the case of the man living in the state of nature" (E 85); it is also the case of the animals who live in the wild (D2 138–139, 149–150); and it is, finally, the situation of children "before prejudices and human institutions have corrupted" their "natural inclinations" (E 85).

To some extent, these two requirements yield overlapping practical prescriptions. One who is substantially unfree (whose activities are sharply curtailed by external constraint) may be unable to adopt a manner of living that enables him to exercise all of his developed faculties of body and mind; and one who acts unjustly (whose activities bring the self-reproach of conscience) also experiences a kind of unfreedom destructive of happiness. Nevertheless, Rousseau's account of happiness implies that one cannot be fully happy or fully alive who does not satisfy both requirements.

Activity of One's Whole Being

To understand the consequences that follow from the requirement of comprehensiveness, we must recognize that human nature contains within

10. In describing himself as idle and eager to savor the pleasure of *"far niente"* Rousseau does not so much reject the idea of activity (for he certainly engaged in a considerable range of different activities during his time on the island) as reject *compulsory* activity—anything that smacks of work or obligation: he does not literally want to do nothing, sitting on his hands in silence; he wants only to do *nothing in particular*, to be free to do as he pleases at any given moment. Indeed, the only activity that he mentions resenting is letter writing, because he felt compelled to answer his correspondents.

itself a dynamic principle, according to which the constitution of man changes over time in accordance with the development of his mind and body.[11] Just as it is natural for human bodies to grow and mature according to a regular pattern, so also is it natural (under certain conditions) for us to cultivate our intelligence, and when we do, our minds develop according to a regular (predictable) pattern, just as our bodies do. At every stage of this natural development, the principle of self-love manifests itself as a different basic motive, depending on the level of intellectual sophistication attained. Initially, we conceive our welfare in terms of what is *pleasant*, and self-love directs us to seek what is pleasant and to avoid what is painful. Later, we conceive it in terms of what is *useful*, and self-love inclines us to seek what we perceive to be advantageous and to avoid what we perceive to be disadvantageous for us. Finally, we conceive our welfare in terms of what is *good*, and self-love moves us to seek what we judge to be good and to avoid what we judge to be bad (E 39). Whereas the primitives seek their welfare in what is pleasant and the savages seek theirs in what is advantageous, civilized man acts on "judgments [he] make[s] . . . on the basis of the idea of happiness or of perfection given [him] by reason" (E 39).

As we develop and become more complex beings, we acquire new faculties over time: the faculty of speech, the faculty of reasoning instrumentally, the faculty of reasoning practically about action, and the faculty of the conscience. Just as an infant learns over time to feel the "sentiment of his own existence" in his limbs and in his organs of sense perception (E 61), so too do we learn over time to feel alive and to sense our own existence in all of these emerging faculties. Rousseau explicitly enumerates "our organs, our senses, [and] our faculties" as among "the parts of ourselves which give us the sentiment of our own existence" (E 42). He who would be maximally alive, who would taste the richness of life to the full, therefore, must exercise *all* of these faculties: he must be physically active, intellectually alive, and morally aware. This is why Emile, reared in the hope that he will live happily at every age of his life, is educated to be physically, intellectually, and morally active as an adult: he works on his farm; he perform practical experiments relative to his agricultural labors; and he takes an active

11. Melzer views Rousseau's conception of human nature as fundamentally static (reading Rousseau as maintaining that "our being *is* . . . our sentiment of existence," *Natural Goodness*, 41) and thus infers from the formality of Rousseau's conception of happiness the radical teaching that "it no longer matters what a man is so long as he is it wholly and consistently;" thus "'unity of soul,' as a purely formal condition becomes (along with 'extent') the sole determinant of existence and thus the primary good. Accordingly, disunity of soul, being the direct negation of existence, becomes human evil itself." *Natural Goodness*, 65. He also sees in Rousseau's work a secondary prescription: that we seek to form emotional and other attachments that would extend our being, but this injunction is to some extent in tension with the first. *Natural Goodness*, 44.

part in aiding his poorer and more ignorant neighbors, striving in every way to act in accordance with the demands of his conscience and reason (E 425, 435–436, 471–473). Two important aspects of our nature make possible this reconciliation between the rational requirements of social existence and our natural longing for our own welfare. The first is our capacity for emotional attachment; the second is the faculty we call the conscience.

The argument of chapter 4 demonstrated that once human beings become sensitive to the presence of other persons as persons, we become capable of forming the emotional attachments constitutive of friendship and love. We find that we can, with the aid of imagination, feel sympathy with others, in effect expanding our sense of our own being by establishing emotional bonds that link us with others. When we make a friend or fall in love, we come to feel that a part of our self and our being exists in our new friend or lover. When we share some activity with our friends and even when we do nothing more than share our feelings with our friends, we put a part of our own being into motion.[12] Rousseau's formal conception of happiness implies that we can increase our ability to be happy by increasing both the range of our desires and our ability to satisfy them, so long as these remain in proportion. He teaches that we will not be as happy as we can be, nor will we live as richly or feel as alive as we might, if we do not put *all* of our being into activity. It follows that we can enhance our own happiness by forming emotional attachments, so long as these remain proportionate to our capacity to maintain them.

At roughly the same point in our intellectual and emotional development that we become capable of friendship, we sense the first stirrings of conscience, experiencing a kind of pain when we have done what we judge in our hearts to have been wrong and taking a kind of satisfaction at having done what we judge to have been right. With the development of the active and moral sensitivity by which we become truly aware of other human beings as *persons* whose opinions and feelings matter to us, and with the development of our capacity to reason practically, we begin to discern moral relationships and begin to have a fully adult sense of right and wrong. In other words, Rousseau sees that it is natural *for civilized human beings* to reason morally, to consider, in general terms, the principles that ought to govern human conduct, and to feel some attachment to what is good, as each of us conceives it. To use the terms introduced in chapter 1, practical reasoning is conditionally natural for human beings, though it is certainly *not* absolutely natural. That it is natural for us, under certain conditions, to engage in moral (practical) reasoning is why Rousseau regards

12. On this point also, Rousseau's account resembles Aristotle's (which it should not do, if the Rousseauian sentiment of existence were the novel passion some scholars take it to be). Compare *Nicomachean Ethics*, 1168a5–10, 1170a13–b10.

the faculty of the conscience as natural. In *Rousseau Judges Jean-Jacques*, "Rousseau" observes that "the voice of conscience can be no more stifled in the human heart than reason can be stifled in the understanding; and moral insensitivity is as rare as madness" (D 242).

To say that all human beings naturally possess a conscience and the power of moral reasoning on which its exercise depends (E 67) is not to say that all human beings naturally reason well about action, nor is it to say that all human beings naturally have well-formed consciences.[13] Conscience is, as Rousseau frequently remarks, an "inner sentiment," but it is a reason-dependent sentiment, as are all the "moral" sentiments. In this respect, the feelings of remorse and the satisfaction of having acted well resemble the feeling of romantic attraction that arises in response to "relations we are not [consciously] able to perceive" (E 214). Neither our feelings of love nor the responses of our consciences necessarily accord with the principles we profess. Consider, for example, the case of Raskolnikov. Before carrying out the terrible deed, Dostoevsky's protagonist convinces himself that it would be right and just to murder the old woman in order to redistribute her money to the needy. Afterwards, however, he is so tortured by conscience that he is ultimately driven to repent. The responses of our consciences do not reflect the current opinions we profess to hold about what is right and wrong; rather, they reflect the settled habits of judgment we have formed over the course of our lives up to the present.

In the body of *Emile*, Rousseau demonstrates how our moral principles and even our moral sentiments (our consciences) can be altered by habituation in society.[14] He invites us to imagine "a young man soberly raised in his father's home in the country" first come to Paris: "you will find that he is right thinking about decent things and even that his will is as healthy as his reason . . . at the very mention of a prostitute you will see scandalized innocence in his eyes" (E 330). This young man's conscience, having been formed in the relatively healthy environment of the countryside, conforms to the requirements of a sound sexual morality, as Rousseau understands them. Rousseau invites us to consider the same young man six months into his career in the capital: "You will no longer recognize him." His "maxims" and "opinions"—in sum, his principles—will have changed, though his heart (and his conscience) will not yet have been "spoiled" (E 330). Associating with fashionable young people, who show nothing but contempt for the principles of his youth, our young man tries

13. Rousseau's suggestions to the contrary in the Profession of Faith of the Savoyard Vicar and the *Moral Letters* to Sophie d'Houdetot notwithstanding.

14. The whole elaborate scheme of education he describes in the first part of book IV can be understood as the process by which Emile comes to acquire a well-formed conscience, but he does not show us in *Emile* anything that suggests Emile's conscience comes to be corrupted.

to fit in among them by living as they do. He speaks as they do and professes the principles they do—even if he does not (yet) really believe them
in his heart: "He mocks good morals before having gotten the taste for bad
ones and prides himself on debauchery without knowing how to be de-
bauched" (E 330). Only after long habituation does he fully abandon the
upbringing of his youth: "his sentiments, slower to alter, will eventually be
spoiled by these opinions, and it is only then that he will be truly corrupted" (E 330). In the end (but only after a considerable interval), his conscience no longer reproaches him for doing things that would have filled
him with horror only a few years before.[15] On this point, Rousseau's analysis agrees with that of Aristotle, who maintains that the mark of the vicious
person is that he has ceased to recognize in any way that anything is wrong
with his base conduct.[16]

Unlike Aristotle, who sometimes seems to treat moral norms as what
Kant calls, "counsels of prudence," Rousseau clearly recognizes that moral
reasoning has its own structure and its own logic. He regards the "law of
reason" as unconditionally binding, even though he makes no effort to
supply any sort of ultimate rational foundation for morality such as one
finds, for example, in Kant's *Groundwork of the Metaphysics of Morals* and
Critique of Practical Reason. Rousseau does, however, indicate repeatedly
(and in his own voice) that he regards the basic moral teachings of the
Christian Gospels as having identified the fundamental requirements of
morality, for example, describing the golden rule as the "perfect" and "sublime maxim of reasoned justice" (D2 154; see E 235n, 251–52, GM 158). In
the Gospels, Jesus articulates the golden rule during his Sermon on the
Mount, and it is presented in the midst of a series of hard moral prescriptions; in St. Matthew's version, it is formulated unconditionally: "*in everything* do to others as you would have them do to you" (Matthew 7:12).
Nowhere does Rousseau suggest that ordinary people ought to depart in
any way from this moral imperative.[17]

15. Rousseau's account is fictional, of course, but those readers who doubt the general
truth that it illustrates can observe a range of similar moral transformations by attending carefully to the character and development of their first-year students.
16. Aristotle, *Nicomachean Ethics*, 1150b29–1151a1.
17. As noted in note 2 of this chapter, Melzer sharply rejects this view, writing that, "In the
very rare cases where injustice, violence, or oppression do not cause corruption [of soul] but
rather prevents it, he *does not condemn* it," *Natural Goodness*, 63. He cites Rousseau's praise of
the Romans and Spartans as inconsistent with imputing to him any sort of Kantian (or Christian) moralism. I argue here in the text that Rousseau does not deny the wrongness of much
of what the Romans and Spartans did, but he does *excuse* it. What Rousseau writes about these
ancient peoples must be understood in terms of his didactic purpose and the rhetorical situation of his remarks. It is always easy for us to condemn our predecessors for doing things that
we now see clearly to have been wrong, but Rousseau refuses to indulge in such criticisms because they are often flavored with unwarranted self-congratulation. Had Rousseau been in a
position to *offer advice* to the Spartans as he was to the Poles, he would likely have told the

The requirement of comprehensiveness states that we will not be as happy as we can be, we will not live as richly or feel alive as we might, if we do not put *all* of our being into activity. To be fully happy, we must use all of our developed faculties: we must exercise our bodies, develop our physical skills, and exercise our minds and our hearts. In virtue of our developed capacity for practical reason, the satisfaction of a clear conscience is a real form of happiness open to us who live in society; he who rejects that satisfaction, seeking instead to ignore or to silence the reproachful voice of conscience within himself, proposes a kind of self-mutilation. Moreover, he who does what he knows to be wrong opens up before himself the prospect of unending remorse and regrets. Rousseau explicitly likens the pains and pleasures of conscience to bodily pains and pleasures, admitting that both sorts of pleasures and pains are equally real and insisting that these are the only true sources of happiness and wretchedness that do not derive their power over us from the opinion of others: "Take away strength, health, and good witness of oneself, all the goods of this life are in opinion; take away the pains of the body and the remorse of conscience, all our ills are imaginary" (E 81). It follows that, insofar as we are appropriately sensitive to the interests of others—that is, insofar as our conscience is well-formed, reliably paining us when we do wrong and giving us satisfaction when we do right—we cannot be fully happy if we do not act justly toward others.

Freedom

Rousseau's conception of happiness implies that one cannot live happily who is not free; only one who has both the power and the freedom to satisfy all his wants can reliably avoid the pains of frustrated desire and hope to delight in putting into motion all the parts of himself in which he senses his life and his being. In the early periods of the state of nature (i.e.,

---

Spartans to abolish slavery, just as he advised the Poles to abolish serfdom. See GP 6 and Ruth W. Grant, *Hypocrisy and Integrity: Machiavelli, Rousseau, and the Ethics of Politics* (Chicago: University of Chicago Press, 1997), 104–110.

More difficult than the case of the Romans and Spartans is the case of the Lawgiver, who does seem to be authorized to do things that the golden rule plainly forbids (for example, he may lie and may perhaps incite and make use of lawless violence) as a part of his effort to establish a new political community. Although Rousseau is fairly indulgent of the founder-Hero's faults in the *Discourse on Heroic Virtue* (insofar as he takes them to be inseparable from that which makes him great), we must recall that Rousseau's own judgment was that that work was "very bad," and that in the *Social Contract*, Rousseau is much more circumspect about the extent to which the Lawgiver might be thought to be free of the normal bonds of morality. That Rousseau does not mention the Lawgiver at all during the summary of the *Social Contract* that he presents in *Emile* may suggest that we—the ordinary men and women, living in established societies, who are the bulk of Rousseau's readers—should not think too long about what might be permitted to the extraordinary founder, lest our own commitment to our duties be thus undermined.

during the primitive and the savage states), when our powers sufficed to enable us to satisfy all our desires, our natural freedom effectively guaranteed our happiness (E 85). In the last stage of the state of nature, however, human needs and desires so expanded that the forces at any individual's command ceased to be proportionate to his needs (SC 49). As a consequence, this was a time of instability, violence, and chaos; Rousseau concludes that this state was so bad that "humankind would [have] perish[ed]" if it had not changed "its way of being" (SC 49) by abandoning the state of nature for the civil state.

The establishment of civil society can be understood as a simple exchange of freedom for security: all agree to abandon the limitless but insecure freedom characteristic of the state of nature in favor of a secure but limited freedom, guaranteed by the laws and protected by the coercive force of the community. If security were the sole compensation for the sacrifice of our natural liberty, however, it would be an unsatisfactory—albeit necessary—exchange. In the *Discourse on Inequality*, Rousseau tells us that "even the wise" see this transaction as akin to the decision to amputate an arm in order to save one's life (D2 173). To sacrifice one's freedom amounts to a kind of self-mutilation because it entails a permanent loss of a part of our natural capacity for happiness: as long as he feels that his freedom is limited by the laws (as the bourgeois does), civil man enjoys only an imperfect freedom: and an imperfectly free being is, as Rousseau observes, an imperfectly happy being.

Rousseau's assessment in the *Discourse on Inequality* does not represent his final judgment regarding the relative merits of the civil state and the state of nature, however. In the *Social Contract*, Rousseau offers this much more favorable view:

> This transition from the state of nature to the civil state produces a most remarkable change in man by substituting justice for instinct in his conduct, and endowing his actions with the morality they previously lacked. Only then, when the voice of duty succeeds physical impulsion and right succeeds appetite, does man, who until then had looked only to himself, see himself forced to act on other principles, and to consult his reason before listening to his inclinations. Although in this state he deprives himself of several advantages he has from nature, he gains such great advantages in return, his faculties are exercised and developed, his ideas enlarged, his sentiments ennobled, his entire soul is elevated to such an extent, that if the abuses of this new condition did not often degrade him to beneath the condition he has left, he should ceaselessly bless the happy moment which wrested him from it forever, and out of a stupid and bounded animal made an intelligent being and a man. (SC 53)[18]

18. It should be noted that in the "Geneva Manuscript" of the *Social Contract* Rousseau is even more enthusiastic about the benefits the civil state makes possible. In that (unpublished)

Rousseau adds that although the establishment of the civil state does entail the loss of our natural freedom, it makes possible the attainment of two new forms of freedom, unknown in the state of nature: civil freedom and moral freedom.[19] We misunderstand Rousseau's account entirely if we fail to recognize that the "remarkable transformation" to which he refers in the passage just quoted does not occur only when a man becomes a citizen of a well-constituted state. Rather, the passage describes the transformations that *necessarily* occur in the constitution of the (adult) human soul when political orders constituted by political right succeed the spontaneous order of the state of nature, which was constituted by natural right. It is entry into the civil state *as such* that causes man to substitute "justice for instinct in his conduct" and thus endows "his actions with the morality they previously lacked."

The "remarkable transformation" that entry into the civil state occasions in the constitution of man raises the possibility that the loss of our natural freedom need not entail an absolute loss of happiness. Civil freedom, however, cannot serve as a sufficient foundation for the happiness of a civilized man. This sort of freedom is, Rousseau writes, "*limited* by the general will" (SC 54, emphasis added). In other words, civil freedom is the liberty one enjoys as a member of a political society to do with one's person and property whatever the laws do not forbid. "Moral freedom," in contrast, offers a more promising basis for the happiness of the civilized man. This kind of freedom, Rousseau cryptically explains, "alone makes man truly the master of himself; for the impulsion of mere appetite is slavery, and obedience to the law one has prescribed for oneself is freedom" (SC 54). There are two ways of interpreting the idea of moral freedom, however. The first is to view it as a political ideal embodied in a certain form of political life;[20] in the *Social Contract* Rousseau reveals what would be required to realize this aspiration. The second possibility is to view moral freedom as an ethical ideal, realized and embodied in a certain form of individual character—a form of character that may come to exist in any of a wide variety of decent political regimes; the aspiration to realize moral freedom as an ethical ideal lies at the heart of Rousseau's educational project in *Emile*. In either case, freedom and thus also happiness, are attainable only for those who possess virtue.

---

work, he observes that the "one essential vice" of the state of nature is that it is "harmful to the progress of our most excellent faculties"; had we remained in that state, he conjectures, "we would never have tasted the most delicious sentiment in the soul, which is the love of virtue" (GM 154).

19. My interpretation of civil and moral freedom owes much to Frederick Neuhouser's extraordinarily helpful article, "Freedom, Dependence, and the General Will," *Philosophical Review* 102 (July 1993): 363–396.

20. Ibid., 365–366.

HAPPINESS, FREEDOM, AND VIRTUE IN THE *SOCIAL CONTRACT*

Earlier in this chapter, it was noted that Rousseau's *First Discourse* and *Discourse on Political Economy* depict the virtuous citizen of antiquity as being not only more just than the bourgeois, but also happier—even as he is shown less completely happy than the Rousseauian savage. In the *Social Contract* Rousseau offers a more detailed account of the virtuous republic that reveals both the solidity and the limits of the foundation on which the citizen's freedom, and thus also his happiness, is constructed. We fail utterly to make sense of Rousseau's account of freedom in the *Social Contract* if we do not attend carefully to the specific question he wrote that work to answer: "I want to inquire," he writes, "whether in the civil order there can be some legitimate and sure rule of administration, taking men as they are, and the laws as they can be: In this inquiry I shall always try to combine what right permits with what interest prescribes, so that justice and utility may not be disjoined" (SC 41). In other words, he wants to know whether one can discover, among the many possible shapes political societies may assume, a particular form of political organization[21] such that the demands it makes on its subjects will be morally binding ("legitimate") and be reliably supported by the natural (i.e., predictably arising) dispositions of those subjects ("sure").[22] Both aims turn out to be *equally fundamental*: because the basis of moral obligation is reciprocity, the laws cannot generate valid obligations to obey unless they are securely grounded in the hearts of the citizens (see SC 81). The "legitimate and sure rule of administration" he identifies is the general will, which is brought into being by the social contract.

Recognizing that human nature is not limitlessly malleable, Rousseau proposes to take "men as they are," and to construct his "rule of administration" on the basis of "what interest prescribes." The most fundamental desire in the human heart is the desire for one's own well-being and self-preservation (i.e., self-love); thus Rousseau insists that men form political societies when they find themselves unable to survive any longer in the state of nature (SC 49). It is true that men will agree to sacrifice some of their liberty if they see that they will perish otherwise, but it is impossible to erect a stable political order on this basis. As long as men sense that the laws are limitations on their freedom (and thus on their ability to live happily) they will look for ways to evade the demands of the law. To be even remotely stable, a regime that requires its subjects to part with a measure

21. One might recall in this connection that the subtitle of the "Geneva Manuscript" of the *Social Contract* is "Essay about the form of the republic."

22. For further evidence that Rousseau regards stability as an essential feature of a good system of laws, see also SC 79–81; GP 179–182.

of their freedom must rely on some additional motive to induce subjects to obey the law; for Hobbes, that motive is fear, and for Locke, it is avarice. By contrast, Rousseau in the *Social Contract* asks whether it is possible to establish a political society *without* demanding the sacrifice of the members' freedom and without requiring a supplemental motive such as fear or greed to induce subjects to obey the law. Is it possible, he asks, "to find a form of association that will defend and protect the person and goods of each associate with the full common force, and by means of which each, uniting with all, nevertheless obeys only himself and *remains as free as before?*" (SC 49–50, emphasis added).

Rousseau offers a unique solution to this problem: "*Each of us puts his person and his full power in common under the supreme direction of the general will; and in a body we receive each member as an indivisible part of the whole*" (SC 50). The social contract demands that we cease to view ourselves as individuals who grudgingly accept the limits imposed on our freedom by the demands of others, obeying the law for the sake of some private and exclusive advantage—for example, gaining profits that improve my standing in relation to others or preserving my own life without regard for, and perhaps at the expense of, others. In the bourgeois society, whose foundation is depicted in the *Discourse on Inequality* (D2 173–174), all men will that the laws should protect property, but their pursuit of wealth also necessarily sets them at odds with one another since each desires to be accounted better off than all the rest. Their inflamed *amour-propre*, which in one respect moves them to obey the law (since they wish that their own property be protected), in another moves them to look for ways around the law (since they resent the law forbidding unjust means of acquiring from others).

In contrast, the genuine social contract demands that we reconceive ourselves as members of a community, who devote ourselves to the pursuit of goods that are truly common (such as the security and independence of our community) and to the pursuit of those private goods whose enjoyment is consistent with the enjoyment of like goods by others (for example, delighting in the company of our family and friends). We must cease to see ourselves as independent *men* who define ourselves by our differences from (and superiority to) others and instead see ourselves as *citizens* and co-legislators working together to forge a life in common under laws that we as citizens will as our general will. This is what it means to say that the establishment of the social-contract state demands that all citizens possess civic virtue, understood as the conformity of particular wills to the general will (PE 13).

The social-contract state thus rests on a far more secure foundation than the bourgeois society. In the latter, individuals obey the law for idiosyncratic and internally contradictory reasons—each obeys for the sake of the particular, exclusive benefits he alone hopes to reap thereby, but since his heart is divided, with his *amour-propre* and natural self-love in conflict with each other, he cannot wholeheartedly support the laws that he nevertheless cannot live without. In the social-contract state, however, every citizen obeys the law for the same reason—everyone sees that the social order established by the laws conduces to the general welfare of the community, which each one cherishes as the foundation of his own happiness.[23] In the hearts of the citizens, moreover, *amour-propre* reinforces the dictates of self-love: taking pride in their city, the citizens ground their self-esteem on their membership in and dedication to their community, the flourishing of which they also see as constitutive of their own well-being.[24] The precise content of the common good to which citizens collectively dedicate themselves is not exactly the same for every community (SC 79; GP 179–182; CP 901–905). Rousseau indicates, however, that the common good must include some right to property (duly regulated by law in the interest of the common good) and some right to personal security, since without the protection of these basic rights no individuals and no community could conceivably thrive.

Where all see what regulations would be in the common interest and where all unanimously abide by them, all can be said to possess what Rousseau calls moral freedom, each obeying (or acting in accordance with) only laws he has literally given to himself. In the idyllic community of Swiss peasants, whom Rousseau pictures as gathered around an oak tree to settle their affairs amicably, we see the image of a community in which the citizens do not feel the demands of membership to be anything other than a constitutive element of their own well being (SC 121). Independent-minded men such as Rousseau's Neufchâtelois, all sharing the same way

23. Thus my account differs subtly from the position developed in Joshua Cohen, "Reflections on Rousseau: Autonomy and Democracy," *Philosophy and Public Affairs* (Summer 1986): 275–297, 286. Cohen imagines that Rousseau's argument for the general will is directed to a "self-consciously free" agent who must choose whether to "have and act on a general will" or "to conform to the requirements of the general will only instrumentally"; he argues that the citizen should choose to will the general will because his interest in freedom can only be advanced by willing generally. Cohen is right that the instrumental view of the social contract is unsatisfactory, but wrong to suggest that the citizen's interest in freedom is the fundamental consideration: the citizen's interest in his own well-being is what motivates his attachment to the contract; freedom is valuable only insofar as it is a condition of well-being. It should also be noted that no agent can literally face the choice Cohen imagines between willing generally or refraining from doing so because the two attitudes toward the polity he envisions are not directly matters of choice at all but are instead states of character (corresponding to having civic virtue and lacking it) that are only brought into being by long sequences of choices and actions over time.

24. The idea that the social-contract state does not require the eradication of self-interest in its members was first made persuasive to me by Hilail Gildin, *Rousseau's "Social Contract": The Design of the Argument* (Chicago: University of Chicago Press, 1983), 59.

of life and having the same material interests, would gladly recognize one another's right to their own property and would recognize immediately the personal rights of all the others. To do anything less than this would be to fail to be the sort of men they know and wish themselves to be. In other words, both their material interests and their *amour-propre* jointly underpin their willingness to abide by whatever rules they collectively deem necessary for the advancement of their common welfare.

To see how a small group of peasants might unanimously settle their affairs is not, however, to say that it would be possible to order any real polity in accordance with the general will of its members. Rousseau recognizes two ways of falling short of the unanimity that the general will seems to require. First, some, viewing themselves primarily as independent beings and only secondarily as citizens, shall decline to do what the law prescribes (SC 52–53). Rousseau insists that those who do not wish to obey the law must be "constrained by the entire body" to do so because the enforcement of laws "alone renders civil engagements legitimate" (SC 53). The difficulty here is not to see why the laws must be enforced: were the laws not enforced, respecting the rights of others would be utter folly; absent the reciprocity of obligation, no polity nor any moral duty can be said to exist at all.[25] The difficulty, rather, is to see how those "constrained" to obey can nevertheless be understood *as free*; how is it possible, in short, for anyone to be "forced to be free"? (SC 53). The second problem is closely related to the first. Just as some are tempted for more or less selfish reasons to disobey the laws, others disagree on principle about what the law ought to prescribe; this possibility leads Rousseau to ask, "How are the opponents both free and subject to laws to which they have not consented?" (SC 124).

Why Freedom Is "the greatest good of all"

Rousseau's solution in both cases depends on the notion that the general will is "the citizen's own constant (and therefore true) will," so that being constrained to obey it in effect amounts to being enabled to do something that the structure of his own desires commits the citizen to wanting to do already.[26] The basic idea here is that to be a member of any community is to aim at some good or end common to the members of that community. Thus, to be a member of a community of scholars is to aim at the advancement of knowledge; to be a member of a soccer team is to want what is good for the team (to win, perhaps, or for everyone to have fun and to improve their skills).[27] To be a member of a political community—to be

25. Even the society brought into being by the fraudulent contract described in the *Discourse on Inequality* requires the enforcement of laws (D2 173).

26. Neuhouser, "Freedom," 372. See SC 123, 124.

27. Compare Aristotle, *Politics*, 1252a1–5; *Nicomachean Ethics*, 1159b25–1160a31.

a citizen—is to aim at what is good for the community.[28] According to Rousseau, "the greatest good of all," which "ought to be the end of every system of legislation" is the freedom and equality of its members. He explains that equality is necessary "because freedom cannot subsist without it," which seems sensible enough; he adds, however, that freedom is necessary "because any individual dependence is that much force taken away from the State" (SC 78). At first sight, this answer does not seem at all helpful. We are left to wonder: Why is maximizing the force of the state an end to which we are committed by the mere fact of citizenship? and, What does maximizing the force of the state have to do with the preservation of freedom?

The most straightforward answer to these questions conceives the force of the state as its military power with respect to foreign states. Since we form political societies to enhance our own security and our well-being, we are committed to viewing the survival of our polity as an independent, self-governing community as its highest good. Political independence is plainly a common good: none can enjoy the benefits of national independence unless we all do, and no one can be excluded from the benefits of independence except by being excluded from membership in the community. As good citizens, we must wish that our state be as powerful as possible, relative to other states that might threaten ours. Rousseau supposes that the only sort of power a state can command is the power of its people (SC 49); where that is true, the strongest state of any given size will be the state that all of its members wholeheartedly support, one where no citizens find themselves at cross-purposes with themselves or with others. The only state that can attract such wholehearted support is one where the citizens regard the laws as the embodiment of its freedom.

A second sort of force, the internally binding force of the law, is also of concern. The state and its laws are at their strongest when they are supported wholeheartedly by all the citizens; indeed, the state has its only existence in the disposition of its citizen-subjects to subordinate their particular wills to the general will. "Individual dependence" weakens the laws by creating motives in the heart of both master and servant that are at cross-purposes with the commands of the law. An example may help to clarify this point. The desperate man who has borrowed money from a loan shark has powerful motives that incline him to do whatever is necessary, legal or otherwise, to repay his debt; the loan shark, too, has no interest in seeing the laws enforced since the laws would rob him of the illegal gains he hopes to accrue by lending money at usurious rates of interest. More-

28. Jason Andrew Neidleman, *The General Will Is Citizenship: Inquiries into French Political Thought* (Lanham, Md.: Rowman & Littlefield), 30.

over the sight of others disregarding the commands of the law has a corrosive effect on other citizens: if the loan shark is seen to wear fancy clothes and to drive an expensive car, those who see him might easily be mislead into thinking that securing private wealth is the best way to live happily. Ceasing to love what is common to the citizens and beginning to love goods that are exclusive, they reorient their wills and hearts away from *amour-propre* as patriotism toward a form of *amour-propre* that is closer to avarice. It follows, therefore, that any individual's being in a state of dependence on the will of any other is not only bad for the persons directly involved; it is bad for everyone in the polity. That virtue reigns in the hearts of all the citizens is a common good.

To put the same point in other terms: the freedom of each in society is the condition of the freedom of all. Because my own most fundamental desires (for my own preservation and well-being) commit me to seeking the protection of my own freedom in a well-constituted republic (so that I am ruled only by laws that I recognize as stemming from my own will), they also commit me to desiring that all members of the community be able to recognize the laws as self-willed in the same way. Rousseau elaborates this point in *Emile*. Early in that work, he contrasts "dependence on men," which is "without order" and "engenders all the vices" with "dependence on things," which "is in no way detrimental to freedom and engenders no vices." He continues: "If there is any means of remedying this ill in society, it is to substitute law for man and to arm the general wills with a real strength superior to the action of every particular will; if the laws of nations could have an inflexibility that no human force could ever conquer, dependence on men would become dependence on things again" (E 85). Just as we do not sense the physical laws of nature as limitations on our freedom but rather as the conditions under which we can experience any freedom at all, so also, Rousseau suggests, it is possible to conceive (some of) the claims others make on us not stemming from the arbitrary wills of others, rather deriving from a kind of rational necessity. Were we to feel that the laws operate with an irresistible force, we would find it as easy to limit our desires to what is lawful as we find it easy to condition our desires on what we know to be physically possible. Were all to desire only goods that could be realized in common with others, all could see all of their desires satisfied: all would be free.

How It Is Possible to Be "forced to be free"

It should now be clear why being constrained to obey the general will amounts to being forced to be free.[29] Not to obey the general will is to place

29. The discussion in this paragraph is deeply indebted to Neuhouser, "Freedom," esp. 372–373.

oneself in a condition of personal dependence on another individual. This is precisely the consideration to which Rousseau himself appeals to explicate his paradoxical suggestion that one can be *forced* to be free: "whoever refuses to obey the general will shall be constrained to do so by the entire body: which means nothing other than that he shall be forced to be free; for this is the condition which, by giving each Citizen to the Fatherland, guarantees him against all personal dependence" (SC 53). It may happen that one may very much want to do this; to return to the example introduced previously, we can easily imagine that someone unable to pay his debts might very much want to borrow money from a loan shark. The law that forbids him from doing so certainly frustrates his immediate desire. But to be dependent on another's will is to find oneself in a state that is necessarily inimical to one's freedom, virtue, and happiness.

As Frederick Neuhouser describes it, Rousseau's legitimate republic establishes "a social order in which the ineliminable relations of dependence among individuals are preserved but *mediated* by a system of well-founded law and thereby made less injurious to freedom."[30] Where there exists a system of rights that are protected by law, he explains, individuals cease to live at the mercy of other individuals and instead depend for their well-being and preservation on the community as a whole. The laws transform personal dependence into dependence on the community by providing a degree of material equality to all citizens, preserving the formal equality of all citizens before the law, and by guaranteeing to all citizens equality of respect.[31] Neuhouser is right to spell out the ways in which the preservation of equality may conduce to the protection of our freedom, but he does not attend sufficiently to the moral transformation citizenship both demands and occasions. It is true that the man who, having been prevented from borrowing money from a loan shark and is instead forced to seek the legal protections of bankruptcy and public assistance, is preserved from a state of personal dependence that is necessarily inimical to freedom and happiness. But as long as the constraint of the general will reaches only his external actions, the frustrated borrower (who still wishes he had been able to borrow from the loan shark) is not really free: he is only less unfree than he might otherwise have been. But it is not Rousseau's aim to make our ineliminable dependence on others "less injurious to freedom," as Neuhouser indicates; Rousseau aims, rather, to show how the laws are not really limitations on our freedom at all, but instead are *constitutive* of our freedom.

Steven Affeldt offers an account of "forcing to be free" that settles the difficulties that remain unresolved by Neuhouser's account.[32] He focuses

30. Ibid., 386.
31. Ibid., 386–390.
32. Steven G. Affeldt, "The Force of Freedom: Rousseau on Forcing to Be Free," *Political Theory* 27 (June 1999): 299–333.

precisely on the moral or spiritual dimension of citizenship, rightly emphasizing the extent to which Rousseau conceives citizenship as an *activity* that makes constant demands on us: "one is a citizen if one is continuously engaged in the effort to constitute a general will."[33] Because a republic can exist only where citizens reciprocally respect one another's rights and where all work together to advance the common good, one's own activity of citizenship is inseparable from the effort to elicit similarly civic dispositions from others. "Forcing individuals to be free," writes Affeldt "is . . . part of what is involved in continuously constituting a general will."[34] One important way that citizens elicit others to act virtuously is by the force of their example.[35] The desperate debtor is truly "forced to be free" only when he is brought by his friends and fellow citizens to recognize and feel in the depths of his heart the wrongness of his desire to borrow money from the loan shark. He will only truly liberate himself when he learns to detach his heart from the passions that led him to feel that he could only secure his own well-being by enslaving himself to the usurious lender; he must rediscover and find himself truly satisfied by the compensations available to any decent and law-abiding soul in a well-ordered polity. This moral transformation will not be at all likely, of course, unless certain institutional prerequisites are met: legal protections must be available to protect our insolvent debtor from his creditors, and reasonable public provisions made for his welfare and for those of his dependents, and he must have a reasonable chance of finding suitable employment so that he may re-establish himself on a sound economic footing (see PE 16–20, 23; SC 78–79). Though such institutional guarantors of equality are necessary, they do not suffice to sustain the citizen's sense of himself as an equal and free citizen: that must come from within. He must know and feel in his heart that the general will is the sole basis on which a community of men may live together as free and equal citizens. He must, in short, possess civic virtue.

The Freedom of the Minority Voter

To the second query, which asks, How one can be free who obeys a law to which he did not consent? Rousseau replies that "the question is badly framed" (SC 124). In virtue of his continued membership in the polity, "the citizen consents to all the laws, even to those passed in spite of him." This

33. Ibid., 308.
34. Ibid., 314.
35. Affeldt further suggests that, "in the *Social Contract*, Rousseau proposes the kinds of philosophical instruction, critique, and self-presentation that the text itself contains as forms of the force that constrains to freedom." "Force of Freedom," 318ff. Perhaps he is correct, but it seems a considerable stretch to suggest that the *Social Contract* presents his own life as "exemplary" of a turn away from private goods and towards the common good. The *Social Contract* is the work in which Rousseau least of all brings himself forward to the reader's attention; in this respect, it differs markedly from *Julie* and *Emile* and even from the various *Discourses*.

may seem to claim too much on behalf of the state, but it must be recalled that Rousseau does not mean that the citizen by the mere fact of his continued membership consents to whatever the polity should do. He insists only that the citizen consents to follow *the general will* in all things. When the laws cease to be acts of the general will they cease to be binding in conscience (i.e., we are no longer bound to do what the laws command *because it is the law*, although we may have other moral reasons for going along with what the law requires). The obligation to obey the general will in all things follows directly from the terms of the social contract (SC 50). Rousseau justifies this posture of deference to the law by explaining that the object of the general will is the common good; when the citizens vote on a measure, they are asked for their opinion about what would be best for the community (SC 122). Ideally, we would all reach the same judgment about every such question to arise, but in the actual practice of any remotely complex community there will be disagreement.

A concrete example will help to clarify Rousseau's point: the majority, let us suppose, may believe that our fundamental laws should forbid burning our national flag, and I may disagree. If I should find myself in the minority, Rousseau insists, I must conclude (if I am to be a good citizen) that "I made a mistake and that what I took to be the general will was not" (SC 124). I must, in short, acknowledge the law banning flag burning as legitimate and binding in conscience on me. David Estlund takes issue with this response because he deems it to entail a violation of the Rousseauian principle that "no one's reason should be subordinated to anyone else's."[36] But that is not quite right. Rousseau does not insist that the minority voter defer to the majority in his judgment about the goodness or wisdom of the statute under consideration; he knows perfectly well that majorities do not always recognize what would really be best for their community (SC 68). The minority voter must, however, recognize that he was wrong *about the content of our general will*; he holds a conception of what would be good for the community that the majority does not share. As a citizen, the minority voter also recognizes that no statutory enactment can be good for the community if it is not willed by the community as its general will; the citizens are not free unless they can, in fact, recognize the law as stemming from their own conception of the common good, their own general will. I may believe that prohibiting the burning of our national flag in protest may be unwise and even unjust; but that belief is consistent with my believing that the community as a whole has the basic right to decide such matters for itself and that I ought to go along with the majority decision. The minority

36. David Estlund, "Beyond Fairness and Deliberation: The Epistemic Dimension of Democratic Authority," in James Bohman and William Rehg, ed., *Deliberative Democracy: Essays on Reason and Politics* (Cambridge, Mass.: MIT Press, 1997), 173–204, 184.

voter must recognize that his interest in preserving the laws as an embodiment of the citizens' freedom is more fundamental than his interest in seeing his own conception of what is just prevail.

If my view were to have become law, not because my fellow citizens believed that a ban on flag burning would harm the common good, but for some other reason (perhaps they were bribed by some enormously rich civil libertarian, or felt constrained by elite opinion not to voice their true convictions) then, writes Rousseau, "I would have done something other than what I had willed, and it is then that I would not have been free" (SC 124). Notice that in thus fraudulently defeating the measure that would have criminalized flag burning, I would not have been free—even if it is true that the rejected measure would have been unjust according to the law of reason and even if it is also true that our community would, in the long run, be better off if we allowed our citizens to protest actions of the government or sovereign by burning the national flag. If my opinion had fraudulently prevailed, a measure would have been enacted into law that did not, in fact, correspond to or stem from the general will of the citizens. Those who had voted for the measure although not recognizing its requirements as according with "the general will, which is theirs" would be unable to recognize the law as anything other than an infringement of their liberty, an imposition (SC 124). For me to compel others to go along with my vision of what is just (even if I am right about what practical reason in truth demands) would be to deny the status of my fellow citizens as my equals; it would be to insist that they subordinate their wills to mine. Moreover, in conforming my actions to the requirements of the law, I would be making myself dependent on the particular wills of those who had fraudulently supported its enactment (i.e., who had voted for the measure for the sake of particular goods they expected to receive as a consequence of its enactment instead of voting in the hope of realizing some common good for all of us in society).

Once again, we find that moral freedom can be realized in the political community, but only on the basis of equality: only one who truly accepts his fellow citizens as his equals and who is truly committed to living with them on a footing of equality is able to conform his particular will to the general will on those occasions when his own judgment tells him that his polity is doing something that is unwise. The general will does indeed solve the problem Rousseau introduces it to address. In the republic of virtuous citizens, where the laws are nothing other than acts of the general will, it is true that the citizens are perfectly free. They never experience the laws as a constraint on their desires; they instead recognize the laws as stemming from their own wills. Recognizing that the laws make possible their well-being and happiness, they want to obey the laws: rather than eliciting resistance to themselves, the laws invite citizens to obey them. For this reason, the Rousseauian social-contract state is the most perfect political community—the polity that most perfectly realizes the aspiration to create a community of free and equal citizens.

Civic Virtue, Public Education, and the Happiness of the Citizen

The Rousseauian social-contract state is not necessarily the best or happiest place for a human being to live. It creates equality and reciprocity among the citizens, thus enabling them to live under laws that they can recognize as stemming from their own wills, and it effectively advances the common good of the citizens, but these benefits must be purchased at a high price. To be a citizen is to be constantly engaged, together with one's fellow citizens, in the construction of a general will; to be a citizen is to condition one's desires and interests on the general will so that one has no desires that would set one's heart at odds with itself or with the wills of one's fellow citizens. Because citizenship demands so much of us, Rousseau insists, a virtuous republic cannot endure unless a scheme of public education exists that cultivates virtue in the citizens (PE 20–23; SC 81,141–151; GP 189–193, 239–248). The virtuous citizen must learn to love his "fatherland" (*patrie*), but civic virtue requires more than simple patriotism: the citizen's own sense of himself must also be so transformed that he "love[s] the country *exclusive of himself*" (E 40, emphasis added). The virtuous citizen must feel himself to be so completely a part of his city that he cares more about the flourishing of the community of which he is a part than he cares about his own prosperity or even his own life. That is what Rousseau means when he observes that the citizen is "denatured" by his civic education (E 40). Rousseau expresses a similar idea in the *Social Contract*, where he observes that the Lawgiver makes citizens by "transforming each individual who by himself is a perfect and solitary whole into part of a larger whole from which that individual would, as it were, receive his life and his being; [and by] substituting a partial and moral existence for the independent and physical existence we have all received from nature" (SC 69).

To see clearly what we may be called on to sacrifice for citizenship, it must be remembered that whereas the social contract state necessarily establishes a measure of justice among its citizen-subjects, no guarantee exists that the social-contract state will act justly toward neighboring states (PE 7). Indeed, the states to which Rousseau points as exemplary fatherlands *characteristically* acted unjustly towards foreign states. To cite the most notorious example, Rousseau himself reminds us that the freedom that existed among the Spartan citizens was erected on the foundation of the enslavement of the Helots (SC 115). One could not be a virtuous Spartan without accepting and supporting the laws that codified the servile status of the Helots: one could not, in short, be a virtuous Spartan without being an unjust human being. The virtuous citizen is enabled to identify closely with his fellow citizens, but his identification with them as friends is predicated on his relegating the rest of humanity into the categories of strangers and enemies. Although it is possible for the citizen to retain a measure of intellectual detachment from the opinions that prevail in his city, such detachment is difficult to sustain. Citizenship does not require philosophy, and it is to an extent hostile to philosophy: it is easier to be wholeheartedly devoted to one's city if one does not suspect that the justice it embodies is defective from the standpoint of reason.

The citizen is happier than the bourgeois because his most fundamental desires do not put him at cross-purposes with himself, nor do they set him in conflict with his fellows. He is less happy than the savage, however. The limit on his happiness is not necessarily that he is less free—it is possible, at least in principle, to live in a regime where the laws embody his moral freedom; the limit on his happiness is that the requirement of comprehensiveness cannot be satisfied. Citizenship requires the cultivation of certain aspects of one's body and soul, to the exclusion of others. The citizen must condition his desires on what is accounted good in his city. The Spartan citizen, for example, must be a soldier; he does not have the option of remaining a Spartan and devoting himself, say, to poetry. If his education succeeds in making him love the military life, he will no longer be troubled by the yearning to be a poet. It is possible that he will then put into motion all the parts of himself in which he senses his life and being. But he will have lessened himself by effectively excising the poetic part of himself. Had he been able to be a soldier-poet, he might have lived more happily; but this option the laws of Sparta have foreclosed. Civic virtue is thus necessary for the citizen's happiness, but his devotion to the city is also what limits the range of goods and pleasures he can realize.

The extraordinary difficulty he imputes to civic education tends to obscure a crucial feature of Rousseau's conception of civic virtue, namely that it amounts to a simplification of morality, whose merit is that it brings an approximation of moral virtue within the reach of ordinary men who would not otherwise be able to attain it. A few rare souls, Rousseau admits, can attain perfect virtue even in a very defective regime—as Socrates seems to have done in the "most tyrannical aristocracy governed by learned men and orators" that was classical Athens (PE 8). But such men are rare. What sets Socrates apart from the rest of us is his extraordinary wisdom: "Socrates' virtue is that of the wisest of men," Rousseau writes in the *Discourse on Political Economy*, adding that "a worthy disciple of Socrates would be the most virtuous of his contemporaries . . . [and his] virtue would make for his own happiness" (PE 16; DV 306). Following

Plato, Rousseau presents Socrates as a figure who does not need to struggle with himself to do what is right; rather, his desires reliably accord with
the demands of justice and thus he does not experience the demands of
morality as an oppressive yoke. On the contrary, he derives a profound
sense of satisfaction from his attachment to morality; never having to be
ashamed before others nor even before himself, he can savor the delightful approbation of his own conscience. Thus he is, in effect, the man of full
Aristotelian virtue, the *phronimos*.

In the *Discourse on Inequality*, Rousseau hints at the nature of the difference between Socrates and the rest of us; in that work, he distinguishes
"Socrates and minds of his stamp" from ordinary mortals, observing that
the former "may be able to acquire virtue through reason," whereas the rest
of us cannot do so (D2 154). The problem is not that most of us are too stu-
pid to understand what morality requires of us: it does not take a genius
to understand the golden rule. What is difficult is the application of moral
rules to our conduct. The problem is that reasons do not very effectively
move us to act; we are primarily moved by our desires and our passions,
and these are stimulated above all by our imagination. When we deliberate about what to do, we imagine the likely consequences of our actions,
parading before our inner eye the different pleasures and pains we think
will be associated with the different courses of action open to us. But the
imagination is unruly and deceptive, and by tempting us with images of
the happiness we fancy we might taste if only we were to violate our moral
principles, it recurrently threatens to undermine our capacity to do what
is right. It is the imagination that makes the goods of opinion appear to be
so overwhelmingly desirable as to make the bourgeois way of life appear
to be so powerfully attractive. That is what Rousseau means when he says
that we have an "unstable judgment" and "easily seduced hearts" and why
he is right to assert that, "there is more weakness than malice in our vices"
(DV 315).

Socrates' great wisdom immunized him against such illusions, but most
of us are not so fortunate.[37] We do not so easily see things as they truly are,
and as long as we live in societies marked by great inequality and injustice,
we are particularly susceptible to the illusion that money and power are
the greatest goods and vulnerable to all of the foolish prejudices to which
our upbringing necessarily exposes us. Even if we should live in a substantially just society, we would still face almost irresistible temptations.
That is why civic education as Rousseau conceives it does not end with
childhood but lasts throughout the whole of life. Civic festivals, military

---

37. Not even Emile is free of "deceptive opinions," as Socrates is; rather, he is "the *con-
queror*" of such opinions, including (most important) "the opinion that places so great a value
on life" (E 446, emphasis added).

exercises, and public service continue to reinforce the lessons learned in childhood. In the *Discourse on Political Economy*, Rousseau argues that a civic regime predicated on a system of public education is the best regime we can hope to attain because "no one has ever made a people of wise men" (PE 16). He adds that it is not impossible, however, to design a regime in which most people are preserved from the aimlessness and futility of the bourgeois way of life; it is not impossible "to make a people happy"—by establishing a well-ordered polity (PE 16; DV 306–307; D2 118).

"FREEDOM IS FOUND IN . . . THE HEART OF THE FREE MAN"

Although Rousseau's account of human nature implies that it is possible to live happily in a republic that is well ordered in accordance with the general will of its citizens, that possibility will be little consolation for those of us who do not live in a genuine republic. In *Emile*, Rousseau bluntly observes that "public instruction no longer exists and can no longer exist, because were there is no longer [any] fatherland, there can no longer be citizens" (E 40). Much as Rousseau admired Geneva he recognized plainly enough that, even in the idealized form in which he depicts it in the dedication to the *Discourse on Inequality*, it was no Sparta (LA 67, 134). Compared to the ancient republics, Geneva was, as Judith Shklar has observed, "only a semi-civic order."[38] It may have been a city full of patriots, but it was not a polity composed of citizens.

In *Emile*, Rousseau describes a third sort of relationship between the polity and the individual. To the denatured citizen, whose education has made him into a perfect part who contributes to the success of a well-ordered whole, the laws of his fatherland are the embodiment of his will. To the bourgeois, the laws are a regrettable limitation on his freedom that he obeys only for the sake of his own exclusive advantage. Emile neither sees the laws of his state as the embodiment of his freedom, nor as an arbitrary fetter on his will. He sees the laws as the necessary precondition of the exercise of freedom, and his attachment to the laws is based on the development of his nature as a (conditionally) rational and reasonable being. He finds his freedom, not (directly) in obeying the laws of the political community he inhabits, but in enslaving himself to the moral law. To Emile, Jean-Jacques declares: "the eternal laws of nature and order do exist. For the wise man, they take the place of positive law. They are written in the depth of his heart by conscience and reason. It is to these that he ought to enslave himself to be free. The only slave is he who does evil, for he always does it in spite of himself. Freedom is found in no form of government; it

38. Shklar, *Men and Citizens*, 94.

is in the heart of the free man" (E 473). Emile generally obeys the law of his state, but he does so because he recognizes the great moral good that is made possible by the rule of law: "The mere appearance of order brings him to know order and to love it. The public good, which serves others as a pretext, is a real motive for him alone. He learns to struggle with himself, to conquer himself, to sacrifice his interest to the common interest. It is not true that he draws no profit from the laws. They give him the courage to be just even among wicked men. It is not true that they have not made him free. They have taught him to reign over himself" (E 473). The existence of positive law—even in highly imperfect regimes—teaches an important moral lesson. Wherever the government aims to induce the people to obey the laws voluntarily, it must at least create the pretense that the laws aim at some genuinely common good. This hypocrisy is the tribute that civic vice pays to civic virtue, and from this tribute the careful student of politics can learn to love the common good which thus becomes "a real motive for him alone." Rousseau implies that the idea of a perfect moral order (and thus the idea of moral freedom) could not arise until human beings became acquainted with the imperfect moral order constituted by the laws of imperfect political regimes. The rule of law benefits the virtuous man in another way also: where there is no law, where there is no security in one's person and one's property, it is simply madness to live according to the golden rule. Where the tension between self-preservation and the law of reason is too great, Rousseau suggests, virtue is simply impossible.[39]

Although Emile's France is no republican "fatherland," it does enjoy the main benefits of the rule of law. The laws of France have made it possible for Emile to know and to practice virtue, and recognizing this moral good the laws make possible, he holds himself morally obligated to obey the laws in all things, except when obedience would require him to do something positively immoral. The virtuous man respects the imperfect laws of his own community just as Socrates respected the imperfect laws of Athens. Socrates refused to violate the laws in order to save his own life, even from an unjust sentence; but he would not obey the unjust command of the Thirty Tyrants to arrest Leon of Salamis: he would not allow himself to be made an instrument of injustice.

39. Here again, as with the case of the great founding-Legislator, we discover the limits of Rousseau's insistence on the absolute quality of our obligation to obey the golden rule. It should be possible on the basis of the Rousseauian arguments developed in this chapter to mark the limits of morality, at least in a rough and ready way, but Rousseau generally declines to do so because any such inquiry would risk undercutting the forceful moral teaching his principal works aim to impart. For a more philosophical defense of excluding from consideration the sorts of moral problems that almost never arise in ordinary life, see R. M. Hare, *Moral Thinking: Its Levels, Method, and Point* (Oxford: Oxford University Press, Clarendon Press, 1981), 135, 163–164.

How is it possible to be free if one "enslaves oneself" to the law of reason? For Rousseau, the essence of unfreedom is being prevented from doing what one wants to do by a will alien to one's own: "the truly free man wants only what he can do and does what he pleases" (E 84). Thus the citizen finds the laws as the embodiment of his freedom because he makes all of his life projects subordinate to the general will. He does not allow himself to formulate any desires that would necessarily set him at odds with others (e.g., the desire to have more money or more influence than others). Nor does he set his heart on attaining anything the laws forbid. The Spartan does not, for example, allow himself to want to be a poet: he makes himself love the army and the warrior's life. Having been molded by the regime of public education established by the laws, the citizen has only desires that are consistent with the requirements of the law. The moral man (the man of human virtue) does something similar, but rather than make all his life projects subordinate to the general will, he subordinates all his loves and desires to the law of reason. Thus Jean-Jacques advises Emile: "Do you want, then, to live happily and wisely? Attach your heart only to imperishable beauty. Let your condition limit your desires; let your duties come before your inclinations; extend the law of necessity to moral things. . . . Be courageous in adversity, so as never to be miserable; . . . be firm in your duty so as never to be criminal. Then you will be happy in spite of fortune and wise in spite of the passions" (E 446). When others make unjust claims on him, he resists insofar as he is able to do so, consistent with the requirement of doing what is right, but if he fails, he accepts his fate without complaining.[40] He can part with things because they are not the foundation of who he is; he can even (although this is extremely difficult) make himself part with those whom he loves, because he sees that what is most truly lovable is the perfection of goodness ("imperishable beauty"). As long as he cleaves steadfastly to virtue, retaining the good witness of himself, he can never be "miserable": there will always be one real good in his possession and one real source of delight to console him in his suffering. To say that virtue is necessary for happiness is not to say, however, that it suffices for happiness; Rousseau was sure that it did not (LO 264–265).

The perfectly wise man would have no difficulty in enslaving himself to the law of reason, but Rousseau supposes that only God possesses so perfect a degree of wisdom that he need only do what he wants to do what is good. Throughout his whole body of work, Rousseau insists over and over that virtue demands self-restraint. Indeed, Rousseau often seems particu-

---

40. This is precisely how he behaves when he leads the slave revolt in Algiers in the fragmentary sequel, ES 920–923.

larly to relish the *self-sacrifice* involved in virtue. To M. de Franquières, he wrote: "Brutus causing his children to be put to death may have been more than just. But Brutus was a tender father; to do his duty he tore up his insides, and Brutus was virtuous" (LF 281). It is not that Rousseau expects the virtuous man to be in a constant struggle against his inclinations: no one can constantly resist temptations. But in those cases where one does what is right despite the strong inclination to do otherwise, one most forcefully demonstrates one's own moral agency—one's freedom.

When the citizen limits the range of his desires to the domain of goods compatible with his duty as a citizen of a particular country, he prevents himself from experiencing the full range of goods open to us in virtue of our human nature. In contrast, the moral man need not limit the range of his activities in the same way. If he should be fortunate enough to live in reasonably favorable circumstances in a reasonably decent regime (as Sophie's parents do, for example, in the French countryside), there is no reason why he should not be able to exercise the whole range of his moral and physical capacities. That is why Emile's way of life is preferable to that of the virtuous citizen and even to that of the savage; it is his way of life that most perfectly combines "all of the advantages of the natural state" with "those of the civil state" (E 85).

Now that we have seen why the aim of education must be virtue, it is time to consider how the method of education developed in *Emile* proposes to cultivate it.

6 Emile's Moral Education

IF ALL PEOPLE WERE AS WISE as Socrates, moral education would not be difficult. In the ordinary course of growing from childhood to adulthood, we would discover for ourselves the requirements of the law of reason. Able to see and feel the force of the practical reasons that justify our moral duties, we would feel in our hearts that we could know no lasting happiness on earth if we should fail in any significant way to do what justice requires. Repelled by the prospect of doing evil and free of those illusions that make death seem so terrible, we would easily follow the Socratic maxim that it is better to suffer wrong at the hands of another than to do wrong oneself. Unfortunately, all people are not as wise as Socrates, nor is it possible for more than a handful of us to become so. We, therefore, "need to be raised," and in *Emile*, Rousseau depicts the education of an ordinary man with "a common mind" as an example of how an ordinary soul might be educated to virtue (E 52). Rousseau imagines an idealized version of himself in the educator's role, imbuing his literary alter ego with the wisdom and all the virtues (including many that the real Jean-Jacques Rousseau lacked) that are required for the success of his educational project (E 51).

Jean-Jacques does not succeed in literally making Emile wise: that project is foreclosed by the limits of Emile's nature. But he does nevertheless shape his young friend's conscience so that it is well ordered in accordance with the demands of a substantially rational morality, and he teaches his friend to love and to practice virtue. Having a good heart, Emile is rarely tempted to do wrong, but when he feels the inclination to do something his conscience and reason forbid, he finds the strength of character to cleave to the path of righteousness. The means by which Jean-Jacques accomplishes this remarkable feat have not as yet been properly understood, however. Allan Bloom has influentially argued that Emile's love for Sophie is the decisive influence on the young man's moral development. It is true that Emile's romantic passion does much to determine the eventual shape of his character, but there is a more fundamental influence on him than his love for Sophie—one that has heretofore gone almost completely unnoticed by scholars. That influence is Emile's friendship with his wise tutor, Jean-Jacques. Emile falls in love with Sophie because she embodies ideals his friend had already taught him to love before he has even met her, and his education is not accounted a success until he proves that he continues to love the ideals Sophie represents more than he loves the living, breathing woman.

The education Rousseau devises for Emile may be divided into two parts, corresponding to these two aims, the formation of conscience and the cultivation of virtue. The first part of Emile's education lasts roughly from his birth until the time when, as a young man of twenty, he receives from Jean-Jacques an account of all that his tutor and friend has done on his behalf (E 317). During this time, Jean-Jacques labors first to preserve Emile's natural goodness by means of a "negative" education, which aims primarily (though not exclusively) to protect Emile from the baleful influences of society. Once his pupil has entered adolescence, Jean-Jacques works much more actively to cultivate the goodness of Emile's nature, by making him compassionate and by teaching him to derive satisfaction from doing good works for others (E 211–253). Throughout this process, he shapes Emile's conscience, so that the young man is pained when he does things that are morally wrong and is pleased when he does things that are morally praiseworthy (E 253). The second part of Emile's education aims to perfect the first, raising Emile above mere goodness to attain that virtue without which no ordinary soul can expect to live happily in human society. No perfectly sharp chronological division occurs between the two educations; rather, Emile is given his first lessons in subordinating his desires to his duties even before he is ready to be introduced to the idea of virtue.

Bloom has proposed a somewhat different principle of division between the two parts of Emile's education, distinguishing between a "Socratic" education in books I–III and a "romantic" education in books IV and V. In his view, the first part is Socratic not so much in virtue of the educational method followed as on account of the lessons learned: "The moral education of the young Emile is . . . limited to the effective establishment of the rule that he should harm no one. And this moral rule cooperates with the intellectual rule that he should know how to be ignorant."[1] By making puberty the point of division between the two educations, Bloom's account highlights the moral significance Rousseau attributed to sexuality and love. In his view, it is the sexual passion that is made to "provide the link between the individual and disinterested respect for law or the rights of others" (15). Emile is taught to love a woman for her virtues so that he may eventually come to love virtue itself. Bloom's account of *Emile* suggests that

---

1. Allan Bloom, "Introduction" to *Emile*, by Jean-Jacques Rousseau, translated by Allan Bloom (New York: Basic Books, 1979), 15. Citations that follow appear parenthetically in the text.

the tutor's role in his pupil's education is limited and akin to that of a midwife: the tutor facilitates the process of learning, but the pupil performs all the educational labor for himself. He draws his own conclusions from his experiences, discovering all of the truths most important for living a good life, until at the end of his education he emerges from the tutor's hands, "intellectually and morally self-sufficient" (27). In Bloom's view, Jean-Jacques "appears on the scene as an authority" only once during the course of Emile's education, and that exercise of authority "annihilate[s] the influence of authority on him" (27). The decisive moment, in his view, occurs when Jean-Jacques commands Emile, very much against the latter's inclination, to delay his marriage to Sophie. Emile obeys, and during the period of separation, he becomes passionately devoted to virtue, preferring to remain true to his ideal rather than give in to any inclination that would cause him to betray it.

Although Bloom's account of Rousseau's educational method is extraordinarily illuminating, his view of the limited role of the tutor is doubtful. In a variety of ways, Rousseau suggests that Emile never attains moral self-sufficiency, thus outgrowing his need to be governed by the tutor's authority. First, Rousseau himself never claims that Emile's education accomplishes the task he sets for it: he introduces the educational project of *Emile* as a question, "What will a man raised uniquely for himself become for others?" leaving the reader to judge for himself the answer (E 41). Second, Emile's last words indicate that he continues to feel the need of his tutor's wisdom, even after having married Sophie: "remain the master of the young masters; advise us and govern us. . . . As long as I live, I shall need you" (E 480). Finally, the fragmentary manuscript of the sequel to *Emile* indicates that, when he is deprived of his tutor's guidance, Emile's good habits are not enough to enable him to make wise decisions when he is faced with new conditions to which those habits are no longer directly applicable. When Sophie falls into a depression after the death of her parents and daughter, Emile makes a series of unwise choices, which lead to the disintegration of his family and to the loss of his well-being.

An examination of the whole course of Emile's education reveals that the tutor exercises authority over Emile on more than the one occasion Bloom acknowledges. To be sure, Emile does learn a great deal on his own: he learns for himself the use of his senses and the limits of his strength; he learns on his own about the nature of his physical environment; he is even brought to discover for himself the elements of scientific method. These are all lessons any individual could in principle learn without the assistance of any other human being, and the tutor's role in teaching them is duly limited. Bloom is right, therefore, to conclude that Emile matures into an *intellectually* self-sufficient adult. But in teaching Emile to know what is good and to love virtue, the tutor's authority proves decisive throughout the whole of their lives together, not on one occasion only, as Bloom supposes. During the entire course of Emile's education, even during its early, "negative" phase, the tutor serves as an exemplar of moral rectitude for his pupil. From his childhood, Emile imitates his tutor, acquiring in this way a number of his tutor's virtues—or at least acquiring a set of good habits that subsequently become true virtues as he grows in moral understanding.

Jean-Jacques also intervenes on three specific occasions during the course of Emile's education in order to give the young man a sense of how he should react when he finds that his desires are thwarted by the just claims of another person. These lessons stand out from the background of the work because they are both unpleasant and "untimely." Unlike Emile's other lessons, which involve activities that Emile either enjoys immediately (e.g., his games, his lessons in drawing, his scientific experimentation) or comes to enjoy (e.g., his visits to aid the sick and needy), these lessons are *unpleasant* in that they can only be taught by administering to Emile a painful shock that risks provoking him to infantile fury; and they are *untimely* in that they are presented to Emile before the natural development of his faculties has reached the point at which he should be able to learn them on his own. The first is the episode with Robert the gardener in which Emile is taught by the destruction of the beans he had planted to respect the property of others. The second is the episode in which Emile learns to conform the use of his knowledge to the demands of morality as a consequence of being humiliated by the magician-Socrates. The third is Emile's forced departure from his beloved, Sophie, that teaches him to love virtue. Each of these three lessons involves a confrontation between Emile's will and the will of another, and in each case the lesson succeeds on the basis of an implicit appeal to the tutor's role as an authoritative exemplar of right conduct.

Emile must be *taught* to love virtue because he is not able on his own to discover the wisdom to govern his actions in accordance with reason. It is difficult, after all, to see why one ought to resist one's inclinations, especially if one knows them to stem from a good nature. But he cannot simply be told what to do: to insist that he follow some particular course of action would risk provoking his *amour-propre*. He must be guided by some figure whose authority he himself recognizes as valid. That is why he can only be guided to virtue by a *friend*. As Emile lives with Jean-Jacques, he recognizes not only that he has himself lived happily and that Jean-Jacques has looked out for his well-being; he recognizes also that Jean-Jacques himself is happy and respected. He comes to perceive, at first unconsciously and later consciously, that Jean-Jacques's manner of living is the foundation of his

happiness. That recognition is the foundation of the authority that Jean Jacques exerts over Emile. Regarding his friend almost as an extension of his own being, who already embodies everything he hopes himself to become, Emile patterns himself after Jean-Jacques, and in doing so, it is almost as if he were taking direction from himself.

PRESERVING AND CULTIVATING EMILE'S GOODNESS

Emile's education aims to preserve and to cultivate the young man's natural goodness. In order that he be happy at every age of his life, Emile's education is governed by the natural, biological development of his faculties (Rousseau calls this "the education of nature" [E 38]). To describe it in other terms, Emile's activity is animated at each stage of his life by a conception of the human good proportionate to the development of his faculties of mind and body. During his childhood (book II), Emile is moved solely by physical pains and pleasures to exercise his body. Later, as a youth (book III), he learns to perceive what is useful to him and what is harmful; at this stage, he is led by his emerging curiosity to use his mind (the faculty of instrumental reason) and body to secure the material conditions of his own existence. Finally, as an adolescent (book IV), he begins to govern his actions according to the judgments he makes about what he ought to do, grounded in a rational conception of the good (E 39).

Conventional educations fail—indeed they are often affirmatively corrupting—because they disregard this natural order of development and thus fail to respect the natural limits of children's capacity to understand and to feel the force of moral reasons. Rousseau vividly illustrates the difficulty of teaching morality to children by presenting a short dialogue between a well-meaning but unwise master and his pupil, in which the master tries to explain to the lad why he should obey his instructions. It is worth quoting this exchange at some length (E 90):

> Master: You must not do that.
>   Child: And why must I not do it?
> Master: Because it is bad to do.
>   Child: Bad to do? What is bad to do?
> Master: What you are forbidden to do.
>   Child: What is bad about doing what I am forbidden to do?
> Master: You shall be punished for having disobeyed.
>   Child: I shall fix it so that nothing is known about it.
> Master: You will be spied upon.
>   Child: I shall hide.
> Master: You will be questioned.
>   Child: I shall lie.

Master: You must not lie.
 Child: Why must I not lie?
Master: Because it is bad to do, etc.

Such are the only moral lessons within the ken of children, Rousseau claims. Unable to perceive the relations of sentiment and opinion that constitute the moral world, they cannot conceive any reasons other than the instrumental reasons familiar to them from their experience of the physical world. Instrumental reasons cannot, however, ground any genuine attachment to morality, which requires that one be prepared to sacrifice oneself for the good of others. Rousseau's illustration does more than remind us that children do not have the capacity to become truly moral; it also pointedly suggests that anyone who would seek to establish morality based on instrumental (or economic) rationality alone adopts a fundamentally childish perspective.

Rousseau's claim about the ability of children to understand the considerations that generate moral reasons is a fundamentally empirical one, and it is readily confirmed by ordinary experience. It is impossible to get children to comprehend in any deep way the reason behind moral duties because they do not yet have any stable or permanent feeling that the existence of other persons matters to them. Rousseau writes: "To know good and bad, to sense [to feel: *sentir*] the reason for man's duties is not a child's affair" (E 90). To add the threat of punishment to one's unintelligible reasons is only to make the child feel that he is a slave and to fill his little heart with the desire to rebel. To the child, who cannot understand the reasons behind the rules that his tutor would impose on him, all restrictions are tyrannical, and he responds to them all in the same way: with resentment, anger, and defiance—manifestations of *amour-propre* inflamed into the desire to oppress others in the same way as he feels he is being oppressed. "It is thus that we fill up his young heart at the outset with passions which later we impute to nature and that, after having taken efforts to make him wicked, we complain about finding him so" (E 48).

Common educational methods fail because they are based on a misunderstanding of the proper authority a teacher of morals must exercise. To reason with children is to try to dispense with authority entirely; to impose rules on them by threat of force is to mistake bullying for the exercise of genuine, personal authority. Ordinary children who cannot discover the good without guidance require to be led, but insists Rousseau, they must not *realize* that they are being led. As long as Emile is in no position to understand the nature and extent of his tutor's just authority over him, he must never be made to feel the force of the tutor's *will*. Unable to distinguish just claims from unjust, children regard all commands as assaults on

their will, as efforts to enslave them. Rousseau instructs the tutor to "command [your pupil] nothing . . . absolutely nothing. Do not even allow him to imagine that you might pretend to have any authority over him" (E 91). Even an infant responds with anger when he feels that he has been deliberately assaulted (E 65–66), but Rousseau insists that children will not rebel against what they believe to be natural necessities any more than the animals rebel against the physical constraints imposed on them by nature. To that end, Rousseau advises: "Keep the child in dependence only on things" (E 85). The success of this project is favored by the natural intellectual limitations of children. Unable to perceive the moral relations that obtain among men, children (unlike adults) are disposed to view the whole world as a purely physical system, governed exclusively by natural necessity. The tutor's contribution to the child's education is to structure his environment so that the child will want to engage in activities from which he will learn on his own the lessons which the tutor judges it would be good for him to learn (E 120). Thus he designs a variety of games, which Emile plays because he finds them entertaining, but which have as their end the cultivation of Emile's strength, agility, and his ability to use his senses.

Imitation and the Virtues

Rousseau's critique of imitation is well known, and as a consequence, the role imitation plays in Emile's education is not widely recognized.[2] Nevertheless, Rousseau insists several times that tutors must exemplify the virtues they wish to impart to their pupils, and he explicitly observes that imitation necessarily has a role to play in moral education: "[A]t an age when the heart feels nothing yet, children just have to be made to imitate the acts whose habit one wants to give them until the time when they can do them out of discernment and love of the good" (E 104; see also E 95, 194, 195, 202–203, 447). Under the right circumstances, imitation can be good for us, but in society as it now exists, those circumstances generally do not obtain. People whose tastes and judgments have already been corrupted by inflamed *amour-propre* are overwhelmingly likely to choose bad exemplars to imitate. Such people either imitate those whom they believe to be esteemed by others—like the child who, on hearing a soldier's drum, fancies himself a general (E 198)—or mockingly imitate those whom they sense to be better than themselves (E 104). Either way, Rousseau insists, such people "want to make an impression on others or to get applause for their talent far more than to make themselves better or wiser" (E 104).

2. Ernst Cassirer goes so far as to say that "Rousseau categorically denies the educational power of example." *The Question of Jean-Jacques Rousseau*, translated by Peter Gay (New Haven: Yale University Press, 1993) 124.

Aroused *amour-propre* makes them want to imitate others in order to fit into the society of others before whom they are self-conscious; that is what Rousseau means when he writes that "the foundation of imitation *among us* comes from the desire always to be transported out of ourselves" (E 104, emphasis added).

Uncomfortable and self-conscious about who we are, we try to be something else—what we think we are expected to be—in order to escape that discomfort. This is why imitation is so commonly alienating. From the moment we become self-conscious, aware of how we appear to others, we never look at another person without making some sort of unconscious comparison between ourselves and others. These comparisons are dangerous whenever we make them without possessing the wisdom to make good judgments about what we ought to esteem in others. It is dangerous even when we are shown only the lives of great and excellent historical figures to consider. When children are directed to read history, it is often in the hope that the young readers will want to become one of the heroes about whom they read. Rousseau, however, insists that if Emile "just once prefers to be someone other than himself—were this other Socrates, were it Cato—everything has failed" (E 243). Once we want to be something other than we are because we think it is what someone else wants us to be, we subject ourselves to opinion and thus, to the dangerous manifestations of *amour-propre* that prevail in badly ordered societies: "He who begins to become alien to himself does not take long to forget himself entirely" (E 243). In this sense, Emile is not an imitator. He does not want to become any of the heroes of antiquity, nor does he want to become like the other young people he meets when he finally visits Paris (E 331). Peer pressure does not move Emile; he has no desire to fit into society or to win the acceptance of others, nor does he even care whether others might see fit to mock him (E 336). He wants only to be himself, to be happy, and to be good to others.

Imitation is not itself bad, however; Rousseau observes that it is we who make it so, writing: "The taste for imitation belongs to well-ordered nature, but in society it degenerates into vice" (E 104). Paradoxically, imitation turns out to be good for us only to the extent that we do not understand ourselves to be imitators. The key to understanding the role imitation plays in Emile's education is to recognize that Emile never self-consciously mimics Jean-Jacques, nor does he aspire to be anything other than what he is. The tutor's example influences Emile more subtly than that. During Emile's childhood, Jean-Jacques aims to cultivate in Emile a number of good habits and to preserve him from bad ones. He does this, not by instructing Emile to copy everything he does, but simply by embodying the virtues in his everyday life with Emile—in their games, in their adventures, in their experiments, and in their work. If his tutor habitually seeks to do well whatever he attempts, so too (eventually) will Emile. If his tutor habitually works patiently at any challenging task he sets for himself, so too will Emile. If his tutor always remains master of himself, never allowing himself to become enraged, so too will Emile. (At the very least, his tutor's good example should enable Emile to avoid acquiring the vice of excessive wrathfulness).

Although he certainly arranges for the young Emile to learn some unpleasant lessons, Jean-Jacques manipulates events so that Emile never attributes the frustration of his desires to his tutor's will. To be sure, the tutor's manipulative attitude toward the child Emile is inconsistent with the requirements of an adult friendship. But since the tutor's efforts stem from his genuine attachment to the boy's well-being, and since the lad is unaware of them, the tutor's direction of Emile's education does nothing to undermine the boy's attachment for him. Everything changes when Emile reaches the brink of adulthood: at that time, Jean-Jacques renders an account of all his actions to his pupil, and declares that he will not continue as Emile's tutor without the explicit consent of Emile himself. Having lived happily in childhood and recognizing the evident well-being of Jean-Jacques, Emile consents readily to grant Jean-Jacques the authority his tutor had formerly exercised in loco parentis: "I want to obey your laws," Emile declares to Jean-Jacques, "I want to do so always. This is my steadfast will" (E 325). In his early adulthood, Emile continues to learn from the example of his friend, Jean-Jacques, but the lessons he learns now are more sophisticated than before. Now that he has grown in understanding, Emile is better placed to see what transpires in the hearts of those around him and to perceive the "moral" relationships he had been unable to comprehend as a child. His relationship with Jean-Jacques particularly makes it possible to learn from his tutor. Based on expansive self-love, Emile's relationship with Jean-Jacques makes it possible for him to see his tutor as an other who is also in effect a part of himself. Not blinded by *amour-propre*, Emile sees clearly the state of his friend's soul. He sees that Jean-Jacques lives happily and that he owes his contentment to the great virtues he embodies. Seeing his friend's happiness, Emile does not envy Jean-Jacques, or resent him as he might if he felt self-conscious in his tutor's presence. Rather, he learns his own moral lessons from what he sees. Thus Emile does not make any sort of conscious effort to imitate his tutor. He never sees Jean-Jacques and thinks: *I am not like that man; he is better than I am, and I will change what I am so as to be more like him.* Instead, he recognizes in his tutor's soul the fulfillment of his own best aspirations for himself.[3]

3. Affeldt nicely describes the nature of the constraint we feel when we recognize another

Courage, Moderation, and Justice

Jean-Jacques cultivates Emile's natural goodness by sharing a manner of living with his young friend that introduces the lad to good habits that will mature into virtues as he gains in moral understanding. Rousseau divides his account of Emile's education into five books, corresponding to the five ages of his young hero's life: infancy, childhood, youth, adolescence, manhood. To each book after the first, there corresponds a characteristic virtue, to which that period of Emile's education is devoted. The education of childhood is physical, and in childhood (book II) Emile is habituated to the practice of the self-regarding, largely bodily virtues connected with courage (see E 77–78). Emile's body and senses are constantly exercised, so that he becomes strong and agile, and able to use his senses to gain accurate knowledge about the world around him (E 124–125, 161–162). Ordinarily educated children fall into habits and routines that arise out of, and further encourage, laziness and weakness (E 160 and note). Emile is instead hardened by a variety of exercises and outdoor activities of all sorts, at every hour and in every weather (E 63). This habituation to the "hard life" (E 129) teaches Emile "the virtues" of "constancy and firmness" (E 131) that will spare him from a host of pains later in life.

As a youth (book III), Emile is led to discover the notion of utility, and seeking to learn what he needs to know in order to preserve himself, he discovers the scientific method and its fundamental principles (E 172). This part of Emile's education amounts to the cultivation of two related virtues, one of character—moderation—, and one of thought—knowing how to be ignorant (E 207). As he gains in knowledge, the danger he faces is vanity, which is what the humiliation he receives at the hands of the "magician-Socrates" at the fair is designed to inoculate him against (E 175). He looks at the world in terms of his needs, which are not inflamed by imagination into limitless desires; that is why he prefers a simple peasant's meal to the opulent feast of a nobleman (E 190–192). At the end of book III, Rousseau writes: "Emile is laborious, temperate, patient, firm, and full of courage. His imagination is in no way inflamed and never enlarges dangers. . . . In a word, of virtue Emile has all that relates to himself. To have the social virtues, too, he lacks only the learning which his mind is all ready to receive" (E 208).

The acquisition of the other-regarding virtues begins only after the full flowering of emotional sensitivity (*sensibilité*) that arrives with adolescence. When we truly feel the presence of others—when we first become self-conscious—then self-love (the desire to advance one's own welfare)

---

as a moral exemplar: we feel "attraction toward or desire for the currently unrealized state of ourselves." "Force of Freedom," 323.

begins necessarily to manifest itself as *amour-propre*. Emile's education at this stage aims first to cultivate the young man's sensitivity in order to make him compassionate—so that he genuinely feels that suffering is what unites mankind (E 221–231). Only then will he be brought to see men in their differences (E 235–244). Comparing himself to others for the first time, he will not envy the rich and powerful, but pity them. Reading Plutarch's *Life of Augustus*, Emile is struck by the extent of the emperor's cares and by how little genuine happiness all his power brought (E 242–243). From these comparisons, Emile derives ever greater pleasure in being himself. As he sees the miseries to which even the great are subject, the danger he faces is pride: he may come to believe his happiness derives from a superior nature rather than from the education he has received. More adventures such as the one with the magician-Socrates at the fair and the reading of fables will teach him not to feel proud, hard-hearted, or contemptuous of others (E 246–248).

Finally, Emile and Jean-Jacques work to protect the weak and to do such practical good as they are able. Writes Rousseau: "The exercise of the social virtues brings the love of humanity to the depths of one's heart. It is in doing good that one becomes good; I know of no practice more certain" (E 250). He adds that in seeking to right wrongs and to aid the victims of oppression, Emile will acquire a number of specific virtues: he will be "circumspect in [his] conduct, respectful before older people, reserved . . . , modest . . . , hardy in good deeds and courageous in speaking the truth" (E 250). Emile's practical efforts to do good thus enable him to learn about the practical workings of men and their institutions. Most important, Emile's active beneficence trains his heart to love justice: concerning himself with the welfare of others frees him from excessive selfishness and enables him to take real pleasure in the happiness of others. Rousseau writes that this part of Emile's education aims to "extend *amour-propre* to other beings" (E 252). In other words, Emile is to identify so much with his neighbors that he comes to take pride in their welfare (to which he feels that he has contributed). When he sees others suffering because of an injustice he can right, he feels mortified, or even wronged himself by the injustice— and this motivates him to right it.[4] Thus by the conclusion of his period of tutelage, Emile comes to possess the moral virtues of courage, moderation, and justice and a number of lesser virtues besides. To put the same point in other terms, Emile at this time has a substantially well-formed conscience.

Based on the structure elaborated thus far, one should expect Rousseau

---

4. For a slightly different view of this passage, see Dent, *Rousseau*, 144. Whereas I take the extension of *amour-propre* to be the cultivation of a certain motive, Dent takes it to be the adoption of a certain rational end, for which the motive requires further explanation.

to devote book V of *Emile* to the cultivation of the fourth and final cardinal virtue, wisdom. In fact, wisdom is the major topic of book V, but Emile never actually becomes truly wise; he learns, rather, to love an image of wisdom and to be attentive to its teachings (wisdom = *sophia* = Sophie). Wisdom raises particular problems for Rousseau because he supposes both that all people must possess it if they are to live happily in society with others, and that true wisdom is beyond the reach of most persons to acquire.[5] This is the problem to which Rousseau's separation of Aristotelian practical wisdom into conscience and virtue provides the solution. Emile does not become wise, but he does come to possess a sound conscience; because he will never be free of practically unreasonable desires, he must learn how to do what his conscience and reason demand of him, even when he does not want to. He must, in short, perfect his goodness with virtue.

THREE LESSONS IN VIRTUE

It has not as yet been sufficiently appreciated that Emile does not learn to subordinate his desires to his duties all at once. Even during the early, "negative" period of his moral education he is put into circumstances where his will is thwarted by the will of another. He is habituated into the practice of ruling himself just as he is habituated into the practice of the other virtues. Rousseau depicts three specific lessons in virtue, one in book II, one in book III, and the last in book V.[6] As might be expected, these three lessons in virtue are painful to Emile. He learns to respect the property of others by having some of his property taken from him; he learns to respect humanity by being himself humiliated; and he learns to rule over his passions by having to part with his heart's desire.

Given that it is Jean-Jacques who arranges for Emile to suffer in these ways, it can be hard to see how he can be accounted his pupil's *friend*. Most of us would not remain friends for long with someone who tricked us into planting a crop of beans, only to have them dug up. Nor would we appreciate being set up for humiliation, nor would many of us tolerate anyone's making us fear, even for a moment, that some terrible misfortune had befallen someone dear to us. Jean-Jacques, of course, does all of these things to Emile. Measured by the standards of adult friendships, all three actions are difficult to justify. But, especially in the early years, Jean-Jacques's re-

5. Indeed, insofar as he suggests that happiness in society requires that men and women take on distinctly male and female attributes and that wisdom requires an intellectual androgyny incompatible with either masculinity or femininity, the problem is exacerbated even further.

6. The Savoyard Vicar's Profession of Faith is the corresponding lesson in book IV, but the Vicar's instruction is directed only at the readers of *Emile,* not to the lad himself.

lationship to Emile is more complicated than a simple friendship between adults. To the boy Emile, his tutor seems to be nothing other than a companion in his games. But Jean-Jacques is more than a companion; he is also a guide, aiming to lead Emile by the most direct route to a happy and flourishing life. Since Emile comes to judge his education to have been successful, the tutor's early efforts are justified, and on reaching adulthood, Emile accepts Jean-Jacques as a friend (E 323).

Even then, when Emile and Jean-Jacques have become friends, they are not yet equals. Emile recognizes his friend's superior wisdom and begs him to reassert his authority. Given that the third shock is administered as a part of the education that Emile has begged Jean-Jacques to give him (and given that Emile eventually does absorb the lesson it aims to teach), it is even less difficult to see how that incident could count as an obstacle to viewing Emile and Jean-Jacques as friends. Few parents, perhaps, would arrange for their children to suffer the sorts of reverses from which Emile learns to master his passions. But in the real world, as opposed to the world of Rousseau's pedagogical romance, we do not need to arrange for bad things to happen to our children. Some parents may be tempted to shield their children from every kind of hard lesson, but wise parents do not do this: hard lessons allow us to take risks, to learn from our successes and our failures. And, if the parental efforts to cultivate virtues have been successful, the children will appreciate what has been done for them, and the relationship eventually matures into a warm and enduring friendship.

Learning to Respect Property

Rousseau himself warns us at the beginning of this episode that he is introducing his pupil to an important lesson that justifies a departure from the natural sequence of moral development (E 97). Rousseau acknowledges that the child Emile must learn the first lessons of morality: never to harm others either in their persons or in their property. Since Emile will have some interactions with other people, he must learn to respect the most basic rights of others lest he believe "himself master of everything" and thus do "harm to others without scruple and without knowing it" (E 97). Still a child, Emile is moved by self-love as the desire to experience pleasures and to avoid pains; he does not yet have a clear understanding of the ideas of utility or of interest, and he certainly has no conception of moral goodness. Emile must first learn to respect the property of others.[7] The problem is that, according to Rousseau, "there is no true property of any

---

7. The prior lesson—not to harm persons—Rousseau thinks need not be taught. Since his will is never thwarted (so far as he knows) by the wills of others, Emile should have no reason to attack persons. If he does strike anyone, Rousseau insists that he should be struck back in return, forcefully enough so that he will not do it again. E 97n.

kind at that age" (E 106). Emile is in no position to learn the truth about property, that it exists in virtue of consent—when people reciprocally recognize one another's rights to their property. It is not the man who first encloses a piece of earth who invents property; it is the man who does that *"and found people sufficiently simple to believe him"* who truly brought property and civil society into being (D2 161, emphasis added). Ignorant of the wills of others, ignorant even of the requirements of his own survival, a child is in no position to understand what it means to ask or to receive consent to possess a parcel of property. The difficulty goes even deeper: a child's imagination and understanding of time is so limited that the future means nothing to him. For this reason, Rousseau declares that "all commitments of children are in themselves null" (E 101).

The child must nevertheless get a sense of what property means so that he will gain some understanding of why he should respect that of others. Jean-Jacques teaches Emile to respect property by making him feel what it is to have his own property taken away; he must, therefore, begin by teaching the boy what property is. He proposes to teach this lesson by getting Emile to plant some beans in a garden (E 98–99).[8] This project can only successfully teach the lesson Rousseau has in mind because Emile does not perceive Jean-Jacques as having a will or interest distinct from his own. Emile is too small to do the labor of tilling the soil by himself; Jean-Jacques does the actual labor. Nevertheless he explains to the boy that the seedlings he has planted belong to him. The tutor shares in this experience; as far as Emile is concerned, he and Jean-Jacques are both growing the beans for the pleasure of it. Every day they water the beans, and every day Jean-Jacques and Emile together delight in their handiwork. By his tutor's example, Emile learns to feel that he has put his self and his being into the bean plants. Emile will not learn the lesson Rousseau wants to teach unless he feels that the beans are his; he must not think of Jean-Jacques's assistance as in any way diminishing his own possession. And he must certainly not think that he is being forced to undertake this little experiment: he must be unconscious of the tutor as an other, but experience his presence and his teaching as if they were expressions of his own self.

One day Emile and Jean-Jacques return to find their beans uprooted. The boy is pained; he cries. This is his first experience of injustice. The crucial lesson he must learn is how to respond to the destruction of his property. Left to his own devices, the child will just throw a tantrum; his anger will be boundless, unsatisfiable short of vengeance. Seeking to direct that anger (though not, of course, sharing it himself), Jean-Jacques joins Emile's

---

8. My account of this incident owes much to Bloom's account, except insofar as it asserts the necessity of the tutor's friendship to the success of the lesson. "Introduction," 13–14.

search for the culprit. It turns out that Robert the gardener has uprooted their beans. But he too is angry: to plant their beans, Emile and Jean-Jacques had uprooted some rare melon plants Robert had begun to cultivate. A confrontation ensues. As Bloom astutely observes, Emile's anger is deflected by the thought that the uprooted melons were to have been his to eat: in uprooting the melons, he has done injury both to another and to himself. Emile's anger may be deflected, but it is still present. Taking advantage of Emile's momentary confusion, Jean-Jacques replies to Robert, offering an apology for what they have done: "Excuse us, my poor Robert. . . . I see clearly that we did wrong in ruining your work . . . and we will never again work the land before knowing whether someone has put his hand to it before us" (E 99). Jean-Jacques says that *he* sees that he and his pupil have wronged the gardener. Emile, however, does not apologize. He is, however, puzzled by the gardener's rejoinder to his tutor's apology, asking: "Monsieur Robert, are melon seeds often lost then?"

The gardener explains that each respects the property of others so that the others will respect his property in turn. Still the perfect little egoist, Emile replies, "But I don't have a garden." He feels himself excluded from the regime of property; everyone else has some plot of land to call his own, but he has nothing. Having nothing of his own, he has no incentive to respect the property of others. Emile learns from Jean-Jacques a way to settle the conflict. Jean-Jacques proposes a contract on Emile's behalf: he suggests that Robert allow them to cultivate a small portion of his lands, and in return they will give him one half of what they grow. Robert generously grants them the right to a small piece of land without conditions— or rather with the sole proviso that Emile must not dig up what he (Robert) has planted elsewhere. By this arrangement, Emile is allowed to do what he wants to do, namely to grow his beans; and the resulting state of affairs will be one in which he will not have any motive to violate his agreement. The obvious lesson Emile learns from this incident is that he will injure himself if he damages the property of others; this is the lesson Bloom focuses on in his account of the incident.[9]

The less obvious but more important lesson is to learn restraint in anger and moderation in his desires. The first experience of injustice prompts a feeling of limitless anger. At this point the tutor's personal example is crucial: were the tutor to command Robert to give them the land in virtue of the boy's aristocratic blood, the education would evidently be ruined. The whole point of the lesson is to teach Emile that some things do not belong to him. But Emile must not feel that the tutor's response to Robert's counter-accusation is inappropriately mild. He must not feel betrayed by

9. Bloom, "Introduction," 14.

his tutor. Rather, he must feel that the tutor's actions with respect to Robert and that the agreement he reaches with the gardener satisfy his anger. Emile will only be able to feel this way to the extent that he sees Jean-Jacques to be as identified with the beans as he is—he must see Jean-Jacques if not as a friend, then at least as a youthful comrade who shares his pleasures and shares his pains. Of course, he must also feel a kind of respect for Jean-Jacques that he cannot articulate.

Learning to Respect Humanity

During his childhood, Emile's increasing physical strength made him potentially dangerous to other persons, thus requiring that he be taught not to use it to violate the rights of others. During his adolescence, Emile's growing knowledge and the power it gives him over the natural world also make him potentially dangerous to others. Unchecked physical strength might have led Emile to harm others inadvertently. Unchecked intellectual prowess poses a more subtle danger, however: Emile risks becoming proud of his knowledge and contemptuous of those who lack it; the danger to be feared is not that he will unknowingly injure the rights of others but that he will willingly violate them. In order to forestall this development, Jean-Jacques takes Emile to see a magician at a fair (E 173–175). Rousseau himself warns that "each detail of this example is more important than it seems" (E 175); one vital detail has been overlooked by the commentators, however: this lesson succeeds only in virtue of the authority Jean-Jacques exerts over his young friend.

At the fair, Emile and Jean-Jacques watch the magician-Socrates use a piece of bread to lead a wax duck around a tub of water, amazing the ignorant crowd. Returning home, Emile quickly discovers how to duplicate the trick. Having previously been introduced to the principle of magnetism, Emile discovers that by placing a magnet inside the duck, he can cause the duck to follow a metal key hidden in a bit of bread. Thrilled by his knowledge, he returns to the fair and boasts to the crowd that he can do what only the magician has done: he, too, can make the wax duck follow his piece of bread. He replicates the magician's trick to the crowd's enthusiastic applause. In reply, the magician congratulates him, inviting him to return the next day. Eagerly the young man looks forward to demonstrating to all the power his knowledge confers. When the time comes, however, Emile finds that he cannot duplicate the trick. The magician has altered his trick, and Emile is humiliated by the magician's masterful performance.

Emile's lesson does not end with that. The day after Emile's embarrassment, the magician comes to the house where he and Jean-Jacques live.

"Modestly he complains of [their] conduct." What harm has he done to them that they should wish to endanger his livelihood? he asks. To satisfy their curiosity, he explains the secret of the trick they had been unable to penetrate, adding that he knows still more about his craft than he has shared with them. He does not put all of his knowledge on display every time because, "one ought not to be in a hurry to show off giddily what one knows" (E 174). Before he leaves, the magician reproaches Jean-Jacques in front of his pupil:

> "I willingly excuse," he says to me, "this child. He has sinned only from ig-
> norance. But you, monsieur, who ought to know his mistake, why did you
> let him make it? Since you live together, as the elder you owe him your care
> and your counsel; your experience is the authority which ought to guide
> him. In reproaching himself for the wrongs of his youth when he is grown
> up, he will doubtless reproach you for those against which you did not
> warn him." (E 174–175)

Just as it is Jean-Jacques who apologizes to Robert the gardener, so also it is Jean-Jacques who takes the blame for Emile's foolish vanity. Having had his ignorance exposed by the magician, Emile has already come to feel the unpleasant consequences of his vanity. Lest his *amour-propre* be aroused to anger by the magician's reproaches, however, he is shown how the magician was injured by their behavior towards him. Commiserating with the magician for his suffering, Emile does not become haughty or defensive. Lest Emile become angry at Jean-Jacques for having allowed him to embarrass himself, the tutor arranges to be punished by being reproached publicly.

They return once more to the fair to see again the trick to which they now know the secret. Rousseau writes that the "magician-Socrates" performs his tricks, but Emile and Jean-Jacques remain properly silent. The magician is Socratic in that he does to Emile what Socrates does to his interlocutors by means of the elenchus: Emile is publicly revealed as a boaster, who does not really know what he claims to know. Socrates exposes his interlocutors' ignorance not for its own sake, but for a moral purpose: he exposes erroneous moral opinions in the hope that they will learn the truth about virtue. The magician-Socrates teaches a related moral lesson—the lesson that Kant claims to have learned from Rousseau—he teaches Emile to respect humanity. At first, the power that his knowledge of physics confers makes Emile contemptuous of those who lack that knowledge. But the affair with the Socratic magician reminds him that possessing power is not a reason to use it: the exercise of theoretical reason must always be subordinate to the dictates of practical reason.

Leaving Sophie, Finding Virtue

Jean-Jacques's ability to introduce moral notions to the child Emile was limited both by the limits of the boy's understanding and by the limits of their relationship. He was able to teach his pupil only very basic moral ideas and to give him the habits of imitating his acts of virtue. As the boy matures, however, his heart and mind develop. We have already seen how Jean-Jacques trains Emile's conscience by making him sensitive to the ills of others and teaching him to take pleasure in acts of beneficence. In this way, Jean-Jacques brings Emile to the pinnacle of goodness perfected by reason; Rousseau writes that thanks to this education, "the true principles of the just, the true models of the beautiful, all the moral relations of beings, all the ideas of order are implanted on [Emile's] understanding" (E 253). At the age of eighteen, Emile has a healthy and well-formed conscience, and he finds his own happiness in doing good for others. But this natural conformity of tastes to duties cannot last forever. Emile will soon experience sexual desire and sexual passion in all its force; this passion will threaten to overturn all the good accomplished by Emile's earlier education.

The sexual passion is only the first of a series of dangers looming over the horizon: love may be the great moral danger we face in our twenties, but others follow. In our thirties, says Rousseau, we are led "by the pleasures, at forty by ambition, at fifty by avarice" (E 431). Although "each age has its own springs that make it move, . . . man is always the same" (E 431): our imagination always threatens to deceive us into attaching undue importance to some partial good, thus inflaming our *amour-propre* into a passion hostile to our own well-being. If Emile is to retain that unconditional commitment to justice that is prerequisite to the happiness of any civilized man, he must acquire virtue—so that he may triumph not only over the temptations of sex and love, but also prove superior to the corresponding temptations appropriate to the other stages of life.

Allan Bloom has rightly drawn attention to the importance Rousseau attaches to sexuality and to the sex education Emile receives from his tutor. Bloom's account of Emile's introduction to sex and love is flawed, however, because it does not recognize that Emile's education can succeed only in virtue of the boy's friendship for Jean-Jacques. To see why, we must examine the way Jean-Jacques delivers his teaching about sexuality to his pupil and then consider carefully the contrast between Emile's love affair with Sophie and Saint-Preux's love affair with Julie d'Etange. Like Emile, Saint-Preux has a generally well-formed conscience when he falls in love; certainly he has good moral opinions and for the most part acts well. Saint-Preux lacks only the guidance of a tutor such as Jean-Jacques. If we compare Julie to Sophie, we must conclude that Julie's nature is at least as good as Sophie's. But here is a crucial difference: Julie differs from Sophie in that she has no wise parent to guide her. Julie's mother is too indulgent; her nurse, too indiscreet; and her father, too distant. As a consequence, the two love affairs are mirror images of one another: Emile and Sophie demonstrate the happy possibilities of a well-regulated love; Saint-Preux and Julie, the tragic dangers of love unregulated by wisdom.

Sexuality is the final, great problem Emile's education confronts. It is the first and most natural passion we experience; because it is so deeply connected to *amour-propre*, it is also the most dangerous, as Rousseau frequently reminds us (E 415–416, 432). We never forget our first love affairs, claims Rousseau, and we always remember them fondly. If Emile preserves his good tastes and inclinations through his first romance, Rousseau supposes that he will preserve them thereafter; but if they are supplanted by new tastes, his first education will be ruined (E 432). It is easy to see how a man in the throes of passion could willingly violate any law, abjure any duty in order to win his heart's desire (E 444). Rousseau warns that a man whose first taste of love sets him against law and moral duty will most likely never again be whole or at home in society.

Saint-Preux makes himself Julie's slave, but as with any spirited slave, he rebels against his servitude and importunes her to grant him all the favors her love seems to promise. As a result, their affair is a constant struggle that in the end brings more misery than happiness to them both.[10] Rousseau makes clear the extent of Saint-Preux's subservience to Julie by giving him no name; even the name Saint-Preux is only a nickname bestowed on him by Claire. He sees himself only through Julie's eyes, and his passionate love for her leads him to rebel against the moral order represented by her father. He must have her at any cost, and he is willing to do almost anything to get her. When Julie, after her wedding and conversion to virtue, finally terminates their affair, his whole identity collapses: he wants to die, and only Lord Edward's friendship for him saves him from killing himself.

At eighteen, Emile can no longer be preserved from the dangers of love. He must enter society, and once there, he would quickly learn about love and sex on his own, but the lessons he would learn in society would undermine the lessons Jean-Jacques had taught. It would seem that the problem could be solved by a quick marriage. But Rousseau rejects this "most natural expedient" (E 317). The problem with it is that sexual desire is not enough to sustain the moral commitment required of a good husband and father. Not only do men commonly feel sexually attracted to other women

---

10. M. B. Ellis, *"Julie or La Nouvelle Héloïse": A Synthesis of Rousseau's Thought* (Toronto: University of Toronto Press, 1949), chaps. 2–3.

than their wives, but the feelings of sexual attraction do nothing to motivate a man to rear and provide for his children. To take his place in the order of society, Emile must learn how to master his desires, regulating his actions by reason—he must be more than merely good; he must be virtuous. It is not enough, however, for the tutor to tell him plainly what he must do and why; Rousseau insists that reason alone is too weak to move the young man to do what he must. He enjoins tutors: "Never reason in a dry manner with youth. *Clothe reason in a body if you want to make youth able to grasp it.* Make the language of the mind pass through the heart, so that it may make itself understood. I repeat, cold arguments can determine our opinions, but not our actions. They make us believe and not act" (E 323, emphasis added). Jean-Jacques must inspire Emile with a *passion* to do what reason requires of him—that is, with a passion for what Emile will later learn is virtue.

Allan Bloom has rightly pointed out that Jean-Jacques prepares Emile to hear his teaching in much the same way that the Savoyard Vicar prepared the young Jean-Jacques Rousseau to hear his teaching about God.[11] Jean-Jacques carefully selects the time and place for his speech; he calls God and all of nature as witnesses. There the similarities end. The Vicar addresses a young Jean-Jacques Rousseau in order to explain to the younger man how and why he is happy in a world that Jean-Jacques sees as full of misery and despair. The Vicar answers with an account of his faith in God. In contrast to the young Rousseau, Emile has never known unhappiness, and he is not particularly curious about his tutor's motives for speaking. Jean-Jacques, the tutor, speaks because he knows that Emile must still learn how to secure his own happiness. He begins his teaching by revealing not God, but himself, to his pupil. His is the reason that Emile must obey, but Sophie's is the body in which he clothes it so that Emile can love it.

This is the one important speech where Rousseau does not reveal the content; we read only an outline of its contents and a description of its presentation. Rousseau explains that the speech would only be suitable for a man educated like Emile (E 323–324); I speculate on the reasons for this in chapter 7. Jean-Jacques begins this speech by explaining to Emile what he has done for him and why; speaking with emotion, Jean-Jacques seeks to inspire the boy by his example with feelings similar to his own:

> I shall put in my eyes, my accent, and my gestures the enthusiasm and the ardor that I want to inspire in him. Then I shall speak to him, and he will listen to me. I shall be tender, and he will be moved. By concentrating on the sanctity of my duties, I shall make his duties more respectable to him. . . . Then, in revealing to him all I have done for him, I shall reveal that

11. Bloom, "Introduction," 20.

I have done it all for myself, and he will see in my tender affection the reason for all my care. . . . I shall inflame his young heart with all the sentiments of friendship, generosity, and gratitude which I have already aroused and which are so sweet to cultivate. I shall press him to my breast and shed tears of tenderness on him. I shall say to him, "You are my property, my child, my work. It is from your happiness that I expect my own. If you frustrate my hopes you are robbing me of twenty years of my life, and you are causing the unhappiness of my old age." (E 323)

Having explained that his own happiness depends on his friend's happiness, Jean-Jacques continues by telling the young man about sex, love, and marriage, and explaining to him that his happiness depends on his winning the heart of a virtuous woman to be his wife and on his remaining a faithful husband to her and a devoted father to their children.

Jean-Jacques also introduces Emile to the dangers of love and to the possibility that he may find himself required by his duty to act contrary to his desires. Jean-Jacques also makes clear that the happiness of his own life thus far has followed from his devotion to his moral duty. Emile does not need to be reminded that he has been up to this point in his life the happiest of mortals. Now that he is brought to see that his tutor has cared for him out of friendship, Emile sees himself and his tutor in a new light. He recognizes fully for the first time how closely their identities are intertwined. Now for the first time, he really sees himself in Jean-Jacques, and he recognizes that his own well-being is a constitutive part of his friend's happiness. Emile knows also that the tutor has some of himself (Emile) in him: as a consequence, he knows that the tutor can only be happy as long as he (Emile) loves him. Neither man is exactly self-conscious before the other, as lovers are, but their friendship does enable them to gain a certain perspective on each other and a greater depth of knowledge of themselves. Through all of this speech, Emile is as conscious of the wretchedness of the mass of humanity as he is of his own and Jean-Jacques' happiness. This contrast reinforces his *amour-propre* in the direction it has already begun to take: Emile wants to see himself as Jean-Jacques sees himself—as a man who follows duty and reason. Eager for the happiness Jean-Jacques speaks of and wary of the dangers of which he has been warned, Emile begs Jean-Jacques to lead him. At the moment he makes this promise to obey his tutor, he already feels a passionate desire to do only what reason requires. The trick is to make that passion endure in his soul.

All of this preparation is essential to the success of the final phase of Emile's education—in which Emile is prepared to take his place in society as a husband and father. Now that Emile has reached adulthood and has become capable of a true friendship for Jean-Jacques, the older man remains more than ever his protégé's confidant. Although not experiencing the complete intimacy appropriate to a friendship of true equals, they nevertheless approximate it. Emile continues to show himself without disguise to his tutor, although Jean-Jacques does not explain his entire project to Emile. Nevertheless, he speaks to Emile about what the younger man wants to talk about—women, love, pleasures. Emile's own desires supply the motive to continue his education: he will seek a woman to be his wife. Jean-Jacques guides him in this quest by telling him what traits to look for, crafting in speech the portrait of an ideal woman, with whom it is hoped he will fall in love. In this fashion, Jean-Jacques makes "agreeable and dear to [Emile] all the qualities he ought to love" (E 329). He even gives her a name—Sophie. It is easy for Jean-Jacques to inspire his friend with love for this ideal woman because she is the embodiment of an ideal he himself loves. Emile will love Sophie, but Jean-Jacques loves the wisdom she incarnates.

Once Emile has fallen in love with his ideal, it is safe for him to enter society. He will compare the women he finds there to Sophie, and they will never measure up. The real danger of society continues to be *amour-propre*—the desire to be popular in society (E 331). But Emile's friendship with Jean-Jacques protects him from the bad influence of fashionable young men. To see that it is friendship for Jean-Jacques—not love—that protects Emile, one need only compare Emile's experience in Paris to Saint-Preux's. Although he is deeply in love with Julie, Saint-Preux has no tutor to guide him; he falls in with a group of fashionable young officers who take him to a brothel. Afraid of looking like a bumpkin and a prude, Saint-Preux agrees to join his companions and their ladies for supper: he drinks too much wine and ends up spending the night (J 240–244). Nothing of the sort could possibly happen to Emile. He does not fear ridicule, as Saint-Preux does. He feels no need to win the applause of people in society, and he does not grant anything to opinion. Men of bad morals may try to convince him that he would do nothing wrong in behaving as they do, but Jean-Jacques is easily able to demonstrate the fallacies in their moral reasoning. Emile is moved, however, less by the force of the arguments themselves than by the fact that they come from his friend. Jean-Jacques observes: "Emile will never be made to believe that I bored him with vain lessons; and in an honest and sensitive heart, the voice of a faithful and true friend can surely drown out the cries of twenty seducers" (E 331).

During the course of Emile's quest to find Sophie, Rousseau repeatedly draws attention to the effect of the tutor's friendship on Emile. At the beginning of their quest, Rousseau remarks that friendship is the reason for Emile's willingness to do what Jean-Jacques recommends: "He recognizes the voice of friendship, and he knows how to obey reason" (E 332). Emile follows his tutor's advice because he wants to: he trusts his older friend's judgment and values his esteem. When Jean-Jacques leaves Emile alone in society, he tells him confidently: "I entrust you to my friend; I deliver you to his decent heart. It will answer to me for you!" (E 333). He is confident that Emile's desire to remain worthy of Jean-Jacques's friendship will be strong enough to keep him above temptation. After they have left Paris, Emile complains that his friend let him spend so much time in Paris when he knew that Sophie could not be found there: "my time scarcely costs you anything," he charges, "and my ills cost you little suffering" (E 410). This sort of resentment could undermine the entire educational project if it festered, but Emile quickly recognizes a purpose in his friend's delays. Asked by Jean-Jacques whether he believes that his friend is really indifferent to his suffering, Emile responds by embracing his friend silently. This is as close as their friendship comes to the ideal of silent intimacy depicted in the English breakfast at Clarens.

When Emile finally does meet Sophie, Jean-Jacques must be more active than ever. This is the crucial moment for Emile: his passion for Sophie will be the greatest passion of his life (E 416). If this passion causes him to despise virtue, he will never again love it completely. The first effects of love are overwhelming to Emile. He loves Sophie for her beauty, for the goodness of her heart, and for the decency of her sentiments. He yields completely to his emotions for her. In his romantic delirium, the "sweet illusions" of love "make him a new universe of delight and enjoyment" (E 419). In this state, their thoughts turn sometimes to God—"under the illusion which charms them," they imagine each other perfect, and in this state they think of God's love and the reward He promises for the virtuous. Rousseau consistently insists that this first stage of love—when the lovers are full of desire but remain innocent and chaste—is the happiest time of life (E 419, 426; J 71–83). Not only can the lovers delight in the pleasure of anticipating their first moment of intimacy, they also delight in each other's virtue: "their very privations add to their happiness and do them honor in their own eyes for their sacrifices" (E 426).

When he courts Sophie, Emile begs to make her wishes known to him so that he can please her by complying. He is tempted to become as abjectly servile before her as Saint-Preux before Julie, but the interventions of Sophie's parents and his friend prevent it. Having allowed Emile to kiss her in secret, Sophie comes to fear that she will be unable to resist the temptation to yield more to him than she should; she quarrels with Emile. Having consulted her parents about what to do, Sophie nevertheless does not quite know how to make amends. With the aid of Jean-Jacques, the parents have arranged everything: Emile is allowed, in front of everyone, to give her one chaste kiss and then warned about how he ought to behave around an honorable young woman (E 426–427). "Consult your friend about your duties," Sophie's mother tells him: "He will tell you what a difference there is between the games authorized by the presence of a father and mother and the liberties taken far away from them, liberties which abuse their confidence and turn into traps the same favors which are innocent under their eyes" (E 427). Between Julie and Saint-Preux, things begin the same way, but Julie does not consult her mother. Rather, she takes her lover to a secluded grove and kisses him, with her cousin as witness. Without the presence of the parents' restraining authority, Julie's kiss has an effect opposite to that of Sophie's: the two young people burn ever more ardently with desire and quickly liberate themselves from the constraints of traditional morality. In the end, Emile and Sophie remain chaste until their marriage, whereas Julie and Saint-Preux illicitly consummate their affair, with almost disastrous consequences for both.

When Sophie bids Emile to not to come visit her on some particular days, he does not importune her as Saint-Preux does Julie; nor is Emile tempted to disobey. Rather, he "rigorously sticks to his banishment" and never tries to secretly steal a glimpse of Sophie (E 436). In contrast, Saint-Preux spends his days apart from Julie trying to espy her through a telescope from his vantage on a high cliff across the lake from her home in Vevey (J 74). One day Sophie bids Emile to end his visit early; he complies. When he reaches his lodging, he gruffly informs Jean-Jacques that he has come, not out of friendship, but because Sophie had insisted. In this behavior, Jean-Jacques sees two true signs of the young man's friendship—signs that lead him to conclude that Emile is not "only Sophie's lover," but also "his Mentor's friend." The first is that he did not seek to flatter his friend by lying about his motive in returning. The second is that he returned without lingering near Sophie's abode to daydream about her; he walked home as he would have done had Jean-Jacques been with him (E 435).

After almost five months of courtship, Emile wins Sophie's consent to marry; naturally, he wants to be wed at once. Jean-Jacques, however, has other plans. He insists that Emile must first leave Sophie and spend two years traveling abroad before he will be worthy of assuming his duties as a husband. Emile has, during his courtship, preserved his attachment to virtue. He ultimately won her hand by skipping an appointment with her in order to care for an injured peasant in urgent need of aid. By being the Good Samaritan to the man he found lying by the side of the road, Emile demonstrated that his conscience is well-formed in accordance with the morality of the Gospel: he loves his neighbor as himself. But before he is ready to fulfill the duties of a husband and father, Emile must learn two further lessons that require him to travel far from his beloved. First, he must make himself the master of his attachment to Sophie and not be its slave: he must be able to follow the voice of duty even when it commands him to do something he is disinclined to do. Second, he must learn about politics and law: when he becomes a husband and father, he must assume his place in the conventional order of society, and he will have to know how to fulfill his obligations as a citizen. These two lessons turn out to be two sides of the same lesson: Emile must learn how to be free in the "moral" world just as he knows how to be free in the physical world.

Jean-Jacques's arguments do not convince the young man that he should go. His reasons having failed to persuade, Jean-Jacques reminds Emile of his promise and commands him to go. Emile agrees directly. Bloom rightly points out that this episode epitomizes the whole problem of morality to Rousseau. Morality comes down to keeping promises, and the problem is: Why should anyone keep a promise when it would be more advantageous to break it?[12] This episode demonstrates the nature of Rousseau's solution. It is *not* that Emile has an answer to the question, "Why keep a promise?" *Rather, Emile has become the kind of person who would not ask that question.* In response to Jean-Jacques's command, Emile does not think about his alternatives, looking for ways to back out of his inconvenient promise: he asks how soon they will go. In virtue of his friendship with Jean-Jacques, he has already developed a conception of himself that is predicated on his attachment to his duties. To break any promise would betray his own sense of who he is and would betray his friend.

By departing now, the happiness of his five months of innocent love for Sophie—made sweeter by the sacrifices both of them have made to virtue—will be burned into his memory. Jean-Jacques reminds Emile that he has already experienced the greatest happiness known in human life: "before tasting the pleasures of this life, you have exhausted its happiness" (E 447). This memory of happiness and virtue will remain with him for the rest of his life, and Jean-Jacques hopes, will give him the strength he needs to cleave constantly to virtue. Spending time away from Sophie and in his friend's company will reinforce the importance of his friendship to his identity and thereby prevent him from becoming too dependent on his beloved.

Bloom suggests that Emile learns from his final separation from Sophie how to be "intellectually and morally self-sufficient."[13] But the ending to *Emile* and the fragmentary sequel Rousseau composed, *Emile and Sophie, or the Solitaries*, suggest otherwise. When Emile and Jean-Jacques return to Sophie's home, Jean-Jacques resumes the mediating role in their relationship

12. Ibid., 25–26.
13. Ibid., 27.

that he had played during their courtship. He is needed to remind the couple that as long as they are tempted by erotic passion to tyrannize each other, they must strive to preserve a certain independence—loving what is good more than they love even each other. He is also needed to prevent Sophie from exercising her rights over Emile too capriciously and to deflect Emile's anger in the face of her whims. Most important, he is needed to guide the couple as they rear their own children. In the last lines of _Emile_, the soon-to-be father implores his friend: "remain the master of the young masters. Advise us and govern us. We shall be docile. As long as I live, I shall need you. I need you more than ever now that my functions as a man begin. You have fulfilled yours. Guide me so that I can imitate you" (E 480).

CONCLUSION

At the end, the same relationship is re-established as existed before Emile's journey. Jean-Jacques continues to reason wisely for the two young lovers. Remarkably, Rousseau presents this curious arrangement as both happy and stable: Emile and Sophie are happy in their love for each other, both depend on their friend's guidance, and Jean-Jacques takes pleasure in the happiness he brings to the couple. Remarkably, Rousseau indicates that Jean-Jacques is not jealous of Emile: loving wisdom in all its purity, the perfectly wise tutor does not envy his friend's happiness with Sophie. It is unclear whether Rousseau thought such a triangular relationship could ever really work. Some evidence in the _Confessions_ suggests he did. It is, in any case, striking how frequently these triangular relationships appear in Rousseau's works. There are two in the _Confessions_: the first is established among Claude Anet, Mme de Warens, and Rousseau; the second includes Saint-Lambert, Sophie d'Houdetot, and Rousseau. Even _Julie_ is built around one, comprising Wolmar, Julie, and Saint-Preux. These triangles all take the same form: two men and one woman. One of the men is always older and a wise figure of authority whose role is to bring harmony and balance to the passionate love of the other two.

Even as Rousseau describes them, these relationships never really succeed. Claude Anet died, possibly a suicide, shortly after Mme de Warens' seduction of Rousseau turned their relationship into a ménage à trois. Moreover, Rousseau resented Anet so much that he named the one dishonorable character in _Julie_, the valet, after him.[14] Rousseau never convinced the reasonable Saint-Lambert to try such an outlandish relationship, nor did Sophie show any interest in the arrangement. And when Julie de Wolmar dies, she is glad to depart from this earth because she is torn between her

14. Shklar, _Men and Citizens_, 135.

affection for Wolmar and her passion for Saint-Preux.[15] Without even looking at the dark sequel, we know that the happy ending of *Emile* is deceptive: Emile and Sophie will be unable to combine happiness and virtue
without the influence of Jean-Jacques's wisdom. And if it is just possible to
imagine that an individual could have a wise friend to help and guide him
to attain virtue, it is not really credible to suppose that any man could really do what Jean-Jacques is supposed to do at the end of *Emile*.

How, then, are we to account for the oddly happy ending of *Emile*? The
book presents a deeply disturbing teaching. We can only be happy in this
world if we can find some way to generate an intrinsic attachment to
morality in our souls (and even then with no guarantees), but most of us
have neither the wisdom to desire only genuine goods nor the strength of
will to follow the dictates of conscience. The abstract knowledge that we
cannot be happy without virtue is not enough to move us to do what is
right; we need another motive—a passion for virtue. Rousseau sees that
the desire to be worthy of the right kind of person's friendship can motivate the requisite attachment to justice, but he sees also that we are not at
all likely to find a friend as worthy of emulation as Emile's tutor or the
extraordinary Wolmar. The difficulty would be solved if we did not need
to find a real tutor to guide us—if we could somehow draw the necessary
guidance from a work of art, as religious people find direction in certain
sacred writings. In fact, Rousseau offers a glimpse of one potentially successful triangular relationship in his works. In the second preface to *Julie*,
he tells us that he delights in fancying that his work has fallen into the
hands of a provincial couple, who will read his book and, inspired by its
example, take new pleasure in fulfilling their own duties to each other and
to their neighbors (J 16–17). He imagines himself, in virtue of his role as
author, as the imagined tutor of his readers. Whether we, as readers, can
take guidance from the authorial persona of Rousseau as from a wise friend
is the topic of the next chapter.

---

15. This is the tragic consequence of Saint-Preux's "cure" at the hands of Wolmar. As long
as Saint-Preux had been the sort of man who would abjure his duty for the sake of satisfying
his passions, Julie could easily enough convince herself that he was unworthy of her love for
him, and she rightly concludes that the Saint-Preux of parts I–III of the novel could not have
made her as happy as Wolmar subsequently does (J 299). Having triumphed over his fatal passion for her, however, Saint-Preux made himself worthy of winning Julie's love; a Saint-Preux
restored to virtue could indeed have made her happy. Drawn now to Saint-Preux both by his
personal charms and by his virtue, Julie would have to struggle constantly against her inclinations to remain faithful to her husband. Recognizing the dangers of such a struggle, she wel-
comes her death when it comes.

7 The Author as Tutor

THE OPENING SENTENCE of *Emile* expresses both the depth of Rousseau's loathing for his society and the blasphemous height of his literary and philosophical ambition: "Everything is good as it leaves the hands of the Author of things; everything degenerates in the hands of man" (E 35). Seeming to praise God for having made everything good, Rousseau in fact criticizes Him for allowing His works to be so easily depraved. In addition, Rousseau proposes to do what God cannot do, or at least has not done: to cure man of his self-induced depravity. It was noted in chapter 6 that Rousseau presents in *Emile* a theoretically possible solution to the predicament of civilized men: the right kind of education, conducted at the hands of a wise tutor who is his pupil's friend, can enable a man to attain an intrinsic attachment to morality and to avoid the miseries inflamed *amour-propre* causes.[1]

Difficult as Emile's education is—and Rousseau makes certain that we see the impossibility of actually undertaking any education exactly like it—Rousseau has an even greater ambition for his work. The epigraph to *Emile* calls attention to Rousseau's didactic purpose in writing; he quotes Seneca's *De Ira*: "We are sick with evils that can be cured; and nature, having brought us forth sound, itself helps us if we wish to be improved" (E 31 n. 2). This passage does not describe the action of the novel: born with all the goodness of nature, Emile is never sick with any sort of evil and is never cured. He is only made to feel a weak form of the ills from which the rest of us suffer, but that is only in order to inoculate him against the more virulent forms of *amour-propre*.

We, however, are sick; and a symptom of the disease is that we fail to see that we *are* sick even though we sense that we are not well. The whole point of the *Discourse on Inequality* is to make us aware of our moral illness. Rousseau makes us see and feel the contrast between the savage who is happy and knows it and the bourgeois who is wretched but has forgotten that life could be otherwise. Rousseau does not tell us all this only to make

---

1. To be precise, the cultivation of Rousseauian virtue offers only a *partial* solution to the predicament of civilized man: a perfect solution would require the attainment of practical wisdom—but this wisdom is by nature unattainable for all but an extraordinary few, like Socrates.

us feel worse: he thought of his books as genuinely, practically useful. The epigraph to *Emile* expresses the same thought: we who are sick *can* be cured. Rousseau saw that the greatest obstacle to our convalescence is that we do not wish for recovery: we are deeply attached to the vain illusions that *amour-propre* fosters. He writes in *Emile* that the lost golden age is a permanent possibility for us, but for it to be reborn requires "one single but impossible thing: to love it" (E 474). That insight supplies the key to understanding Rousseau's didactic intention in his novels: he aims to make it possible for us to make a partial return to the quasi-natural golden age by making us truly love that state. To love the golden age is to be enabled to live, as does Emile, as a free man and a citizen whatever the nature of the regime governing the place in which one dwells.

This chapter argues that *Emile* not only depicts an ideal education but also aims to make a suitably modified version of this ideal education accessible to the reader. Rousseau hopes that his reader is so moved by his encounter with *Emile* that he will come to see himself and his world differently: attracted by the image of Emile's domestic happiness, the (male) reader is to be inspired to imitate Emile and aspire to the virtue he incarnates. In fact, Rousseau's *Julie* is didactic in precisely the same way as *Emile*, except that the *Nouvelle Héloïse* depicts an ideal heroine, whom its female readers are to want to emulate, but I will not pursue that observation here (J 17–19).

Focusing on *Emile*, we find that Rousseau, the author, endeavors to provide his readers the same kind of guidance in wisdom that Jean-Jacques supplies to Emile. Rousseau the author aims to make himself accessible to his readers as a kind of imagined friend so that he can inspire us to attain virtue just as Jean-Jacques inspires Emile. At the conclusion of his education, Emile cleaves steadfastly to what is right, even in the face of temptation, because he has come to see himself as the sort of person he perceives his friend Jean-Jacques to be: one who bases his self-esteem on his attachment to morality. So also does Rousseau invite his readers to be his friend (to befriend the authorial "persona" he presents in his fictions) so that we come to see ourselves as people who do not ask what advantage can be found in doing what is right, but who instead cleave steadfastly to what conscience and reason require.

Claims about authorial intention are notoriously difficult to establish. Nevertheless, in this case three different kinds of considerations—philosophical, autobiographical, and rhetorical—all point to the same conclusion. First, Rousseau's philosophical doctrines point to the need for a kind of education such as I argue the reading of *Emile* or *Julie* supplies. In particular, both teach that we require a tutorial friend to help us to escape or to overcome the effects of inflamed *amour-propre* in our own souls. Second,

Rousseau's own autobiographical remarks support this reading of *Emile*. Finally, structural peculiarities in *Emile* cannot plausibly be explained if we suppose that work exclusively about the theoretical solution it depicts. An examination of the narrative of *Emile* reveals that Rousseau subordinates the presentation of his philosophical points to the imperatives of his literary and didactic aims.

PHILOSOPHICAL CONSIDERATIONS:
WHY EACH OF US REQUIRES A (FICTIONAL) TUTOR

It must be noted at the outset the great difference between the two projects Rousseau undertakes in *Emile*. To preserve a child in his natural goodness is far from simple, but it is easier than curing those who are sick. We are constituted by our instrumental relations with people around us. We already feel the effects of inflamed *amour-propre*: we love the wrong things, and we care about the wrong people's judgment. The whole orientation of our desires must be altered so that our *amour-propre* supports our attachment to morality rather than undermining it. Before we can see why Rousseau thinks that he, as an author, can appear to his readers as the appropriate kind of friend, it is necessary to review the reasons which lead Rousseau to conclude that those who are already sick with inflamed *amour-propre* can only be cured by the influence of an exemplary friend.

Why Only a Friend Can Cure Us

The same considerations that lead to the conclusion that only a friend can introduce a good child to virtue apply with even greater force to the present case. The tutor seeking to cure men whose *amour-propre* has already been aroused into a concern for money and status must if anything be more careful about further arousing *amour-propre* than Jean-Jacques had to be with Emile. His project is more difficult: our tutor must not only lead us to esteem what is truly estimable, he must dispel the illusions that attach us to the goods we presently value. We must no longer care about our social and economic status vis-à-vis the rest of society; we must instead care only about our happiness, the justice of our actions, and the flourishing of the communities of which we are a part. How can such a transformation of the self be accomplished?

One might suppose that reason should suffice to guide adults. Our minds are fully developed, and every normal adult has some sort of conscience and has achieved at least a basic level of self-control. On this point, however, Rousseau's pessimism is unremitting. When we who see the world through the lens of inflamed *amour-propre* think of reason, we think of instrumental reason. When we deliberate about action, we tend to ask what advantage we will derive from the alternative courses of action before us. If we could be led by moral reasons, we would not suffer so much from ills of our own making. Wise advice may be—and often is—given us, but we do not heed it. Disordered *amour-propre* distorts our understanding so that we do not always hear what the preacher is trying to say. Even when we do hear and understand, it is not so easy to change how we act because how we act depends so much on how we *feel*. Although it may not be too difficult to compel oneself, contrary to inclination, to perform any single action, it is extremely difficult to give up entirely an activity that one enjoys. The problem is that we cannot, by any single act of will, alter what gives us pleasure: we can only change the objects that delight us by changing our habits, which is never easy.

The problem faced by someone seeking to educate an already corrupted adult to virtue is akin to that faced by the great Lawgiver depicted in the *Social Contract*. The Lawgiver seeks to transform the inhabitants of one particular place into a people: he aims to make a disordered mass of individual persons into a body of virtuous citizens. To do so, he must make them desire as individuals what they ought to desire as citizens, and he must do this before they have the experience of citizenship that would give rise to those desires. Unable to persuade the unruly mob to embrace civic virtue's austere demands, the Legislator seeks to "rally by divine authority those whom human prudence could not move" (SC 71). Not every would-be founder can make this trick work, however. For the people to believe that the founder speaks for the gods is not easily accomplished. Apparent miracles can be arranged, but they will not convince the people for long. Only a real miracle will do, and Rousseau specifies what it must be: "the great soul of the Lawgiver is the true miracle which must prove his mission" (SC 71). But there is a problem with this solution also: Rousseau does not say how the people are to judge the Lawgiver's greatness of soul. He indicates only that a Lawgiver's greatness of soul can be perceived retrospectively, by looking to the success of the institutions he created. Unsatisfying as it is, this answer suffices for Rousseau's purposes in the *Social Contract*. He need explain no more because he is not proposing to teach a would-be Lawgiver or to show a populace how to recognize one (SC 73).

We saw in chapter 4 that it can be possible, under certain conditions, for one person to gain knowledge of another's soul—namely when they are friends. We saw that a friend can, through force of personality and the power of example, exert a potent influence on his friend without thereby provoking resistance or inspiring resentment. In virtue of our intimate association, I can have a reasonable degree of confidence that my friend is happy and that he owes his well-being to his virtue; this confidence in turn will give me good reason to trust my friend's judgment and wisdom. His friendship for me will also prove to me that he cares genuinely about my well-being. And the involuntary respect I feel for my friend's virtue (assuming he is so) can fill me with the desire to imitate him. The more I come to define myself in terms of my friend—the more I imagine myself, not as I appear to the crowd, but as I appear to my excellent friend—the more I am liberated from my subjection to opinion. I remain, of course, dependent for my conception of myself on my friend, and I can be virtuous only to the extent that my friend truly is wise and genuinely loves virtue. But these defects are inevitable for most of us: if we could be fully independent of the opinion of others, we would need no tutoring because we would never be corrupted in the first place.

It is, however, hard to see how a person already consumed by inflamed *amour-propre* could come to recognize another person as a real friend. Someone wholly bent on achieving a brilliant success in business or in society will see other people only as they relate to the advancement of his own purposes, not as they are in themselves. Thus a partial, preliminary transformation is required to open an already corrupted soul to the possibility of true friendship. By examining Rousseau's account of the Lawgiver's task, we get a sense of what this preparatory transformation might entail. Rousseau first insists that a people, once corrupted, can never be restored to virtue because their collective identity as a people would have to be too radically transformed. But he modifies this assertion at once, explaining that: "there may . . . also sometimes occur periods of violence in the lifetime of States when revolutions do to peoples what certain crises do to individuals, when horror of the past takes the place of forgetting, and when the State aflame with civil wars is so to speak reborn from its ashes and recovers the vigor of youth as it escapes death's embrace" (SC 72). The Roman Republic was born only after the expulsion of the Tarquins, and the republics of Sparta, Holland, and Switzerland all follow the same pattern. In each case, the people stood at the brink of slavery and ruin, only to be reborn to the possibility of virtue and freedom. In each case, horror at the awful consequences of living under a tyrannical regime prepares the people to embrace the burdens civic virtue requires of them.

Not even the godlike Legislator can cause the crisis that prepares the state for a republican rebirth; neither can the aspiring educator of those already corrupted initiate the first movement away from inflamed *amour-propre* that the education to virtue presupposes. Although such personal crises cannot be directly caused by any outside agency, they seem to occur spontaneously with some frequency: because the goods opinion most values do not really satisfy the deepest longings of our heart, it is only natural that we should, from time to time, grow cognizant of their insufficiency. Moreover, if we should happen (or choose) to distance ourselves from the great cities where the spectacle of inequality does so much to inflame the imagination, we can begin to regain the taste for simpler pleasures and rediscover the impulse of our natural self-love, which inclines us only to seek our own, absolute well-being. Thus when Rousseau describes the ideal readers of *Julie*, he imagines them as "honest people spend[ing] their lives cultivating their fathers' patrimony in the distant countryside" (J 16).

Why an Author Can Be Such a Friend

Rousseau's pessimistic moral psychology leads to the conclusion that those of us already corrupted by living in a society based on inflamed *amour-propre* can only be cured by the beneficent influence of a wise and excellent friend. Two problems surface with this proposal. We have already seen the first: that corrupted individuals must first be awakened to a perception of their "moral" illness before they can be cured. The second problem is that most people never encounter anyone worth imitating in this way because the virtue and wisdom required of a moral tutor are so extraordinary and rare. Both difficulties could be solved at once if it were possible to be sufficiently moved by an encounter with the *image* of a friend, whom we could come to know by means of some literary or other artistic representation.

Rousseau considers carefully the possibilities of two artistic forms, the stage-play, and the novel, concluding that "great cities must have theaters; and corrupt peoples, novels" (J 3). In his *Letter to d'Alembert*, Rousseau argues at length that the modern theater can do nothing to improve morals or to impart virtue. The fundamental problem with the theater is that watching other people perform on stage reinforces the self-consciousness that lies at the root of *amour-propre*. The effect is only exacerbated when the theatre is treated, as it was in Rousseau's day, as a place for the luminaries of high society to see and be seen (LA 63). To engage our attention, moreover, the staged performance must appeal to and flatter our dominant passions (LA 18). "Reason," by contrast "is good for nothing on the stage," according to Rousseau (LA 18). Were an author to try depicting a character who was "entirely wise," the effort would necessarily fail: unable to identify with the wise man or to share his feelings, the audience would dismiss him as "mad" (LA 45). In comedies, where even good people are made to appear ridiculous (this is the heart of Rousseau's critique of Molière's *Misanthrope*), our own fear of ridicule is reinforced (LA 26, 37–47). We enslave ourselves to the tyranny of social appearances. Tragedies are even worse. They make wickedness attractive and even cruelty seem pardonable (LA 23). Worse yet, they make us want to sacrifice everything—honor, virtue, and even duty—to the passion of love (LA 53). Why, then, does Rousseau advise great cities to maintain theatres? Because he supposes that it cannot make the already vicious any worse than they are and that the habit of going to the theater imparts "a soft disposition and a spirit of inaction which will . . . keep the bad from meditating great crimes" (LA 64–65).

When we read novels, by contrast, we are alone, far from the eyes of others. In Rousseau's account, *amour-propre* has its roots in the faculty of sight. We see others and feel the weight of their gaze. Conversely, isolation and solitude weaken *amour-propre*. In fact, Rousseau suggests at one point that reading can be beneficial in this way, even when we are reading otherwise unedifying literature (LA 82). But in the second preface to *Julie*, Rousseau explains that some novels can be affirmatively beneficial to their readers, while others only reinforce society's malignant lessons. The corrupting fictions are those fashionable novels that only inspire people to adopt the wicked maxims of high society (J 13–15). Rousseau proposed therefore to write a different sort of fiction: "If Novels offered their Readers only tableaux of objects that surround them, only duties they can fulfill, only pleasures of their own station, Novels would . . . make them wise" (J 15).

But a novel must be more than merely edifying: we do not read to be improved; we read to enjoy. The trick is to make the novel entertaining enough for people to read it while making sure that the lessons it teaches are morally beneficial. Rousseau solves this problem in *Julie* by beginning with the story of her illicit love and by showing how she is restored to virtue and made even more lovable because of her triumph. Likewise, Rousseau thought that the most important lessons in *Emile* appear in books IV and V, and these are the most engaging parts of the text: the love story of book V is still deeply moving to some readers, and the Profession of Faith of the Savoyard Vicar—which Rousseau said was the "best and most useful writing" of the eighteenth century (LB 960)—was sufficiently appealing to readers that it was widely reprinted and read on its own.

Not only does reading the right sort of fiction not arouse *amour-propre*, such reading can also be uniquely beneficial because it creates—or can create—an intimacy between reader and author that is akin to the intimacy of friendship. This encounter with the author of a book we love is as close as we ever come to Rousseau's ideal of friendship as "two souls in the same body" (C 348). Rousseau felt very strongly that all his works carried the unmistakable stamp of his own, distinctive personality. He makes the depth of that conviction clear in *Rousseau Judge of Jean-Jacques: Dialogues* (hereafter referred to as the *Dialogues*).[2] After the Frenchman has read Jean-Jacques's works, he reports to "Rousseau":

2. In that work, Rousseau presents three conversations between a fictionalized version of himself (the "Rousseau" of the title), who represents the man that Jean-Jacques Rousseau would have become had he never published any books, and an unnamed Frenchman; the

I found the writings of J.J. full of affections of the soul which penetrated mine. I found in them ways of feeling and seeing that distinguish him easily from all the writers of his time and most of those who preceded him. He is, as you said, an inhabitant of another sphere where nothing is like it is here. His system may be false, but in developing it, he portrayed himself so truthfully in a manner so characteristic and so sure that it's impossible for me to mistake it. (D 212)

With this judgment at least, few subsequent readers have been inclined to disagree.

It is hard to see how we can experience in reading anything analogous to the equality and reciprocity we feel in the presence of friends, however. Friends love each other for their own sake and know that they love each other in the same way; because they are not self-conscious before one another, they gain unparalleled insight into the real state of each other's character. This cannot literally be true of an author whose books are widely read. The author does not know his readers and cannot love them as individuals; nor do readers come to know the real person behind the authorial persona they encounter in their reading. But a kind of imperfectly reciprocal affection may nevertheless arise between an author and his readers. Rousseau, for example, insists repeatedly that he loves humanity as a whole, and so in a formal way can be said to love each one of his readers.[3] But Rousseau also attempts to generate a more satisfactory approximation of intimacy with his readers than that. He writes in a highly personal style, revealing his soul to his readers; he invites his readers to love him and makes clear the conditions under which he would love in return. We know from Rousseau's correspondence that he inspired many such "friends" at a distance.[4]

Finally, the problem of equality remains. Friends must be in some sense equal, but it is hard to see how we could imagine ourselves in a relationship of equality with the author of a book we are reading. The equality of

topic of their discussion is J.J., (the "Jean-Jacques" of the title), who is the author of *Julie*, *Emile*, and the other books written by the actual Jean-Jacques Rousseau. At issue in the conversations between "Rousseau" and the Frenchman is whether J.J. deserves the reputation for wickedness imputed to him by society. Jean-Jacques Rousseau explains that he wrote the work in order to demonstrate that, "if someone had given [him] ideas about another man like those [his] contemporaries have been given about [him], [he] would not have behaved toward [that other man] as they do toward [himself]" (D 3).

3. Although he appeared misanthropic to many observers, Rousseau explains that his frequent criticisms of his contemporaries in fact stem from his deep love for them: since he cannot abide to witness human suffering, Rousseau constantly voices indignation at the constant wickedness which is its principal cause.

4. Robert Darnton, "Readers Respond to Rousseau: The Fabrication of Romantic Sensitivity," in *The Great Cat Massacre and Other Episodes in French Cultural History* (New York: Basic Books, 1984), 235–249.

the literary critic to the author is not really the equality of friends, as the second preface to *Julie* makes clear. In that short dialogue, Rousseau talks to an unnamed critic about the literary merits of the letters comprising the *Nouvelle Héloïse*, and he can even explain how one might go about writing them, but the two men are not friends. They are fundamentally never more than competitors. As a man full of the inflamed *amour-propre* endemic among Parisian *bels-esprits*, the critic has nevertheless been deeply moved by his reading of the epistolary record of Julie's life and love. But the possibility that the work is a fiction—that another author like himself has made him feel as he does—distracts him. He demands to know whether Rousseau is the author or only the editor of the letters. That question need not detain the ordinary reader, who feels no need to compete in technical skill with the author.

Nevertheless, the inequality of author and reader persists. This inequality is, however, akin to the inequality that necessarily exists between teacher and student. That inequality does makes friendship more difficult, perhaps, but hardly impossible. It is necessary only for the teacher to find some way to lessen the distance between himself and the pupil. In like fashion, an author may also attempt to diminish the distance between himself and the reader. Rousseau does this in a number of ways: by insisting on his own weaknesses and faults, by revealing himself to us through imperfect literary characters whose lives and virtues are closer to us, and by his evident sympathy for the simple, country life he urges his readers to adopt.

The final difficulty readers today face in conceiving the authorial persona of Rousseau as a teacher of virtue is that we know from reading Rousseau's various autobiographical writings that the man possessed little of the virtue he attributes to his literary alter ego in *Emile*. Jean-Jacques, the tutor of Emile, is a man of wisdom and virtue. In contrast, the real Jean-Jacques Rousseau preserves his natural goodness (which means that he does not wish evil to anyone), but is certainly not a man of virtue. Although he loves virtue with all his heart, Rousseau utterly lacks the strength of will required to make himself act in the face of contrary inclination to do what he knows to be right (D 10, 184; RW 77). Rousseau admits as much in the body of *Emile* when he describes the refined, epicurean life he would adopt if he were wealthy enough to live as he pleased. He would not devote his life to the practice of self-commanding virtue, nor would he attempt to educate a child to virtue. He would live in the country with a small group of friends, delighting in simple pleasures. In such circumstances, his lack of virtue would matter little: his manner of living would substantially protect him from situations in which he would be tempted to wrong another. Nevertheless, Rousseau makes clear that, in the face of temptation, he would succumb. The personal weaknesses of the man, Jean-Jacques Rousseau, however, should serve as a reminder of the aptness of the educational method he adopts: exemplary persons of perfect wisdom and virtue are so rare as to be useless to the vast majority of us who will never meet them, but a writer who can endow a literary persona with the required attributes is able to touch the hearts of many.

AUTOBIOGRAPHICAL CONSIDERATIONS: ROUSSEAU AS HIS READERS' FRIEND

The only two works in which Rousseau discusses at any length how his works are to be read are dialogues, the second preface to *Julie* and the autobiographical *Rousseau, Judge of Jean-Jacques*. In both works Rousseau converses with a reader who has not responded to his works quite as the author would have wished, although there the similarities end. We have already seen that in the dialogue preface to *Julie*, the discussion centers on the appreciation due the work. In the *Dialogues*, the discussion focuses on the man, Jean-Jacques—although both "Rousseau" and the Frenchmen first make his acquaintance by reading his books. Both readers approach the texts in much the same way, but their reactions differ in important respects. From the similarities and differences in their responses, we can get a sense of what Rousseau hoped for from an ideal reader—from "Rousseau," which is to say, from himself—and what he expected from a more typical one—the Frenchman.

"Rousseau" Befriends Jean-Jacques

We have seen that the preface to *Julie* presents inflamed *amour-propre* as the greatest obstacle to appreciating that novel; for that reason "Rousseau" doubts the book will be successful in Paris but hopes it will win the hearts of women in the provinces.[5] In the *Dialogues*, *amour-propre* also obstructs the Frenchman's understanding. He has trouble encountering the author, Jean-Jacques (J.J.), in his works because he has trouble giving up his prior belief in the author's wickedness. When he does read the books with an open mind, he still does not read them as J.J. would wish because he reads them with a primarily intellectual project in mind: he examines the books and evaluates their contents so that he can form a judgment of their author; he does not let himself experience the books and be moved by them in the same way that "Rousseau" is moved. "Rousseau" is the ideal reader of J.J.'s works in two respects: first, he reads the books ignorant of their author's evil reputation, and this ignorance enables him to be open to the books'

---

5. In fact, *Julie* was tremendously successful—particularly among the Parisian women whom he professed to think would be repelled by it.

emotional impact. Second—and this is the more important consideration—he already believes in his heart the teachings J.J.'s works contain.
Reading J.J.'s books affected him powerfully because he "recognized in his
writings the man [he] found in [himself]" (D 52).

"Rousseau" explains that he found his own moral convictions reinforced by the discovery of a person whose thoughts and feelings con-
formed to his own: "his example was useful above all in nurturing my
confidence in the feelings that I alone among my contemporaries had preserved. I was a believer, I have always been one, though not in the same
way as people with symbols and formulas. . . . I found myself alone in the
multitude, as much because of my ideas as because of my feelings. This
solitary state was sad. J.J. rescued me from it. His books strengthened me
against the derision of free-thinkers" (D 53). Not only did "Rousseau's" encounter with J.J. reinforce his attachment to his own moral ideals, it inspired him with the desire to befriend the author. Imagining himself as J.J.'s
friend in turn strengthened him in his devotion to the difficult task of prac-
ticing virtue:

> Based on all these ideas [prompted by reading J.J.'s books], I made a plan
> of living, whose charm would be a relationship with him; and I—for whom
> the society of men has for a long time offered only a false appearance with-
> out reality. . . . I yielded to the hope of finding again in him all I had lost, of
> tasting once again the sweetness of a sincere friendship. . . . That a single
> man thought as I did nurtured my confidence, a single truly virtuous man
> made me believe in virtue, inspired me to cherish it, idolize it, place all hope
> in it. (D 53–54)

"Rousseau's" imagined friendship with J.J. strengthens his belief in God
and his devotion to virtue; these feelings together give "Rousseau" the
courage to do justice in this world and fill him with the hope of "finding
compensation in a better order of things" after death (D 54).

When the Frenchman explains to "Rousseau" that the world deems J.J.
to be the most reprehensible of men, his reaction is equally passionate: the
first news of it cast him into despair: "by taking away this support, you
leave me alone in the world, swallowed up in a chasm of evils" (D 54).
Based on what he feels he knows of the author from his reading, however,
"Rousseau" does not believe what he hears. Instead, his resolve to meet the
man himself is strengthened. He discovers that J.J. does not possess virtue,
although he is good (see, e.g., D 87, 127, 154). He loves virtue, however, but
lacks the strength to master his desires. He lacks also the *amour-propre* that
could inspire him to hate anyone or to commit any crime; he is, judges
"Rousseau," a "man of nature enlightened by reason" (D 158). The discovery that J.J. is good but not virtuous does not lessen "Rousseau's" en-

thusiasm for J.J.'s books or for his ideas. Nor does it diminish his enthusiasm for virtue. Nor does "Rousseau" adopt J.J.'s life of goodness as his own. He does not aim to refrain from action, as J.J. does. He will follow his desire to live in friendship with J.J., and he resolves to faithfully transmit J.J.'s last manuscripts to the future. He will live also in the hope that he will be able to mount a successful public defense of his friend in the future. Finally, he resists his inclinations in a way that suggests he possesses something more like virtue than J.J.'s goodness: he wants very much to enlighten J.J. about the nature of the calumnies spread against him; to do so would be to make possible the fullest intimacy with his friend. But his sense of duty moves him to keep the promise he had given to remain silent.

The Frenchman Honors Jean-Jacques

The Frenchman's reaction to J.J.'s books is rather different. We do not know why "Rousseau" takes up J.J.'s books, but we are told that the Frenchman reads them in order to learn whether their author could possibly deserve the evil reputation he has acquired. We also know how the Frenchman approaches the texts. He read J.J.'s works twice: the first time rather chaotically and confusedly, the second time, systematically. He describes his way of reading as follows:

> In order to judge the true goal of these books, I didn't apply myself to picking apart a few scattered and separate sentences here and there; but rather consulting myself both during these readings and as I finished them, I examined as you desired the dispositions of soul into which they placed and left me, judging as you do that it was the best means to penetrate through to that of the Author when he wrote them and the effect he proposed to produce. (D 209)

His initial response to J.J. is much more moderate than "Rousseau's": "I had found him impassioned for virtue, freedom, order, but with a vehemence that often carried him beyond the goal" (D 211). This first reading made him want to know more about the author, so that he could reach a conclusive judgment regarding him.

In his second reading, the Frenchman tries more earnestly to understand the logic of J.J.'s system. He begins with *Emile*, the book in which he perceives J.J.'s first principles, and reads the books in the reverse order of their publication.[6] When he has finished, he offers a summary of J.J.'s teachings

---

6. We should be careful not to regard the Frenchman's statements about how to read Rousseau's works as the author's authoritative statement on the matter. The Frenchman qualifies his statements significantly: "I had *felt* that these writings proceeded in a certain order . . . I *believed* I saw that this order was the reverse of their order of publication . . . " D 211, emphasis added.

that closely resembles "Rousseau's" account, with one crucial difference. Whereas "Rousseau" had himself been inspired to love virtue more and to become J.J.'s friend, the Frenchman simply perceives that J.J. wants his readers to be thus moved. He writes that J.J.'s "goal is to rectify the error of our judgments in order to delay the progress of our vices, and to show us that where we seek glory and renown, we in fact find only errors and miseries" (D 213).

The Frenchman is not immediately moved with a feeling of friendship for J.J. or even by the desire to befriend him. He now agrees with "Rousseau's" judgment of J.J.: that he is a man of nature enlightened by reason. He declares: "I honor him because I want to be just, because I believe he is innocent, and because I see him oppressed" (D 214). But he does not love him, and he does not know whether he will ever do so. It seems, remarkably enough, that he does not yet know the man sufficiently well (D 214). He ascribes definite limits to his willingness to aid J.J.; he will not defend him publicly, nor does he even agree—at least at first—to visit him. He fears to suffer J.J.'s fate at the hands of the conspiracy: "I have a status, friends to preserve, a family to support, patrons to satisfy. I don't want to play Don Quixote in this" (D 222).

Although the Frenchman perceives the same intention behind J.J.'s works as "Rousseau," he is not moved in the same way. The Frenchman's narrow purpose in reading the works limits his openness to being moved by them, reading as if through the eyes of the conspiratorial Gentlemen, who are (in the world of the *Dialogues* at least) out to destroy J.J. (D 216). "Rousseau" entreats the Frenchman to join with him to form with J.J. "a social group with him that is sincere and without fraud," and the Frenchman agrees. "Rousseau" reports that this friendship is also what J.J. himself desires: "The hope that his memory may be restored someday to the honor it deserves, and that his books become useful through the esteem owed their author is henceforth the only hope that can please him in this world" (D 245, 227).

The *Dialogues* ends on a wistful note: all three characters look forward to a future in which the corruption characteristic of contemporary society is overcome and J.J.'s reputation restored. But Rousseau is also realistic about the likelihood that such a conclusion will come to pass. The only reader who responds exactly as J.J. wishes is "Rousseau;" the Frenchman, who is the best kind of reader to be expected in a corrupt society, understands J.J.'s project, but is not moved by it. Nevertheless, "Rousseau" remains confident that once he seeks to know J.J. out of a disinterested love for the truth, he will be attracted to his society. The promise, though incompletely realized at the end of the *Dialogues,* is of a new form of society in which people are not self-conscious about what conventional society—

personified in the *Dialogues* by the Gentlemen—cares about, but who find their identity bolstered by their intimate friendships with others who love virtue and are therefore able to act rightly in the larger world.

RHETORICAL CONSIDERATIONS: *EMILE* AS DIDACTIC NOVEL

We have seen that Rousseau's philosophical system teaches that individuals already consumed by *amour-propre* require the influence of a wise and virtuous friend to enable them to attain virtue. Rousseau's autobiographical *Dialogues* express a similar ambition. Rousseau's ideal readers encounter the author in his works, they find themselves drawn to his principles, they find their love for virtue strengthened by the discovery of another who loves virtue as much, and they conceive the desire to live with the author in friendship. Since Rousseau insists so clearly that the *Emile* is his "best" and "most important" book, it seems likely that Rousseau wanted his readers to respond in particular to the *Emile* by conceiving the desire to befriend the author (C 473, 480).

Ample evidence within *Emile* itself supports such a reading. Not only does the epigraph point toward the possibility that Rousseau aimed to show how people sick with a disordered *amour-propre* could be cured, but structural peculiarities in the novel can only be explained by supposing that the needs of the reader's education rather than Emile's are being met. Three of them merit particular attention. First is the matter of the happy ending—which, as we noted at the end of chapter 6, is really happier than it ought to be. Second, Rousseau speaks directly to the readers about how they should rear their own children and in a number of places commends particular "moral strategies" to his readers so that they may free themselves from the corrosive morals of bourgeois society. Third is the question of the Profession of Faith of the Savoyard Vicar that takes up roughly half of book IV and which Emile never hears. In contrast, the most important speech that Emile does hear—the speech Jean-Jacques delivers about love and sex—is the one speech Rousseau declines to include for the readers' perusal (E 323–324).

Emile concludes with a happy ending that in effect leads us to believe that we too can attain Emile's happiness if we imitate his virtuous, rustic life with his family. The recommendation that we find our happiness in our families rather than in social or financial success is the idea that links the beginning and the end of the book. It is striking that Rousseau's most famous bit of advice to his readers—that children should be breast-fed by their mothers—is not followed by the tutor, but is (presumably) followed by Emile and Sophie. Because he sees that political disorders have their roots in moral and psychological deformations, Rousseau teaches that the first step in improving regimes is to improve family life (E 46; J 17–18). If men and women take pleasure in fulfilling their duties as parents, he argues, children would be better raised and the parents themselves would be spared from many of the miseries they inflict on themselves. In *Emile*, he writes:

> Do you wish to bring everyone back to his first duties? Begin with mothers . . . let mothers deign to nurse their children, nature's sentiments will be awakened in every heart. . . . This first point, this point alone, will bring everything back together. . . . When the family is lively and animated, the domestic cares constitute the dearest occupation of the wife and the sweetest enjoyment of the husband. Thus, from the correction of this single abuse would soon result a general reform; nature would soon have reclaimed all its rights. Let women once again become mothers, men will soon become husbands and fathers again. (E 46)

By directing men and women to find the happiness of their lives in the domestic sphere—and by depicting the domestic life as pleasantly as possible—Rousseau seeks to diminish the effects of *amour-propre* in their souls.

Easily the most perplexing structural feature of *Emile*, however, is the famous Profession of Faith of the Savoyard Vicar. Scholars have long debated its relation to the main argument of the *Emile*. Roger Masters suggests that it contains the (dualist) metaphysical foundation of Rousseau's system. But this interpretation cannot be correct, first, because Rousseau notes in his own voice that he "found a multitude of objections to make" to the Vicar (E 294), and second, because the system of thought Rousseau develops in the rest of *Emile* is far more sophisticated and less open to objection than the Vicar's. The Vicar teaches that man is naturally social; looking into his soul, he professes to find written there the principle: be just and you will be happy (E 282, 290). By contrast, Rousseau teaches that we are *not* naturally social and that our instincts tell us nothing about justice—only that we naturally wish for our own well-being (though he does hold that the desire for justice can be conditionally natural for human beings).

Allan Bloom rightly identifies the key to understanding the Profession of Faith: he reminds us that Emile does not hear it.[7] It would not matter if he did: he would not understand it.[8] Moreover, Emile has no motive to listen to the speech. Jean-Jacques wants to know the Vicar's principles because he, having been unhappy himself and aware of so much misery in the world around him, cannot understand how the Vicar can live happily

---

7. Bloom, "Introduction," 20.
8. Rousseau reminds us, just before the Profession of Faith begins that "Emile . . . refuses his attention to everything beyond his reach and listens to things he does not understand with the most profound indifference" (E 259).

in his humble estate. "Who knows how to be happy?" asks Jean-Jacques; "'I do,' answered the priest," and by way of elaboration he explains his faith to the young man (E 256–266). His faith is simple and consoling. He believes the conscience is a natural moral instinct that infallibly distinguishes right from wrong (E 286–287); he believes, further, that human beings are naturally torn between our spiritual natures that naturally long to follow conscience, and our bodily natures that are sinful. From the omnipotence of God, he infers God's infinite goodness, and concludes that God has so ordered the world that justice is rewarded and injustice punished (E 282). From the prosperity of the wicked he concludes not that God is dead but that the soul survives the body and is punished or rewarded sufficiently to restore the cosmic order of justice so often flouted on earth (E 283). In contrast, Emile needs no religion to console him for unhappiness; nor will he be tempted to infer the existence of God from the fact of injustice. Rather, the beauty of the natural world and his belief in his own virtue and Sophie's will fill his heart with a belief in the existence of a benevolent and loving God, and that faith will only add to the delight that is the natural effect of his life of virtue (E 426).

If the faith the Vicar professes is not Emile's, neither is it exactly Rousseau's own. Rousseau's own statements about his religious beliefs are not sufficiently clear to say for certain what his views are. He also had a completely justified fear of persecution for unorthodoxy, which gave him ample reason to dissimulate. Rousseau repeatedly asserts that the Vicar's profession is substantially the same as Julie's and that his own faith is substantially the same as theirs, but these rather qualified statements do not tell us very much.[9] A more solid bit of evidence is that Rousseau never categorically affirms the Vicar's teaching as true, although he repeatedly characterizes it as *useful* and consoling. Indeed, in the *Letter to the Archbishop of Paris*, Rousseau insists that the Vicar's teaching is the "best and most useful writing" to be produced in the eighteenth century (LB 960).[10] The Vicar tells his young listener that he would profit from thinking as he does—and Rousseau notes in his own voice that the good priest could have made the same observation with equal truth to the public at large (E 295 and note).

The problem remains: Why include this writing in the middle of *Emile*

9. See, e.g., C 342; RW 34–35; LB 960–961. See also Charles E. Butterworth, "Interpretive Essay," to *Reveries of the Solitary Walker*, by Jean-Jacques Rousseau, ed. and trans. by Charles E. Butterworth (Indianapolis: Hackett, 1992), 174–181.

10. In the same Letter, Rousseau offers some carefully worded praise of his Genevan Calvinist roots: "Happy to have been born into the most reasonable and holiest religion on earth, I remain inviolably attached to the sect of my Fathers: like them, I take Scripture and reason for the sole guides to my belief." Of the Vicar, he writes: "I will always glory in being counted among his flock" (LB 961).

when it has so little connection to the education of the book's eponymous hero? It seems only reasonable to suppose that the Profession of Faith is included in *Emile* because its teaching corresponds to the larger didactic ambition Rousseau has for the work. It is not difficult to see how the Vicar's teaching would be very encouraging to a couple who was aspiring to live a life of rustic virtue in accord with Rousseau's teachings. The Vicar's teaching is the link between Rousseau's teaching and traditional religious views; one who accepts the Vicar's version of Christianity (and who suspects Rousseau of accepting it—as many and perhaps most readers have done) will be much more willing to let himself be moved by the example of Emile.

Thus the education we, the readers, are to receive is based on the same principles as Emile's education, although it is not exactly his education. Imitation is central to both educations. We saw in chapter 6 that Emile learns by imitating his tutor's virtues. We are to learn by imitating Emile and by imagining Rousseau as our own, personal tutor and friend; we are to adopt the Vicar's creed as our own and find in the hope of life after death a motive to sacrifice our own happiness for justice. We are to live in the country with our families and to make the rearing of our children the center of our lives. It is of course extremely unlikely that any reader could—in virtue of his encounter with Rousseau's *Emile*—fully live up to the virtue he incarnates. His virtue is worth aspiring to, however, because even if we fail to live up to it fully, we can in falling short of that ideal, approximate its excellence. In his final speech to Emile, Jean-Jacques directs his pupil to do what he cannot do himself: "You who have not taken on the sad job of telling the truth to men, go and live in their midst, cultivate their friendship in sweet association, be their benefactor and their model. Your example will serve them better than all our books, and the good that they see you do will touch them more than all our vain speeches" (E 474).

8 Rousseauian Virtue and Contemporary Liberalism

> On the whole, the institution of laws is not such a marvelous thing that any man of sense and equity could not easily find those which, well observed, would be the most beneficial for society. . . . But this is not the only issue. The problem is to adapt this code to the people for which it is made and to the things about which it decrees to such an extent that its execution follows from the very conjunction of these relations.
>
> —*Letter to M. d'Alembert on the Theatre*

ALTHOUGH HE WAS a brilliant prose stylist, Rousseau constantly found that his readers did not understand him. What he never sufficiently appreciated, however, was how much his own literary artfulness contributed to his readers' difficulties. Recognizing that few human beings have the natural gifts to become wise, Rousseau often wrote as the founding Lawgiver acts, in order "to persuade without convincing" (SC 71). He hoped to inspire all his readers to repent of their "mercenary morality" and to set forth on the path of virtue he marked out for them—even those who could not comprehend the details of his intellectual system. As a result, vivid images spring from the pages of his works and live on in his readers' imaginations long after the details of his argument have begun to fade from memory. The remarkable liveliness of Rousseau's images of corruption and virtue may indeed do much to advance his didactic purpose, but it does so at the cost of making a careful assessment of his system of social thought considerably more difficult.

This book has argued that Rousseau's greatest contribution to the study of human beings and human society is his account of the principles of the passions—his dynamic model of the human soul with *amour-propre* at its center. What makes Homo sapiens distinctive, according to Rousseau's account, is the emergence of this reflexive and reason-dependent form of self-love, which moves us to desire to be esteemed by others according to the value we place on ourselves. By positing the existence of *amour-propre* in the soul, Rousseau solves two crucially important puzzles to which his predecessors had been unable to devise satisfactory answers. First, rather than accounting for the existence of human evil by tautologically positing a natural principle of evil in the soul, Rousseau probes more deeply. He asks why it is that human beings, apparently alone in nature, are capable of moral action at all. Only after having accounted for the emergence of a moral order from the amorality of the physical world does Rousseau try to explain why human beings so often choose to do what is morally evil rather than what is morally good.

Rousseau explains that, although the cultivation of reason is a necessary condition for the emergence of morality, it is not sufficient: reason perceives relationships, but it does not create them. Morality enters human affairs only after our developing reason interacts with our natural and organic sensitivity to produce the active and moral sensitivity lying at the root of *amour-propre*. Once *amour-propre* has emerged in us, we are permanently connected to the wills of others, dependent on the esteem of others for a measure of our own well-being. Emotionally connected to others, and enmeshed in a complex web of "moral" relationships, we constantly make claims on the wills of others—both explicitly in what we say and implicitly in how we live—and they make reciprocal claims on us. Only insofar as our being is constituted by our relationships with the wills of others are we capable of morality at all. We do evil when we voluntarily do to another, with whom we are thus related, what we must will that he *not* do to us.

Second, rather than accounting for the existence of political societies by tautologically positing a natural principle of sociability, Rousseau once again asks a deeper question than his predecessors had attempted to answer. Because it is clear that human beings have not always lived in political societies, the establishment of those societies cannot be explained adequately by making reference only to some natural instinct of sociability. In contrast to his predecessors, Rousseau explains how naturally asocial human beings *become* social. His account of the establishment of political society evidently resembles his account of the genesis of morality. Once again, *amour-propre* is the central concept. Human beings form stable political orders when they recognize and come to feel in their hearts that their most important material and psychological needs can only be satisfied by establishing a reciprocal relationship with others of their kind. This is what it means to say that all political societies come into being and are sustained by acts of the human will.

Rousseau's point is not that every society is sustained by the active and conscious voluntary endorsement of all its members. That condition can only be satisfied in fully legitimate regimes. Even bad regimes, however, are constituted and sustained by acts of will. Rousseau's point is that we create and sustain political orders by all of our particular acts and choices, when and insofar as our particular aims are such that they cannot be realized except within the constraints of an ongoing political society. Rousseau illustrates his point in the *Discourse on Inequality* by describing the origins of a right to property, but the point is a general one. What binds us (with all of our socially acquired needs) into civil society is that, regardless of what we want out of life, we require property to realize our goals. The demand that others respect our property—that they recognize the legitimacy of our proprietorship—can only be reliably satisfied by recognizing the rights of others to the legitimate possession of their property and thus by recognizing the legitimacy of some authority to adjudicate conflicting claims of right.

The discovery of *amour-propre* also enables Rousseau to explain both the human tendency to choose to do what is morally evil rather than what is good and our propensity to form oppressive political orders rather than legitimate states. More than anything else, what determines whether we are moved to wrong others or to treat them justly is the basic orientation of our *amour-propre*. If we seek the esteem of others based on our superiority in wealth or power or fame, we are inclined to wrong our fellows and thus tend to contribute to an oppressive political order. If, however, we found our sense of self-esteem and seek the esteem of others based on some common good (such as our devotion to the welfare of our particular political community or to the welfare of humanity) then we will be disposed to treat our fellows as we would wish to be treated and thus help to sustain a free political order—one in which no one takes advantage of any other. In short, Rousseau teaches that the love of exclusive goods lies at the root of all vice, and the love of common goods is the foundation of virtue.

Rousseau's account of the human soul also enables him to explain precisely the interrelationship of politics and ethics. Once again, *amour-propre* is the key. The nature of the political order within which we live does much to determine the sorts of people we grow up to become. Where great inequality of fortune and little security of status exists, we are likely to become inordinately devoted to the pursuit of wealth and status; we are likely, in short, to acquire the vices of greed and ambition.[1] The more people who devote themselves to the pursuit of wealth and the more wholeheartedly they embrace this project, the more inequality is likely to grow and the farther the vices are likely to spread. The problem is that the disposition to take advantage of others is hard to limit to the economic sphere. The desire to maximize profit, which can drive economically productive innovation, can also lead to less socially desirable behaviors. The recent wave of financial scandals nicely illustrates Rousseau's point. The desire to maximize profits led a great many businesspeople to skirt the edges of

---

1. For an extreme case of this phenomenon, see CP 939–940.

legality by using "creative" accounting techniques to deceive investors about the true financial condition of their companies. Others, more consumed by greed or less restrained by concern for others, acted more directly against the aims of the law by manipulating markets to reap windfall profits or to secure themselves in the possession of monopolies by illegally attacking their competitors. The greediest and most unrestrained had recourse to the simplest expedient for satisfying their desires, namely theft.

It is not enough to say that public institutions must enact regulations to restrain private greed. Widespread compliance with such regulations is likely only where another motive than greed—such as the love of virtue—is active. The threat of external sanctions may be enough to motivate (most) actors to avoid the sorts of easily proved, obvious wrongs that can readily be punished. But the threat of external sanctions is not enough to restrain actors from taking every effort to find ways to defeat the point of regulations by subtle and complex stratagems that are hard to detect and where criminal liability is harder to establish. Worse still, the thoroughly greedy soul has every interest in using every means at his disposal to undercut the regulators, whether by lobbying for the enactment of lax standards or by aiming to bring to power an administration that will not enforce them. Punishing wrongdoing after the fact suffers from another drawback also: when the authorities finally do manage to discover the wrongdoing they had been unable or unwilling to prevent, typically it is the ordinary workers who find themselves penniless and unemployed while their corrupt bosses not only escape the prison sentences they deserve but also retain the profits derived from their immoral enterprises.

Rousseau adds that those who are accustomed to using others for financial gain rarely stop at this. Vices acquired in the marketplace have a way of spilling over into personal life and into the political sphere as well. It may be possible to be avaricious and domineering at work while being equitable and mild at home, but it cannot be easy. It is no easier to prevent the desire for limitless wealth from becoming the desire to use governmental power to facilitate this ambition. When unchecked, inflamed *amour-propre* produces a vicious circle of increasing corruption, increasing inequality, and increasing desperation that ends eventually in despotism.

Conversely, where equality and a shared civic identity exist, it is easier for citizens to devote themselves to the pursuit of common goods, promoting the welfare of their community. When the community flourishes in such a way that all citizens benefit from its prosperity, it is easier for the citizens to love their community and to treat their neighbors as themselves: thus can the (relatively) benign manifestation of *amour-propre* as patriotism generate something approximating a virtuous circle. It is vital to recognize, however, that a well-ordered society can never be simply self-sustaining, on Rousseau's account. A well-ordered society will have fewer structural incentives to injustice than a disordered society, but the seeds of vice are present in every individual heart. These seeds could be eradicated and temptation to injustice effectively suppressed if all could be made wise, but Rousseau sees that since such wisdom requires extraordinary gifts of nature, it will always be rare. The public cultivation of virtue could help suppress the persistent temptations to injustice, but public moral education can succeed only under limited circumstances—circumstances that do not generally obtain in modern, commercial republics.

It may be objected that Rousseau's account of human nature is far more pessimistic than I have acknowledged. At the end of the *Discourse on Inequality*, for example, we are left with the impression that European society is already so thoroughly corrupt, at the middle of the eighteenth century, that it is headed inevitably toward the worst form of tyranny. In the *Preface to Narcissus*, Rousseau adds that the societies based on the principle of economic self-interest which were then succeeding the monarchies of the ancien régime would fare no better than their predecessors—and indeed would likely fare worse. Rousseau thus seems to predict that modern, commercial societies like our own will necessarily fail to protect rights and necessarily degenerate into tyrannies; Arthur Melzer, for example, interprets Rousseau in precisely this way.[2] We know, of course, that modern commercial republics do exist and that the citizens of such republics (including the contemporary United States) enjoy a degree of material well-being and a range of liberties scarcely imaginable in the eighteenth century. It would seem, therefore, that Melzer has rightly concluded that "in these respects, Rousseau, even more than Marx, stands refuted by history."[3]

If Rousseau's account of human nature and his political principles in fact entailed the dire conclusions Melzer draws from them, then his negative assessment would be correct. But the application of Rousseau's model of human nature to politics is more complex than Melzer recognizes. It is tempting to say that the application of Rousseau's principles to politics demands more careful and impartial judgment than Rousseau himself managed to employ. Allan Bloom has wisely observed that Alexis de Tocqueville's analysis of politics and culture derives its central insights from Rousseau's political philosophy.[4] This observation suggests the extraordinary level of subtlety and care required to apply Rousseau's highly

2. Arthur Melzer puts the point most strongly: "Rousseau's philosophical system necessarily culminates in the view that there was no political hope for the West and that 'modernization,' the emerging order of liberal, welfare-capitalist, representative, mass democracy, could not possibly work." *Natural Goodness*, 290.

3. Ibid., 290.

4. Allan Bloom, "The Study of Texts" in *Giants and Dwarfs: Essays 1960–1990* (New York: Simon and Schuster, 1990), 312–313.

abstract insights about human nature and the foundations of political society to concrete social conditions.

Rousseau conveys the impression that there can be no hope for the commercial societies of the modern West because he so often writes as if the only genuine human possibilities are those that lie at the extremes: either a person is devoted to virtue or is a morally bankrupt bourgeois, either a citizen, or savage, or slave; either the general will is ascendant, or the polity is sustained by avarice and fear. These extremes are ideal types, however, introduced by Rousseau to illustrate the consequences of the different psychological principles they embody. The history of the last two centuries gives us no reason to doubt that the effect of inflamed *amour-propre* is necessarily bad, and that a regime sustained *wholly* by the avarice and ambition of its citizens would be headed swiftly toward despotism.[5] The truth is, however, that that few people are so devoted to the pursuit of wealth that they base all of their self-esteem on the amount of money they possess, just as few are so perfectly dedicated to virtue that they care only about the judgment of their own consciences and of other wise judges of character. Most people, in most regimes, fall somewhere between the extremes represented by the bourgeois and the man or woman of virtue. Although it may be logically incoherent for us to love incompatible goods, the "philosophically deeply annoying" truth is that "most of us can live comfortably with wholly contradictory beliefs."[6]

As a consequence, most regimes are similarly muddled: the liberal and democratic republics of the modern West are not wholly based on the principle of self-interest, and the level of social inequality they exhibit is far less than one would conclude by focusing on economic inequality alone. It is true that vast disparities exist between the richest and the poorest in the contemporary United States, but that economic inequality is less than obtained in ancien régime France and moreover coexists with a substantial *equality* of basic rights. Most of us are moved by an unstable mixture of pas-

5. Although I have been unable to pursue this idea in sufficient depth to be certain, I conjecture that Rousseau's account of human nature may be usefully linked with Robert Putnam's analysis of the production and effects of "social capital" in the United States and Italy; Rousseau gives us an account at the level of the individual soul that enables us to understand why human beings act in the ways that Putnam and his colleagues observe. Putnam's account of the civic dispositions seems closely to resemble Rousseau's account of virtue (closer, however, to Emile's human virtue than to the truly civic virtue of the Spartans). Putnam shows, based on considerable empirical evidence, that social capital (the prevalence of virtue) correlates strongly with the prosperity, freedom, and happiness of the citizens, and that the lack of social capital (the absence of virtue) correlates strongly with the converse. See Robert D. Putnam, *Making Democracy Work: Civic Traditions in Modern Italy* (Princeton: Princeton University Press, 1993), and *Bowling Alone: The Collapse and Revival of American Community* (New York: Simon and Schuster, 2000).

6. Judith N. Shklar, *Legalism: Law, Morals, and Political Trials*, 2d ed. (Cambridge: Harvard University Press, 1986), x.

sions, including some desires for wealth, celebrity, and power but also incorporating more benign manifestations of *amour-propre* such as the desire to be esteemed for good character, a patriotic devotion to our country's best ideals, and perhaps also the desire to fulfill as best we can God's expectations for us (as we conceive them). Some of the forces in our lives certainly reinforce that aspect of our *amour-propre* oriented toward the pursuit of celebrity, power, and profit. But other, countervailing forces also tend to reinforce the healthier manifestations of *amour-propre*.

The great problem of statesmanship is to discover how to reinforce the latter while diminishing the former. To be sure, Rousseau often expressed very pessimistic sentiments about the possibilities for reforming whole cultures, but occasionally these remarks are counterbalanced by no less remarkably optimistic statements.[7] For example, early in *Emile* Rousseau writes that, if only mothers would "deign to nurse their children, morals will reform themselves, nature's sentiments will be awakened in every heart. . . . This first point, this point alone, will bring everything back together. The attraction of domestic life is the best antidote for bad morals" (E 46).[8] Rousseau seems overly enthusiastic about breast-feeding, but his larger point is sound: the right kind of love for one's family is an important counterweight to consuming ambition and avarice. My desire for the absolute well-being of my family can be satisfied in conjunction with my neighbors' desire that their families flourish; indeed, the flourishing of my neighbors' families can readily be seen to contribute to my own (and my family's) well-being. Those who want to be richer or more powerful than others, however, necessarily set their interests in opposition to those of their neighbors.[9] Even in the *Social Contract*, Rousseau cryptically holds out hope that a disordered political regime will be altered for the better when "invincible nature has resumed its empire" (SC 80). Neither the dark pessimism nor the wild optimism represents the full story of a Rousseauian approach to politics. The truth, rather, lies somewhere between these ex-

---

7. It is not clear that Rousseau is wrong to be pessimistic about the prospects for increasing the degree of civic virtue in a given community. One of the most striking findings of Putnam's work is the persistence over time of civic (or non-civic) dispositions. Those regions in Italy (or in the United States) that were least civic in centuries past (such as southern Italy and Sicily or the States of the Old Confederacy) are those that remain least civic today. *Making Democracy Work*, chapter 5. *Bowling Alone*, chapter 16.

8. "Antidote" has been substituted for Bloom's rendering of *"contrepoison"* as "counterpoison."

9. He insists so strongly that mothers should breast-feed their own children because the likely alternative was not that the mother (or father) would feed the child with a bottle, as is common today, but that the mother and father would send the child off to a nurse, who would care for him; by sending the child away to a nurse, the parents miss out on an important period of development in their child's life and habituate themselves to remaining aloof from and indifferent to the child's welfare.

tremes. Rousseau's proof that injustice and vice can never be eradicated demands that we recognize the limits of what we can hope to attain in politics; but our knowledge that human beings naturally long for happiness and that this natural longing can only be satisfied by those who attain virtue entitles us to a measure of hope. As long as that hope remains duly chastened, we are entitled to cherish it.

ROUSSEAUIAN LIBERALISM AND THE LIMITS OF POLITICS

Some of Rousseau's political ideas are inevitably disconcerting to orthodox liberals, but much in his thought is welcome to more moderate friends of liberalism—above all, his unwavering dedication to protecting "the rights of humanity" (E 441). In his moments of greatest enthusiasm for the unity of ancient Sparta, Rousseau's political vision can seem totalitarian. Indeed, the time is not long past when he was widely understood as the father of totalitarianism. But that reading was made plausible only by making a fundamental mistake about the nature of the project Rousseau undertakes in the *Social Contract*, namely to conflate the idea of the general will with the concept of reasoned justice. In that much maligned work, Rousseau is *not* primarily concerned to discover what justice requires; he aims, rather, to discover a "legitimate and sure rule" according to which a political society may be ordered "so that justice and utility may not be disjoined" (SC 41). Rousseau always maintained that discovering what justice requires is not the difficult aspect of any political inquiry. In the passage from the *Letter to d'Alembert* that stands as the epigraph to this chapter, Rousseau observes that "the institution of laws is not such a marvelous thing that any man of sense and equity could not easily find those which, well observed, would be the most beneficial for society" (LA 66).

The most difficult political problem is to find some way to motivate everyone to do more or less what justice requires. Rousseau in the *Social Contract* does not show us how to create a perfectly just state—a perfectly just state would require universal wisdom, a condition he thinks impossible to meet. He shows us instead how to create a perfectly ordered polity that is nevertheless reasonably just. "Every legitimate government is republican," Rousseau announces, thus answering the question with which he begins his inquiry (SC 67). Where the government acts only in accordance with fundamental laws that are willed by the community as its general will, that is, where the government acts only to promote goods that the citizens recognize (or, at a minimum, are willing to accept) as common goods, the citizens experience the laws not as a limitation on their freedom, but rather as the embodiment of their freedom. The laws, as acts of the general will, do not chafe and incite resistance as do those regulations we sense as impediments to our freedom because they derive from the arbitrary will of others. If the legitimate state does not pursue substantive ends that are truly good and therefore embodies an imperfect degree of justice, at least the citizens of a republic nevertheless do justice to one another. Being virtuous makes them free, and their freedom is a necessary condition of their happiness.

In *Emile*, however, Rousseau announces that "there are no longer any fatherlands," which is to say that there are no more fully legitimate states in the modern world (E 40). No modern political societies—not even his beloved Geneva, as he would soon discover—retain the degree of social solidarity, ethnic and religious homogeneity, and civic virtue required for the general will to correspond reliably to the will of all (see SC 121–122). Of the reasons why no fatherlands persist into the contemporary world, the most important is the rise of commerce. The problem with commerce is not exactly that it is governed by the profit motive. The problem is that we so readily come to desire profit in the wrong way: the legitimate desire to improve one's own absolute well-being all too easily degenerates into the vicious desire to be better off than others. This disordered manifestation of *amour-propre* makes us more likely to attempt to use the power of government to advance our own, partisan agendas, while at the same time making it more difficult for us to appreciate even the just claims of others to be working toward the common good.

Modern liberal and democratic regimes contain admixtures of good and bad, however. They advance some common goods, for example: defending the nation from foreign attack, securing the individual rights of all, protecting the natural environment, providing a measure of economic security for the sick, aged, and unfortunate, and sustaining the electoral institutions by which we choose our rulers. They also promote some private or exclusive goods, for example: taxing some for the arbitrary and unjust enrichment of others, benefiting certain favored sectors of the economy or regions of the country at the expense of others. We recognize the laws as legitimate only to the extent that we recognize them as advancing some common good—as stemming from the general will that is ours. To the extent that the laws seem nothing other than the means by which some powerful group is using the public force to take advantage of the rest of us, the more difficult it is to perceive any moral reason why one should obey.[10] The lib-

10. Rousseau indicates that it is only the "political laws," or as we would say today, constitutional laws, that constitute his subject in the *Social Contract* (SC 80–81). His point is that only the constitutional laws need be willed by the people as its general will (and endorsed by a vote in which all of the citizens are eligible to participate). When we view our society's basic law as the embodiment of our freedom, it will be possible for us to take a long view of the vast number of specific actions our government takes. So long as we see that the whole suite of policies pursued by the government is broadly consonant with the general will, it will be possible to reconcile ourselves easily enough to the occasionally unequal benefits and burdens that the administration of any government necessarily imposes.

eral societies of the modern West remain relatively decent and are sub-stantially legitimate because (and insofar as) the general will of each soci-ety continues to be heeded, albeit imperfectly.

Because Rousseau himself offers little direct guidance about what insti-tutional forms would be appropriate for modern commercial republics, we must use his principles to draw our own inferences.[11] As we have seen, Rousseau expressed a considerable degree of pessimism about the pros-pects of such regimes to resist the vicious circle of increasing inequality and increasing corruption. In *Emile*, however, he offers an account of how an individual may live happily and well even in an imperfect regime. One who possesses human virtue can live in an imperfect state almost as if he were a citizen in a legitimate republic. The great difficulty is that virtue must be cultivated and most of us are not so wise that we perceive on our own the emptiness of the goods valued by opinion, which is why we re-quire some beneficent and wise friend to aid us.

It is difficult to escape the feeling that there is something fanciful and extravagant about Rousseau's hope that his books might contribute to a re-vival of personal virtue in his readers. Nevertheless, if we abstract from the details of his educational project and look only at its structure, it is clear that Rousseau correctly understood the problematic conditions char-acteristic of modern, commercial republics and recognized an appropriate remedy. Such republics can only escape the vicious circle of increasing in-equality and corruption as long as sufficient sources of moral health are available to counteract the ill effects of unchecked commercialism. The problem, however, is that the government, being itself at least partially in-fected by the inflamed *amour-propre* that is endemic in any commercial so-ciety, can do little directly to foster the civic dispositions—the virtues—on which its preservation depends. Hence arises the need, which Rousseau's didactic novels attempt to meet, for extra-political sources of moral edu-cation.

Moral education can succeed, Rousseau explains, only when the recip-ients of the education feel, throughout the whole process of learning, that their teachers embody virtues that they already inchoately and imperfectly value. This constraint is doubly restrictive: the teachers must in fact pos-sess the virtues they aim to impart, and the students must recognize the teachers' virtues as somehow connected to their own understandings of how they themselves aspire to live.[12] It is difficult to see how these condi-

11. At SC 114, Rousseau rejects the British doctrine of parliamentary sovereignty, on the grounds that acts of sovereignty (i.e., changes in a nation's constitutional laws) cannot legiti-mately be entrusted to representatives.

12. In the *Government of Poland*, Rousseau argues that secondary education should be su-pervised by those who have already distinguished themselves in some place of public re-sponsibility. In this way, Rousseau hopes to guarantee that they will be conspicuous for virtue

tions can possibly be met in any scheme of public education that one could implement in a society at all resembling our own. Our teachers are not selected for virtue but for intellectual competence. If we wished to select teachers for their virtue, could we agree on the standards by which the morally excellent would be selected? Nor are students free from inflamed *amour-propre*. When institutions whose authority they do not recognize address openly paternalistic teachings to our young people ("just say no to drugs," for example), they are likely only to arouse the *amour-propre* of those whose values they wish to alter.[13] The danger of moral corruption cannot be easily avoided—even by adopting the expedient of avoiding ostensibly moral instruction. Teachers who aim only to impart the basic skills that define academic competence risk cultivating intellectual vanity in their cleverer students and inflaming the more mercenary ambitions of the rest.

Government action can, however, foster the conditions under which citizens are able to perceive themselves as sharing common goods: it can protect rights for all; it can guarantee a measure of economic security for all; it can encourage or even require citizens to take part in the kinds of common enterprises that nurture feelings of community. In all of these cases, the government acts with the aim of producing a certain set of virtues in the citizens, even though it must proceed by indirection. Like Rousseau, Rawls allows that a government may legitimately "encourage certain moral virtues," in particular the political virtues of "civility and tolerance, of reasonableness and the sense of fairness."[14] Rousseau's account of the human soul, however, leads him to reject Rawls's distinction between the deliberate cultivation of political virtues (which is permitted) and the deliberate attempt to shape citizens' conceptions of what is good (which is forbidden as inconsistent with liberal neutrality).[15] Whether we are disposed to respect the rights of others depends, in Rousseau's account, on the basic orientation of our *amour-propre*. Rousseau's account of human nature gives us no reason to think that we can be reasonable in political life while being fundamentally unreasonable and vicious in our private lives. Because it cannot in any other way hope to prevent malign forms of *amour-propre* from

---

and will have demonstrated that virtue in an arena which the young (he hopes) will respect. (They will respect success in public service insofar as they themselves desire the goods that such success alone makes possible, and Rousseau proposes mechanisms by which to impart this desire to the pupils). See GP 241.

13. For an instructive example of this phenomenon, consider the story of Vicki Frost's struggle with the Hawkins County (Tennessee) school board. Stephen Macedo, *Diversity and Distrust: Civic Education in a Multicultural Democracy* (Cambridge: Harvard University Press, 2000), 157–165.

14. Rawls, *Political Liberalism*, 194.

15. Ibid., 191–193.

dominating the citizenry, a Rousseauian government will aim to create the conditions under which citizens will acquire the comprehensive human virtue described in *Emile*.

Because he saw that government action can do little to foster this virtue directly, Rousseau perceived that the commercial republic must depend on sources of virtue outside of the political arena. The family can be one such source; the Savoyard Vicar's religion—indeed, any humane and tolerant religion—can be another. Rousseau hoped that his novels would be a third. Rousseau's teachings imply that a government hoping to see its citizens acquire virtue will protect these and other similar institutions, within which the kinds of personal bonds are likely to be fostered that make possible moral education. Whether that protection will take the form of subsidies, public endorsement, or the establishment of legal immunities from governmental interference will naturally depend on the particular circumstances of a given society. Although Rousseau's principles of the passions give us some of the tools we need in order to think deeply about the role of government, they do not obviate the need for political prudence.

Rousseau's books can remind us that as human beings we all have more in common than is recognized. We share the same basic nature, and we share the same twin aspirations: to live happily and be worthy of happiness. Part of our problem is that within the polity no one has a sufficiently strong motive to remind us of our commonality. The desire to win elections too often leads politicians to focus on what divides us. The desire to make money leads businesspeople to excite our desires, to inflame our imaginations, and to arouse our *amour-propre* into an unhealthful concern for wealth and status. Rousseau took it upon himself to remind us of what is common to us all and tried to make it possible for all of us to live as citizens, even where no more than a rough approximation to a truly civic regime exists. Whether or not his effort succeeded in its time,[16] his didactic fictions no longer serve our needs. But Rousseau does illuminate the nature of the problem we face, and his account of the principles of the passions gives us the tools to devise an appropriate solution. Whatever else we must do, the first step on the road toward a better world is easy to see, even as it can be hard to take: it is to practice virtue.

16. James Miller supposes that his democratic dreams in fact helped move the world. *Rousseau: Dreamer of Democracy* (New Haven: Yale University Press, 1984).

Bibliography

Acher, William. *Jean-Jacques Rousseau: Ecrivain de l'amitié*. Paris: Editions A.-G. Nizet, 1971.

Affeldt, Steven G. "The Force of Freedom: Rousseau on Forcing to Be Free." *Political Theory* 27 (1999): 299–333.

Aristotle. *Nicomachean Ethics*. Translated by Terence Irwin. Indianapolis: Hackett, 1985.

——. *Politics*. Translated by Carnes Lord. Chicago: University of Chicago Press, 1984.

Barber, Benjamin. *Strong Democracy: Participatory Politics for a New Age*. Berkeley: University of California Press, 1984.

Bellah, Robert N., et al. *Habits of the Heart: Individualism and Commitment in American Life*. Berkeley: University of California Press, 1985.

Bellenot, Jean-Louis. "Les formes d'amour dans la *Nouvelle Héloïse* et la signification symbolique des personnages de Julie et de Saint-Preux." *Annales de la Société Jean-Jacques Rousseau* 33 (1953–1955): 149–208.

Berkowitz, Peter. *Virtue and the Making of Modern Liberalism*. Princeton: Princeton University Press, 1999.

Bloom, Allan. *Giants and Dwarfs: Essays 1960–1990*. New York: Simon and Schuster, 1990.

——. "Introduction" to *Emile*, by Jean-Jacques Rousseau. Translated by Allan Bloom. New York: Basic Books, 1979.

——. *Love and Friendship*. New York: Simon and Schuster, 1993.

Blum, Carol. *Rousseau and the Republic of Virtue: The Language of Politics in the French Revolution*. Ithaca: Cornell University Press, 1986.

Burgelin, Pierre. *La philosophie d'existence de J.-J. Rousseau*. Paris: Librairie Philosophique J. Vrin, 1973.

Butterworth, Charles E. "Interpretive Essay" to *The Reveries of the Solitary Walker*, by Jean-Jacques Rousseau. Edited and translated by Charles E. Butterworth. Indianapolis: Hackett, 1992.

Cassirer, Ernst. *The Question of Jean-Jacques Rousseau*. Translated by Peter Gay. New Haven: Yale University Press, 1963.

Cobban, Alfred. *Rousseau and the Modern State*. New York: G. Allen and Unwin, 1934.

Cohen, Joshua. "Deliberation and Democratic Legitimacy." In *The Good Polity*, edited by Alan Hamlin and Philip Petit. Oxford: Basil Blackwell, 1989.

——. "The Natural Goodness of Humanity." In *Reclaiming the History of Ethics: Es-*

says for John Rawls. Edited by Andrews Reath, Barbara Herman, and Christine Korsgaard. Cambridge: Cambridge University Press, 1997.

——. "Reflections on Rousseau: Autonomy and Democracy." *Philosophy and Public Affairs* 15 (Summer 1986): 275–297.

Cooper, John M. "Aristotle on Friendship." In *Essays on Aristotle's Ethics,* edited by Amélie Oksenberg Rorty. Berkeley: University of California Press, 1980.

Cooper, Laurence D. *Rousseau, Nature, and the Problem of the Good Life.* University Park, Penn.: Pennsylvania State University Press, 1999.

Cranston, Maurice. *Jean-Jacques: The Early Life and Works of Jean-Jacques Rousseau, 1712–1754.* Chicago: University of Chicago Press, 1982.

——. *The Noble Savage: Jean-Jacques Rousseau, 1754–1762.* Chicago: University of Chicago Press, 1991.

——. *The Solitary Self: Jean-Jacques Rousseau in Exile and Adversity.* Chicago: University of Chicago Press, 1997.

Crocker, Lester G. "*Julie,* ou la Nouvelle Duplicité." *Annales de la Société Jean-Jacques Rousseau* 35 (1959–1962): 113–137.

Cropsey, Joseph. "Justice and Friendship in the *Nicomachean Ethics.*" In *Political Philosophy and the Issues of Politics.* Chicago: University of Chicago Press, 1977.

Darnton, Robert. "Readers Respond to Rousseau: The Fabrication of Romantic Sensitivity." In *The Great Cat Massacre and Other Episodes in French Cultural History.* New York: Basic Books, 1984.

Dent, N. J. H. *Rousseau: An Introduction to His Psychological, Social, and Political Theory.* New York: Basil Blackwell, 1988.

Derathé, Robert. *Jean-Jacques Rousseau et la science politique de son temps.* Paris: Presses Universitaires de France, 1950.

——. *Le rationalisme de Jean-Jacques Rousseau.* Paris: Presses Universitaires de France, 1948.

Derrida, Jacques. "Politics of Friendship." Translated by Gabriel Motzkin. *The Journal of Philosophy* 85 (November 1988): 632–644.

Diamond Jared M., *Guns, Germs, and Steel: The Fates of Human Societies.* New York: W. W. Norton, 1997.

Disch, Lisa. "Claire Loves Julie: Reading the Story of Women's Friendship in *La Nouvelle Héloïse.*" *Hypatia* 9 (Summer 1994): 19–45.

Estlund, David. "Beyond Fairness and Deliberation: The Epistemic Dimension of Democratic Authority." In *Deliberative Democracy: Essays on Reason and Politics,* edited by James Bohman and William Rehg. Cambridge: MIT Press, 1997.

Ellis, M. B. "*Julie, or, La nouvelle Héloïse*": A Synthesis of Rousseau's Thought. Toronto: University of Toronto Press, 1949.

Ellrich, Robert J. *Rousseau and his Reader: The Rhetorical Situation of the Major Works.* Chapel Hill: University of North Carolina Press, 1969.

Fabry, Anne Srabian de. *Etudes autour de "La nouvelle Héloïse".* Sherbrooke, Quebec: Editions Naaman, 1977.

Ferrara, Alessandro. *Modernity and Authenticity: A Study in the Social and Ethical*

Thought of Jean-Jacques Rousseau. Albany: State University of New York Press, 1993.

Finnis, John. *Natural Law and Natural Rights*. Oxford: Oxford University Press, 1980.

Fletcher, George P. *Loyalty: An Essay on the Morality of Relationships*. Oxford: Oxford University Press, 1993.

Freeman, Samuel. "Reason and Agreement in Social Contract Views." *Philosophy and Public Affairs* 19 (Spring 1990): 122–157.

Fried, Charles. "The Lawyer as Friend." *Yale Law Journal* 85 (1976): 1060–1088.

Galston, William A. *Liberal Purposes*. Cambridge: Cambridge University Press, 1991.

Gildin, Hilail. *Rousseau's "Social Contract": The Design of the Argument*. Chicago: University of Chicago Press, 1983.

Gourevitch, Victor. "Introduction" to *The Discourses and Other Early Political Writings*. Edited and translated by Victor Gourevitch. New York: Cambridge University Press, 1997.

——. "Rousseau on the Arts and Sciences." *Journal of Philosophy* 69 (1972): 737–754.

——. "Rousseau's 'Pure' State of Nature." *Interpretation* 16 (1988): 23–59.

Grant, Ruth W. *Hypocrisy and Integrity: Machiavelli, Rousseau, and the Ethics of Politics*. Chicago: University of Chicago Press, 1997.

Grimsley, Ronald. *Jean-Jacques Rousseau: A Study in Self-Awareness*. Cardiff: University of Wales Press, 1969.

Habermas, Jürgen. *Moral Consciousness and Communicative Action*. Translated by Christian Lenhardt and Shierry Weber Nicholsen. Cambridge: MIT Press, 1990.

Hall, H. Gaston. "The Concept of Virtue in *La nouvelle Héloïse*." *Yale French Studies* 28 (1961): 20–33.

Hare, R. M. *Moral Thinking: Its Levels, Method, and Point*. Oxford: Oxford University Press, Clarendon Press, 1981.

Hegel, G. W. F. *Hegel's Philosophy of Right*. Translated, with notes by T. M. Knox. Oxford: Oxford University Press, 1952.

Hendel, Charles W. *Jean-Jacques Rousseau: Moralist*, 2d ed. Indianapolis: Bobbs-Merrill, 1964.

Hobbes, Thomas. *Leviathan*. Edited by Edwin Curley. Indianapolis: Hackett, 1994.

——. *Man and Citizen ("De Homine" and "De Cive")*. Edited by Bernard Gert. Indianapolis: Hackett, 1991.

Hulliung, Mark. *The Autocritique of Enlightenment: Rousseau and the Philosophes*. Cambridge: Harvard University Press, 1994.

Johnston, Steven. *Encountering Tragedy: Rousseau and the Project of Democratic Order*. Ithaca: Cornell University Press, 1999.

Jones, James F. *Rousseau's "Dialogues": An Interpretive Essay*. Geneva: Librairie Droz, 1991.

Jouvenel, Bertrand de. "Essai sur la politique de Jean-Jacques Rousseau." In *Du contrat social: précédé d'un essai sur la politique de Rousseau par Bertrand de Jouvenel.* Paris: Livre de Poche, 1978.

Kant, Immanuel. *Groundwork of the Metaphysics of Morals.* Translated by H. J. Paton. New York: Harper & Row, 1948.

——. *Perpetual Peace and Other Essays.* Translated by Ted Humphrey. Indianapolis: Hackett, 1983.

Kelly, Christopher. *Rousseau's Exemplary Life: The "Confessions" as Political Philosophy.* Ithaca: Cornell University Press, 1987.

Korsgaard, Christine M. *Creating the Kingdom of Ends.* Cambridge: Cambridge University Press, 1996.

——. *The Sources of Normativity.* Cambridge: Cambridge University Press, 1996.

Lane, Robert E. *The Loss of Happiness in Market Democracies.* New Haven: Yale University Press, 2000.

Locke, John. *Some Thoughts Concerning Education.* Edited by John W. and Jean S. Yolton. Oxford: Oxford University Press, Clarendon Press. 1989.

——. *Two Treatises of Government.* Edited by Peter Laslett. Cambridge: Cambridge University Press, Cambridge Texts in the History of Political Thought, 1989.

Macedo, Stephen. *Diversity and Distrust: Civic Education in a Multicultural Democracy.* Cambridge: Harvard University Press, 2000.

——. *Liberal Virtues: Citizenship, Virtue, and Community in Liberal Constitutionalism.* New York: Oxford University Press, 1990.

Machiavelli, Niccolò. *The Prince.* Translated by Harvey C. Mansfield. Chicago: University of Chicago Press, 1985.

Macy, Jeffrey. " 'God Helps Those Who Help Themselves': New Light on the Theological-Political Teaching in Rousseau's *Profession of Faith of the Savoyard Vicar.*" *Polity* 24 (Summer 1992): 615–632.

Manin, Bernard. "On Legitimacy and Political Deliberation." Translated by Elly Stein and Jane Mansbridge. *Political Theory* 15 (August 1987): 338–368.

Mansbridge, Jane. *Beyond Adversary Democracy.* Chicago: University of Chicago Press, 1980.

——, ed. *Beyond Self-Interest.* Chicago: University of Chicago Press, 1990.

Marks, Jonathan. "The Savage Pattern: The Unity of Rousseau's Thought Revisited." *Polity* 31 (1998): 75–105.

Marshall, David. "Rousseau and the State of Theater." *Representations* 13 (Winter 1986): 84–114.

Masters, Roger D. *The Political Philosophy of Rousseau.* Princeton: Princeton University Press, 1968.

Melzer, Arthur M. *The Natural Goodness of Man: On the System of Rousseau's Thought.* Chicago: University of Chicago Press, 1990.

Miller, James. *Rousseau: Dreamer of Democracy.* New Haven: Yale University Press, 1984.

Montaigne, Michel de. *The Complete Essays of Montaigne.* Translated by Donald M. Frame. Stanford: Stanford University Press, 1943.

Montesquieu. *Persian Letters.* Translated by C. J. Betts. Harmondsworth: Penguin Books, 1973.

——. *The Spirit of the Laws*. Translated and edited by Anne M. Cohler, Basia Carolyn Miller, and Harold Samuel Stone. Cambridge: Cambridge University Press, 1989.

Moon, J. Donald. "Constrained Discourse and Public Life." *Political Theory* 19 (May 1991): 202–229.

Nagel, Thomas. "What Makes a Political Theory Utopian?" *Social Research* 56 (Winter 1986): 903–920.

——. "Moral Conflict and Political Legitimacy." *Philosophy and Public Affairs* 16 (Summer 1987): 215–240.

——. *Equality and Partiality*. Oxford: Oxford University Press, 1991.

Neal, Patrick. "In the Shadow of the General Will: Rawls, Kant, and Rousseau on the Problem of Political Right." *Review of Politics* 49 (Summer 1987): 389–409.

Neuhouser, Frederick. "Freedom, Dependence, and the General Will." *Philosophical Review* 102 (July 1993): 363–396.

Neidleman, Jason Andrew. *The General Will is Citizenship: Inquiries into French Political Thought*. Lanham, Md.: Rowman & Littlefield, 2001.

Plato. *The Republic of Plato*. Translated by Allan Bloom. New York: Basic Books, 1968.

Plutarch. *Lives of the Noble Grecians and Romans*, 2 vols. Translated by John Dryden. Edited and revised by Arthur Hugh Clough. New York: Modern Library, 1992.

Price, A. W. *Love and Friendship in Plato and Aristotle*. Oxford: Oxford University Press, 1989.

Putnam, Robert D. *Bowling Alone: The Collapse and Revival of American Community*. New York: Simon and Schuster, 2000.

——. *Making Democracy Work: Civic Traditions in Modern Italy*. Princeton: Princeton University Press, 1993.

Rawls, John. *Political Liberalism*. The John Dewey Essays in Philosophy. New York: Columbia University Press, 1993.

——. *A Theory of Justice*. Cambridge: Harvard University Press, Belknap Press, 1971.

Reisert, Joseph R. "Justice and Authenticity in Taylor and Rousseau." *Polity* 33 (Winter 2001): 305–330.

Riley, Patrick. *Will and Political Legitimacy: A Critical Exposition of Social Contract Theory in Hobbes, Locke, Rousseau, Kant, and Hegel*. Cambridge: Harvard University Press, 1982.

Robinson, Philip. "Literature versus Theory: Rousseau's Second Preface to *Julie*." *French Studies* 44 (October 1990): 403–416.

Rorty, Amélie Oksenberg. "Rousseau's Therapeutic Experiments." *Philosophy* 66 (October 1991): 413–434

Rousseau, Jean-Jacques. See "Works by Rousseau," under Abbreviations, page vii.

Rosenblatt, Helena. *Rousseau and Geneva: From the First Discourse to the Social Contract, 1749–1762*. Cambridge: Cambridge University Press, 1997.

Rosenblum, Nancy L. *Another Liberalism*. Cambridge: Harvard University Press, 1987.

——, ed. *Liberalism and the Moral Life*. Cambridge: Harvard University Press, 1989.

Sandel, Michael J. *Liberalism and the Limits of Justice*. Cambridge: Cambridge University Press, 1982.

Scanlon, T. M. "Contractualism and Utilitarianism." In *Utilitarianism and Beyond*, edited by Amartya Sen and Bernard Williams. Cambridge: Cambridge University Press, 1982.

Schmitt, Carl. *The Concept of the Political*. Translated by George Schwab. Comments by Leo Strauss. New Brunswick, N.J.: Rutgers University Press, 1976.

Schwartz, Joel. *The Sexual Politics of Jean-Jacques Rousseau*. Chicago: University of Chicago Press, 1984.

Shell, Susan Meld. *The Rights of Reason: A Study of Kant's Philosophy and Politics*. Toronto: University of Toronto Press, 1980.

Shklar, Judith N. *The Faces of Injustice*. New Haven: Yale University Press, 1990.

——. *Legalism: Law, Morals, and Political Trials*. 2d edition. Cambridge: Harvard University Press, 1986.

——. *Men and Citizens: A Study of Rousseau's Social Theory*. Cambridge: Cambridge University Press, 1985.

——. "Rousseau's Images of Authority." In *Hobbes and Rousseau*, edited by Maurice Cranston. Garden City, N.Y.: Anchor Books, 1972.

Starobinski, Jean. *Jean-Jacques Rousseau: Transparency and Obstruction*. Translated by Arthur Goldhammer. Chicago: University of Chicago Press, 1988.

Strauss, Leo. *Natural Right and History*. Chicago: University of Chicago Press, 1950.

——. "On the Intention of Rousseau." In *Hobbes and Rousseau*, edited by Maurice Cranston. Garden City, N.Y.: Anchor Books, 1972.

Strong, Tracy B. *Jean-Jacques Rousseau: The Politics of the Ordinary*. Modernity and Political Thought. Thousand Oaks, Calif.: Sage, 1994.

Taylor, Charles. *The Ethics of Authenticity*. Cambridge: Harvard University Press, 1991.

——. *Sources of the Self: The Making of the Modern Identity*. Cambridge: Harvard University Press, 1989.

Tisserand, Roger, ed., *Les concurrents de J.-J. Rousseau à l'Académie de Dijon pour le prix de 1754*. Paris: Boivin & Cie., 1936.

Viroli, Maurizio. *Jean-Jacques Rousseau and the "Well-Ordered Society."* Translated by Derek Hanson. Cambridge: Cambridge University Press, 1988.

Weiss, Penny A. *Gendered Community: Rousseau, Sex, and Politics*. New York: New York University Press, 1993.

——. "Sex, Freedom, and Equality in Rousseau's *Emile*." *Polity* 22 (Summer 1990): 603–625.

Williams, Bernard. *Ethics and the Limits of Philosophy*. Cambridge: Harvard University Press, 1985.

——. *Shame and Necessity*. Berkeley: University of California Press, 1993.

Wingrove, Elizabeth Rose. *Rousseau's Republican Romance*. Princeton: Princeton University Press, 2000.

Wokler, Robert, ed. *Rousseau and Liberty*. Manchester: Manchester University Press, 1995.

Yack, Bernard. "Community and Conflict in Aristotle's Political Philosophy." *Review of Politics* 47 (January 1985): 92–112.

——. *The Longing for Total Revolution*. Princeton: Princeton University Press, 1986; reprint, Berkeley: University of California Press, 1992.

——. *The Problems of a Political Animal: Community, Justice, and Conflict in Aristotelian Political Thought*. Berkeley: University of California Press, 1993.

Index

Acher, William, 85 n. 10, 101 n. 35
Aemilius, Quintus, Roman consul, 9
Affeldt, Steven G., 130–131, 149 n. 3
Amour-propre: as basis of virtue, 19–20,
109, 112, 161; defined, 16, 19–20, 40,
185; emergence in adolescence, 65–66;
emergence in the savage state, 40–41;
"extend . . . to other beings," 151; as
foundation of society, 43–53, 187–188;
inflamed, 22, 24, 46, 48, 58, 69–70, 69,
72, 75–78, 86, 89, 91, 100, 106, 112, 125,
146–149, 157, 162, 168–174, 181–182,
193–196; opposition between friendship and, 24, 99–100, 144; as patriotism,
55, 109, 126, 129, 168; reason-depen-
dence and malleability of, 19–20, 23,
109, 185–187; and romantic love, 80,
101, 103
Anet, Claude, 166
Anger, 19, 64, 146–147, 155–156, 166
Apology of Socrates (Plato), 2
Aristotle, 4, 12, 16 n. 45, 50 n. 23, 56, 67 n.
9, 74 n. 11, 74 n. 12, 79–84, 89–94, 110–
111, 120, 127 n. 27, 136, 152
Athens, 1–2, 135
Augustus, Gaius Octavius, Roman emperor, 73, 151
Author of Things, 53, 141. *See also* God
Authority, 23–24, 143–147, 149, 153, 156
Autobiographical argument, 28–29

Bellah, Robert N., 61 n. 6
Berkowitz, Peter, 2–4
Bloom, Allan, 9, 25 n. 57, 25 n. 58, 78–79,
85–90, 100–101, 141–144, 154 n. 8, 155,
158, 160, 165, 182, 189
Blum, Carol, 11–12, 108 n. 2
Boétie, Etienne de la, 79, 100–101
Bomston, Lord Edward (character in
Julie), 91, 96 n. 29, 97 n. 31, 98, 105, 159
Bourgeois, 53, 58–62, 67–75, 78, 104, 109,
111–114, 122, 124–125, 135–137, 168,
190
Bravery. *See* Courage
Breakfast "in the English manner," 94, 97–
99, 163
Breast-feeding, 23, 181–182, 191
Brutus, Lucius Junius, 113, 140
Buffon, Georges Louis Leclerc, Comte de,
30
Burke, Edmund, 7

Cassirer, Ernst, 147 n. 2
Catiline (Lucius Sergius Catalina), Roman
conspirator, 107–108
Cato, Marcus Porcius, the Younger, 110,
112–113, 148
Children, 1–2, 23, 31, 60–64, 72–73, 115,
145–150
Citizen, 1–11, 22, 24, 52, 165, 169, 171,
193–194, 196; virtuous citizen
(Rousseauian ideal type of) 54–56, 69,
78, 107–114, 124, 127–140, 190
Civil right. *See* Political right
Claire (character in *Julie*), 91, 95, 101 n. 36,
102, 105, 107, 159, 164
Clarens (Julie's estate), 76, 94–5, 98, 102–
103, 163
Clinton, William J., 76
Cohen, Joshua, 126 n. 23
Commiseration. *See* Pity
Confessions, 12–13, 22, 24 n. 55, 29, 53, 72,
78, 85 n. 11, 93, 96 n. 30, 97–98, 100, 102,
166, 181, 183 n. 9
Conscience, 2, 16, 26, 71, 75, 108, 111, 118–
119, 121, 132, 136–137, 141, 151–152,
158, 164, 167, 169–170; defined, 20–21
Consent, 31, 43, 46, 48, 50, 52, 127, 131–
132, 149, 154, 164
Considerations on the Government of Poland,
11 n. 22, 24 n. 55, 121 n. 17, 124 n. 22, 126,
134, 194 n. 12